Springer Series in Operations Research

Editor:
Peter Glynn

Springer
New York
Berlin
Heidelberg
Barcelona
Budapest
Hong Kong
London
Milan
Paris
Santa Clara
Singapore
Tokyo

Springer Series in Operations Research

Drezner (Editor): Facility Location: A Survey of Applications
  and Methods
Fishman: Monte Carlo: Concepts, Algorithms, and Applications
Olson: Decision Aids for Selection Problems
Yao (Editor): Stochastic Modeling and Analysis of Manufacturing
  Systems

David L. Olson

Decision Aids for Selection Problems

Springer

David L. Olson
Texas A & M University
Department of Business Analysis
College of Business Administration
   and Graduate School of Business
College Station, TX 77843-4217
USA

Series Editor:
Peter Glynn
Department of Operations Research
Stanford University
Stanford, CA 94305
USA

*Sci
T
58.62
.O35
1996*

Library of Congress Cataloging-in-Publication Data
Olson, David Louis.
    Decision aids for selection problems / David L. Olson.
      p.   cm. − (Springer series in operations research)
    Includes bibliographical references and index.
    ISBN 0-387-94560-1 (hardcover : alk. paper)
    1. Decision support systems. I. Title. II. Series.
  T58.62.O35   1995
  658.4′03 − dc20   95-34191

Printed on acid-free paper.

Production managed by Frank Ganz; manufacturing supervised by Jeffrey Taub.
Photocomposed pages prepared from the author's files.
Printed and bound by R.R. Donnelley & Sons, Harrisonburg, VA.
Printed in the United States of America.

9 8 7 6 5 4 3 2 1

ISBN 0-387-94560-1 Springer-Verlag New York Berlin Heidelberg

This book is dedicated to Sang M. Lee, who has provided so much guidance over the years, and because I couldn't work goal programming in.

Preface

One of the most important tasks faced by decision makers in business and government is that of selection. Selection problems are challenging, because they require the balancing of multiple, often conflicting objectives, criteria, or attributes. Over the past few decades, a number of interesting tools to support selection decision making have been presented. A popular European term for this class of decision support tool is decision aid. Sources for these tools are spread throughout the world, incorporating different ideas.

The intent of this book is to compare some of these decision aids. There are three groupings of chapters: Chapters 1 and 2 present general ideas, Chapters 3–12 focus on specific decision aids and demonstrate some of the software implementing these ideas. Chapter 13 concludes with a comparative analysis. A classified bibliography concludes the book.

Chapter 1 discusses some general thoughts on the importance of considering multiple criteria. The source material for the first chapter is an aggregation of notes I have worked on throughout my academic career. This is followed by Chapter 2 on hierarchy development, a means of organizing criteria of importance into a logical structure for analysis. The material for this chapter draws heavily from Ralph Keeney's book, *Value Theory*.

The next four chapters present techniques using the general idea of a value function defining the relative importance of criteria and measuring relative attainment of the alternatives being analyzed on these criteria. The standard approach in the U.S. is value theory. The software package *Logical Decision* is used in Chapter 3 to demonstrate how value theory can be implemented. There have been many reported applications of multiattribute utility theory (MAUT), or multiattribute value theory. These terms have special significance to some practitioners. Here they are used synonymously. *SMART* is a very usable, practical implementation of MAUT, and is covered in chapter 4. Chapter 5 presents Analytic Hierarchy Process (AHP), a more recent development initially presented by Thomas Saaty. AHP is also very popular, with many applications reported in the literature. But AHP includes some features that some researchers have questioned. Chapter 6 presents methods implementing the geometric mean as well as other changes in the implementation of the general AHP idea. Freerk Lootsma of Delft University in the Netherlands has presented the *REMBRANDT* system that is demonstrated in that chapter.

Chapter 7 presents a different idea, the use of preference cones. This approach is highly popular in the literature, with fewer real applications, although there have been some implementations. The preference cone concept is the product of joint US/European work, combining the talents of Stanley Zionts of the U.S., Jyrki Wallenius and Pekka Korhonen of Finland, and many others.

Chapters 8 and 9 are based on the concept of partial order, seeming to have started initially with Bertram Roy in France. The French *ELECTRE* method has been followed by the Belgian *PROMETHEE* software, demonstrating a radically different approach to the value function concept of multiattribute value theory and AHP. Chapter 8 presents the how these methods work with demonstrations. Oleg Larichev of the Russian Academy of Sciences worked with Roy around 1970. Larichev and his colleagues have subsequently developed *ZAPROS* (Chapter 9), a method implementing Larichev's views on acceptable preference elicitation methods, yielding a partial order for large sets of alternatives. Positive features of the material presented in Chapter 9 are due to a great deal of help received from Alexander Mechitov and Helena Moshkovich of the Russian Academy of Sciences.

Two methods focusing on giving decision makers tools to learn about decision tradeoffs are presented in the next two chapters. Chapter 10 presents *AIM*, an implementation of a number of multiple criteria concepts. While preference cones are available for decision closure, the intent of *AIM* is to help the decision maker explore the possibilities of different aspiration levels. The idea of *VIMDA* in Chapter 11 is a reliance on graphical presentation of information to decision makers, allowing them to make their selections after exploring the tradeoffs among alternatives displayed through graphs of relative attainment. *VIMDA* incorporates the idea of eliminating dominated solutions, identifying those solutions nearest the to target attainment levels of the decision maker, and allowing the decision maker to learn about the possible combinations of attainment in available alternatives. *AIM* and *VIMDA* are based on the same basic concept of using computer systems to aid decision maker learning about tradeoffs.

Chapter 12 presents two techniques that allow decision makers to express preferences less precisely, using ranges rather than specific values for weights or alternative performance on attributes. *ARIADNE* uses a multiattribute value theory framework, while *HIPRE 3+* uses an AHP framework.

Chapter 13 concludes with a relative comparison of techniques, focusing on the four characteristics of task type, task dimensionality, task uniqueness, and decision maker cognitive effort required. The material in this chapter is the product of joint work between Alexander Mechitov and Helena Moshkovich of the Russian Academy of Sciences and myself.

Decision aids are very interesting tools, offering a great deal to contemporary decision making. It is hoped that this book can encourage further use of these tools, as well as possibly open debate on some of the issues involved in their implementation.

Contents

Preface   vii

1 **Introduction**   1
   Multiple Criteria Decision Making   2
   Value   4
   Software Sources   7
   References   8

2 **Developing Criteria Hierarchies**   9
   Hierarchies   9
   Attributes   11
   Hierarchy Development Process   11
   Suggestions for Cases where Preferential Independence is Absent   12
   Energy Hierarchies   13
   Conclusions   18
   References   18

3 **Multiattribute Utility Theory**   19
   Case: Nuclear Depository Siting   19
   Multiattribute Utility Theory   20
   Tradeoff Analysis   22
   Nuclear Dump Site Selection   26
   House Selection   28
   Conclusions   32
   References   33

4 *SMART*   34
   The *SMART* Technique   34
   Independence   36
   Nuclear Dump Site Example   36
   House Selection Example   39
   SMARTS   42

Nuclear Site Selection with *SMARTS* 44
SMARTER 45
House Selection Example Using *SMARTER* 46
Summary 47
References 48

5 The Analytic Hierarchy Process 49
Description of AHP 49
Hierarchy Development 50
Subjective Pairwise Comparisons 51
Calculation of Implied Weights 52
Consistency Measure 53
Synthesis 55
Calculations for the Nuclear Waste Disposal Siting Problem 56
Calculations for the Housing Selection Decision 60
Real-World Applications of AHP 61
Computer Support for AHP 65
Summary 66
Appendix: Calculation of Maximum Eigen Value and Eigenvector 66
References 67

6 Geometric Mean Technique 69
Geometric Mean Solution 69
REMBRANDT 71
Nuclear Disposal Site Selection Problem 73
House Selection Calculations 76
References 80

7 Preference Cones 81
Procedure 82
Basing Objective on Current Best Choice 83
Basing Objective on Worst Choice to Date 84
Adjacency Formulation 85
Cellular Manufacturing Example 85
Basing Objective on Current Best Choice 86
Basing Objective on Worst Choice to Date 88
Automation Example 89
Nuclear Dump Site Selection 92
Conclusions 94
References 95

8 Outranking Methods 96
ELECTRE 96
Cellular Manufacturing Example 98
Automation Example 101
Nuclear Dump Site Selection — *ELECTRE II* 106

PROMETHEE 109
GAIA Output 114
Nuclear Dump Site Selection — *PROMETHEE* 115
Applications of Outranking Methods 117
Conclusions 117
References 118

9 *ZAPROS* 119
Demonstration Model 120
Nuclear Dump Site Selection 127
House Selection 128
Conclusions 130
References 130
Appendix: Input Files 131

10 **Aspiration-Level Interactive Model** 134
Methodology 134
Nuclear Dump Site Selection 136
Cellular Manufacturing Example 141
Summary 143
References 144

11 **Visual Interactive Method** 145
VIMDA Overview 145
VIMDA Procedure 146
Nuclear Dump Site Selection 147
Cellular Manufacturing Example 148
Summary 149
References 150

12 **Models with Uncertain Estimates** 151
ARIADNE 151
Parking Example 152
Nuclear Waste Disposal Siting Problem 153
Uncertain Value Contributions 154
House Buying Example 155
HIPRE 3+ 157
Parking Example 158
Nuclear Dump Site Example 159
Summary 160
References 161

13 **Comparisons** 162
Task Type 162
Task Dimensionality 163
Task Uniqueness 165

Decision Maker Cognitive Effort 165
Human Subject Responses 168
Aid to Decision Maker Learning 169
Synthesis 172
Conclusion 172
References 172

Bibliography 173

Author Index 189

Topic Index 193

1
Introduction

The term "decision aid" comes from Europe, where a number of computer systems designed to help decision makers select from a finite set of alternatives have been developed. Other terms apply, such as "decision analysis," a term more widely used in the U.S., although usually reserved for multiattribute utility theory application. The term "decision support system" has also been used, but in the U.S. that term is usually used for a broader set of computer tools to less specific problems. Whatever they are called, a wide variety of systems have been developed to help humans select from a given set of alternatives. In this book, the European term "decision aid" will be used.

A number of effective decision aids supporting selection problems under conditions of multiple criteria have appeared in the last few decades. The primary techniques in the field are multiattribute utility theory (implemented in short form by the *SMART* approach, and in its fuller form on computer by *Logical Decision*) and analytic hierarchy process (implemented by *Expert Choice* and *Criterium*). In Europe, outranking techniques (*ELECTRE* and *PROMETHEE*) are quite popular. Preference cones have been developed by international teams. *AIM* is a software system using preference cones. *ZAPROS* is a system recently developed in Russia based on ordinal preference input. *REMBRANDT* is a system recently developed in the Netherlands seeking to correct shortcomings its developer sees in analytic hierarchy process. *HIPRE 3+* is a system based on AHP but allowing uncertain inputs, while *ARIADNE* is an American system allowing uncertain inputs in the multiattribute utility theory framework.

This book is intended to show how these major decision aids work, concluding with a comparison of techniques with respect to practical implementation. Chapter two discusses how multiple criteria can be organized into a hierarchical structure. In the subsequent chapters, software support for each of the techniques is demonstrated with applications. A selection problem concerning nuclear waste disposal siting is used with each technique to provide a basis for comparison. Other examples are used for different systems, seeking to demonstrate specific features of each system. The emphasis is on how each technique works, with some discussion of that technique's features. All of these systems aid selection decisions, but of different types. Multiattribute utility theory, analytic hierarchy process, and *REMBRANDT* are considered more appropriate for short lists of alternatives (less than five to nine). Outranking methods, preference cones, and *ZAPROS* require a large list of alternatives before their implementation makes sense. *AIM* and *VIMDA* can be applied to either size of problem.

Multiple Criteria Decision Making

The study of decision making has progressed in a variety of disciplines, including psychology, business, engineering, and operations research/management science. As society has grown more complex, the need to consider multiple, conflicting objectives has grown. Government has always needed to balance conflicting objectives, such as growth, employment, and general welfare. Businesses are finding that they need to consider multiple objectives as well. While short run profit remains important, long run factors such as market maintenance, product quality, and development of productive capability often conflict with measurable short run profit.

Conflicts

Conflicts are inherent in most interesting decisions.

Profit

Because it has the apparent advantage of providing a measure of worth, **profit** has become a valuable concentration point for many decision makers. One of the functions of money, after all, is to provide a scalar value of worth, determined theoretically by the market place. However, profit itself can have multiple aspects. The time value of money is crucial in business. Net present value is a useful concept, because it allows you to convert a stream of cash flow, over a prolonged period, into that stream's net worth today. Given alternative investments, the theory is that people will invest in such a way as to maximize net present value. But we observe that not all people invest in the same things. There is a lack of perfect information in reality.

Risk

There are also varying levels of risk associated with alternatives. People have different views (and the same person's views change with time and circumstance) relative to risk. **Risk** becomes a second dimension for decision making. Further,

TABLE 1.1 Business objectives

Profit	short run cash flow
	short run after tax profit
	long run
Risk	
Market Development	
Capital Replenishment	
Labor Relations	
Other	

there are cash flow needs which become important in some circumstances. Historically, insufficient cash reserves have been a major cause for the closing of U.S. businesses. The net present value of an operation may be very attractive, but if there is insufficient cash to get to the payoff ten years from now, the investment does little good. Further, U.S. income tax laws have played a major role in business decision making, especially when tax law is used as a means to motivate actions desired by the government. Analysis based upon after tax profit may lead to different decisions than analysis based upon pretax calculations. So profit itself has a number of dimensions.

Market Development

There are other factors business decision makers need to consider as well. Businesses need **developed markets** to survive. A naive approach would be to spend all of ones efforts on developing a super product, and wait for the market to come to you. The advertising industry in the U.S. is enormous. The reason for its prosperity is that it pays to advertise. There are so many products available that people are not going to spend effort to compare the value of all products on the market. The impact of advertising expenditure is often very difficult to forecast. Yet decision makers must consider advertising impact. This often forces decision makers to supplement the objective of profit, and consider market development, even if there appears to be a temporary sacrifice to profit. Japanese decision makers seemingly place a higher emphasis upon market share. Recent history indicates that this can have very positive impact upon long range profit.

Capital Replenishment

Another decision factor which requires consideration of tradeoffs is **capital replenishment**. The greatest short run profit will normally be obtained by delaying reinvestment in capital equipment. Many U.S. companies have been known to cut back capital investment in order to appear reasonably profitable to investors. If there were perfect knowledge of the risk involved in retaining equipment that is wearing out, or in the productive improvements available from acquiring new technology, profit (in net present terms) would serve as a very good scale of value. But precise measures of such factors are not available. Judgment is required. Replenishment of capital can be viewed as an objective in itself. It has been called an investment in tomorrow.

Labor Relations

Labor policies can also have impact upon long range profit. In the short run, profit will generally be improved by holding the line on wage rates and risking a high labor turnover. In fact, in some industries, temporary employment is viewed as the norm. There are costs which are not obvious, however, in such a **labor relations** policy. First, there is training expense involved with a high turnover environment. The experience of the members of an organization can be one of its most valuable assets. Secondly, it is difficult for employees to maintain a positive attitude when their experience is that short run profit is always placed ahead of employee welfare.

Innovative ideas are probably best found from those people who are involved with the grass roots of an organization—the work force.

The point is that there are a number of objectives which are important to a business. Decision makers need to consider multiple, often conflicting, objectives in many decisions.

Value

Scientific support for decision making has been of interest for a long time. As stated above, value theory is directly interested in the need to make decisions when facing tradeoffs. The value of a good is determined by a number of characteristics. Water is highly necessary, but it has little market value. Diamonds have some industrial use, which produces valuable output, but in general are not particularly necessary. Yet diamonds hold a tremendously high market value. Supply and demand have a great deal to do with market value. In a decision making context, however, the scale of market value is not representative of utility. Monetary value has a residual purpose of reflecting exchange worth. But even this scale does not suffice in all cases.

Theory of Utility

Attempts to explain human behavior in decision making led to valuable work in development of a theory of utility. This avenue of research continues, and it is not the intent of this book to discredit that research. As with all scientific pursuits, each gain in knowledge generally leads to more questions, however. While there have been useful techniques presented which are based upon the concept of utility, they require some assumptions that may not be acceptable in all cases. Multiple objective analysis provides an alternative route in some sense, with its own set of assumptions.

The theory of utility dates back over a century. Utility and value are synonyms for most of us. In this book we will use the term utility. However, in the last two decades, theorists in the field of risk analysis have used the term to specifically refer to the tradeoff between risk and return. Therefore, tradeoffs among a variety of criteria other than risk and return are sometimes referred to as **value** tradeoffs. Rather than seeking utility functions, when factors other than risk and return are considered, it is often safer to refer to **value functions**. The simplest *value* function is

$$Value = \sum_{k=1}^{K} w_k v_{ik}$$

for alternative i of N alternatives, K is the number of criteria, w_k is the relative weight of criterion k and v_{ik} is the scaled value alternative i has on criterion k. This function is an increasing function, is linear (convex), and is continuous.

The form of utility functions (and parallel value functions) are expected to be quite complex. Debreu [1959] developed a rigorous mathematical system reflecting utility. He assumed that utility would have a number of features, including a monotonically increasing function that is convex and continuous. Keeney and Raiffa [1976] utilized lottery comparisons to identify utility. MacCrimmon and Toda [1969] provided an example of a basic experiment to identify *utility*. That process, however, requires decision makers to conduct preference analysis over often an imposing number of goods combinations.

Criticisms of the Theory

There has been a great deal of self-criticism in economics relative to the theory of *utility*. Georgescu-Roegen [1954] considered the assumptions made in the theory of utility to be far too unrealistic. He also discussed an almost ancient debate concerning the **cardinalist** view that utility can be measured in scalar form versus the **ordinalist** view that humans can generally only identify relative preference. Morgenstern [1972] presented an imposing research agenda of issues requiring clarification before utility could be generally applicable. There have also been very interesting phenomena observed in human decision making not explained by the concept of utility. Simon [1979] observed the phenomena of **satisficing**. Satisficing (satisfactory and sufficient) behavior runs counter to the assumption that firms maximize profit. Individual decision makers were seen to often reject apparent optimal solutions for solutions which provided some sufficient level of profit. March [1978] and Simon both noted that decision making involves a **bounded rationality**, in that;

1. decision makers do not have the perfect information that is assumed in theory;
2. decisions have to be made within limited time frames;
3. decision makers do not know all they want to know; nor
4. do they realize all of the things they should want to know.

One explanation of satisficing behavior would be laziness, or lack of concern. Another would be that decision makers realize that all information is not available, and that optimal solutions to a limited model generally involve greater risk. There is no rational justification for laziness or lack of concern, and when information is not available, it should be sought out. However, decisions have to be made with what is available. A very interesting theory was developed by Lindblom [1959], with the label of **muddling through**. Lindblom not only noted that decision makers tend to prefer incremental improvement over optimal solutions, but proposed that this approach was preferable. The argument would be that every model of a decision problem, formal or informal, lacks important elements. The intuitive feel for the decision background in the decision maker's mind is an example of an informal model. Informal models very often are more complete than formal models. Therefore,

TABLE 1.2 Utility

1) Utility is **an increasing function**
   (more of a good is better than less)
2) Utility is **convex**
   (more of a good is valuable,
   but at a decreasing rate)
3) Utility is **continuous**
   (there are no satisfaction levels)

while it is useful to apply models leading to a better state than currently exists, it is best to hedge somewhat, and make decisions that marginally change systems.

This discussion of alternative views of how decisions should be made is not to open a debate on relative merits of positions for or against utility/value theory. The only purpose was to point out that there are alternative views of what should be done in this field. One position, strongly held by those who support it, is that decision aids should be normative, and should lead decision makers to better decisions than they would have made without the decision aid. This position seems very logical and sound, except that it is almost impossible to establish that the types of decisions that are suggested by such systems are superior to what humans do without the systems. The other extreme position is that decision aids should help decision makers learn more about the decision they are facing, so that they can apply the judgment they normally would, but in a more informed way.

Various Decision Aid Approaches

We will look at a variety of decision aid approaches. Some (MAUT, AHP, *REMBRANDT* and preference cones) are intended to select the best choice from a given set of alternatives. Others (outranking methods, *ZAPROS*) are based on the idea of developing a partial order, useful for sorting out large lists of alternatives down to a short list among which the decision maker can select. In practice, methods used for these two problem types are not that distinct, in that outranking methods have been modified to allow identification of a best choice, and MAUT and AHP have been modified to deal with large sets of alternatives. MAUT is the most theoretically accepted approach. *Logical Decision* is a software implementation of MAUT, and is covered in Chapter 3. *SMART* is a straightforward implementation of MAUT, covered in Chapter 4. AHP is a popular system in practice, and although there have been theoretical questions raised about its validity, Chapter 5 discusses AHP. *REMBRANDT* is a decision aid designed to overcome some of the theoretical questions about AHP. Chapter 6 is about geometric methods, of which *REM-BRANDT* is an implementation. Preference cones apply mathematical programming and utility logic to selection problems. This approach is only useful if there are a lot of alternatives, and is practical only if there are few criteria. Preference cones are discussed in Chapter 7. The French idea of partial order is implemented in outranking methods, covered in Chapter 8. This idea has also been implemented in decision aid *ZAPROS*, a Russian system covered in Chapter 9. Methods intended to help decision makers explore available tradeoffs are discussed in chapters 10 and 11. Chapter 12 reviews two methods allowing uncertain estimates on preference information, and discusses two decision aids. *ARIADNE* uses MAUT principles, while *HIPRE 3+* is AHP based.

Techniques and Proponents

The proponents of each of the ten decision aid techniques discussed here claim that their technique fully follows the normative principle and that their technique leads to better decisions. For some of the techniques, this opinion is not universally shared.

It is not my purpose to establish any one technique as superior to any of the others. My own view is that all ten of the techniques reviewed in this book are useful to somebody. The final chapter seeks to identify those individual types who might find one method more suitable than another.

At a national professional conference I heard a presenter, discussing expert systems, use the definition that an expert is the person in the world that knows more than anyone else about a specific topic. Aside from the fact that I think this view is erroneous, let me be clear in stating that I am not an expert on any one of these techniques. There are a large number of experts in the field of multiattribute value theory, with Ralph Keeney, Craig Kirkwood, and James Dyer the most visible. *Logical Decision* is the software used as the basis of solving problems in the MAUT chapter. Ward Edwards has been proactive in the application of MAUT through *SMART*. Thomas Saaty is the developer and leading proponent of analytic hierarchy process. Ernest Forman has marketed *Expert Choice* in conjunction with Saaty. *Criterium* is another software supporting AHP. Freerk Lootsma developed *REMBRANDT* theory. Bernard Roy is a leading figure in *ELECTRE*. J. Pierre Brans has developed *PROMETHEE*, and Bertrand Mareschal has done a great deal to report its use. Stanley Zionts, Jyrki Wallenius, and Pekka Korhonen all have contributed to the development of preference cones, and Murat Köksalan has refined that theory a great deal. Stanley Zionts provided the *AIM* software used. Another software product, *RADIAL* by Malakooti, probably applies preference cones. Pekka Korhonen provided *VIMDA*. Computer support for preference cone analysis was done with a code I wrote for myself (as was *ELECTRE* support). Oleg Larichev is the leading theorist of *ZAPROS*, with assistance from Helena Moshkovich in its development. Ambrose Goicoechea was kind enough to provide me with *ARIADNE*, and Raimo Hämäläinen and others have developed *HIPRE 3+*, two decision aids allowing uncertain preference inputs.

There are many other experts for each of these techniques, not including me. But I am familiar with all of the systems. I have enjoyed working with a few of the people mentioned, and corresponded with or met many of the rest. I have used all of the systems on the problems presented in the book, as well as many other problems. They offer what I think are some very interesting possibilities to support decisions. The purpose of this book is to seek to share that interest.

The software products mentioned above are available from their developers. Addresses to contact each source is given below. Buede [1992a][1992b] has reviewed this class of software, including other systems, and is recommended as a source of relative evaluation.

Software Sources

AIM—Professor Stanley Zionts, Department of Management Science and Systems, State University of New York at Buffalo, 325 Jacobs Management Center, Buffalo, NY 14260-4000

ARIADNE—Doctor Ambrose Goicoechea, STATCOM Inc., 7921 Jones Branch Drive, Suite 445, McLean, VA 22102

Criterium—Sygenex, 15446 Bel-Red Road, Suite 450, Redmond, WA 98052

ELECTRE—Professor Bernard Roy, University of Paris-Dauphine, Place du Marechal Del Lattre de Tassigny, 75775 Paris Cedex 16, France

Expert Choice—Decision Support Software, Inc. 4922 Ellsworth Ave., Pittsburgh, PA 14213

HIPRE 3+—Professor Raimo Hämäläinen, System Analysis Laboratory, Helsinki University of Technology, Otakaari 1M, 02150, Espoo, Finland

Logical Decision—Logical Decisions, 1014 Wood Lily Drive, Golden, CO 80401

PROMETHEE—Professor J.P. Brans, Vrije Universiteit Brussel, Pleinlaan 2 B-1050, Brussels, Belgium

RADIAL—Professor Behnam Malakooti, Department of Systems Engineering, Case Western Reserve University, Cleveland, OH 44106

REMBRANDT—Professor Freerk Lootsma, Faculty of Technical Mathematics and Informatics, Delft University of Technology, Delft, The Netherlands

VIMDA—Professor Pekka Korhonen, Department of Mathematics and Statistics, Helsinki School of Economics, Runeberginkatu 14-16, 00100 Helsinki, Finland

ZAPROS—Professor Oleg Larichev, Institute of System Studies, Russian Academy of Sciences, Prospect 60 let Octiabria, 9, Moscow 117312 Russia

References

Buede, D.M. 1992. Software review: Overview of the MCDA software market. *Journal of Multi-Criteria Decision Analysis* 1:1, 59–60.

Buede, D.M. 1992. Software review: Three packages for AHP: Criterium, Expert Choice, and *HIPRE 3+*. *Journal of Multi-Criteria Decision Analysis* 1:2, 119–121.

DeBreu, G. 1959. *Theory of value: An axiomatic analysis of economic equilibrium.* New Haven, CT: Yale University Press.

Georgescu-Roegen, N. 1954. Choice, expectations, and measurability. *Quarterly Journal of Economics* 68, 4, 503–534.

Keeney, R.L. and H. Raiffa. 1976. *Decision with multiple objectives: Preferences and value tradeoffs.* New York: Wiley.

Lindblom, C.E. 1959. The science of muddling through. *Public Administration Review* 19, 2, 79–88.

MacCrimmon, K. and M. Toda. 1969. The experimental determination of indifference curves. *Review of Economic Studies.* (October).

March, J.G. 1978. Bounded rationality, ambiguity, and the engineering of choice. *The Bell Journal of Economics* 9, 2, 587–608.

Morgenstern, O. 1972. Thirteen critical points in contemporary economic theory: An interpretation. *Journal of Economic Literature* 10, 1163–1189.

Simon, H.A. 1979. Rational decision making in business organizations. *The American Economic Review* 69, 4, 493–513.

2
Developing Criteria Hierarchies

Analysis of problems with multiple criteria requires steps of identifying objectives, arranging these objectives into a hierarchy, and then measuring how well available alternatives perform on each criterion. The validity of the process requires a good start to this process—identification of what the decision maker or decision makers want to accomplish.

The process of structuring multiple criteria *value* hierarchies has received a great deal of merited attention. Von Winterfeldt [1980] calls problem structuring the most difficult part of decision analysis. Structuring translates an initially ill-defined problem into a set of well-defined elements, relations, and operations. This chapter presents procedures centering around those published by Keeney [1992]. Note that the presentation in this chapter is greatly simplified from that which Keeney presented, and is filtered through the biases of this author.

Before we discuss hierarchies and their structure, we should give some basic definitions. Following Keeney and Raiffa [1976], the following definitions are used:

- **Objective**—the preferred direction of movement on some measure of value
- **Attribute**—a dimension of measurement

Keeney and Raiffa distinguish between **utility** models, based upon tradeoffs of return and risk found in the von Neumann-Morgenstern utility theory and the more general **value** models allowing tradeoffs among any set of objectives and subobjectives. Finally, **preferential independence** concerns whether the decision maker's preference among attainment levels on two criteria do not depend on changes in other attribute levels. **Attribute independence** is a statistical concept measured by correlation. **Preferential independence** is a property of the desires of the decision maker, not the alternatives available.

Hierarchies

The simplest hierarchy would involve value as an objective with available alternatives branching from this value node. Hierarchies generally involve additional layers of objectives when the number of branches from any one node exceeds some certain value. Cognitive psychology has found that people are poor at assimilating large quantities of information about problems. Saaty [1988] used this concept as a principle in analytic hierarchy development, calling for a maximum of from five to nine branches in any one node in AHP. People cope with cognitive overload by employing heuristics that simplify the problem. Brownlow and Watson [1987] note that this can lead to selection of suboptimal alternatives. Structuring by decomposition tends to yield better decision performance.

Desirable characteristics of hierarchies given by chapter 2 of Keeney and Raiffa [1976] include:

- **Completeness**—Objectives should span all issues of concern to the decision maker, and attributes should indicate the degree to which each objective is met.
- **Operability**—Available alternatives should be characterized in an effective way.
- **Decomposability**—Preferential and certainty independence assumptions should be met.
- **Lack of Redundancy**—There should not be overlapping measures.
- **Size**—the hierarchy should include the minimum number of elements necessary.

Keeney [1992] and Saaty [1988] both suggest starting with identification of the overall fundamental objective. In the past, business leaders would focus on profit. Adam Smith long ago cited the desire to gain profit as the motivating force in the economy. However, while it is possible that this is the basic driving force for business organizations in a free-market economy, individuals have a need to consider a more fundamental value function, trading off profit and other considerations (Dyer and Sarin [1979]). Keeney [1992] states that the overall objective can be the combination of more specific fundamental objectives, such as minimizing costs, minimizing detrimental health impacts, and minimizing negative environmental impacts. For each fundamental objective, Keeney suggests the question, "Is it important?"

Subordinate to fundamental objectives are means objectives—ways to accomplish the fundamental objectives. Means objectives should be mutually exclusive and collectively exhaustive with respect to fundamental objectives. When asked "Why is it important?", means objectives would be those objectives for which a clear reason relative to fundamental objectives appears. If no clear reason other than "It just is" appear, the objective probably should be a fundamental objective. Available alternatives are the bottom level of the hierarchy, measured on all objectives immediately superior. If alternative performance on an objective is not measurable, Keeney suggests dropping that objective. Value judgments are required for fundamental objectives, and judgments about facts required for means-ends objectives.

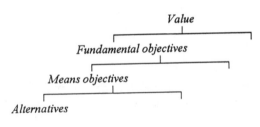

A fundamental premise of Keeney's book [1992] is that decision makers should not settle for those alternatives that are thrust upon them. The conventional solution process is to generate alternative solutions to a problem, and then focus on objectives. This framework tends to suppose an environment where decision makers are powerless to do anything but choose among given alternatives. It is suggested that a more fruitful approach would be for decision makers to (1) take more control over this process, and (2) use objectives to create alternatives, based on (3) what the decision makers would like to achieve, and (4) why the objectives are important. For more complete consideration of this intriguing and promising approach, it is suggested that you read Chapter 3 of Keeney's 1992 book.

Attributes

Measurement of objective achievement may require creation of intermediate or indirect attributes. Attributes should be measurable. They should also describe possible consequences in order to provide a sound basis for value judgments about the desirability of objective attainment levels. Attributes should also be understandable to the decision maker.

Keeney calls those attributes that are commonly understood by all as natural attributes. An example of a natural attribute minimizing loss of pine forest would be acres of pine forest lost. But there may not be a natural attribute for all objectives.

Sometimes intermediate objectives can be constructed. For example, if the objective is to improve the image of the corporation, some other attribute can be constructed for this specific decision context. Keeney notes that the Dow Jones industrial average and the Richter scale started out as constructed attributes, although they have become so commonly used that they now are natural attributes.

If it is difficult to identify either a natural or a constructed attribute, a third alternative is a proxy attribute, or indirect measure. For instance, a useful objective is to minimize damage to historic buildings from acid rain. It is difficult to find a natural or constructed attribute for this concept. A proxy attribute for this case could be sulphur dioxide concentration measured in parts per million.

Hierarchy Development Process

Hierarchies can be developed in two basic manners: top-down or bottom-up. The most natural approach is to start at the top, identifying the decision maker's fundamental objective, and developing subelements of value, proceeding downward until all measures of value are included (weeding out redundancies and measures that do not discriminate among available alternatives). At the bottom of the hierarchy, available alternatives can be added. It is at this stage that Keeney [1992] suggests designing new and better alternatives. Keeney, et al. [1987] suggest the following phases in employing the top-down approach:

1. Ask for overall values.
2. Explain the meanings of initial value categories and interrelationships:
   (a) *What is meant* by this value?
   (b) *Why is this value important?*
   (c) *How do available options affect* attaining this *value?*
3. Get a list of concerns—as yet unstructured.

The aim of this approach is to gain as wide a spectrum of values as possible. Once they are attained, then the process of weeding and combining can begin.

The bottom-up approach also has relative advantages. This approach starts with given alternatives, and asks the decision maker to identify those features which make these alternatives good or bad choices. For instance, the decision maker would be asked for a list of those criteria that distinguish between available alternatives. The bottom-up approach will generate a large unstructured list of criteria of what makes a good or a bad choice. This leads to generation of a list of attributes, which can be clustered into groups of common elements, leading to potentially the same hierarchy as the top-down approach.

Buede [1986] discusses conditions under which either approach would be most advantageous. The top-down approach is most likely best when dealing with strategic decisions, where the available alternatives are not necessarily yet identified. The bottom-up approach works well when the set of alternatives are fairly well fixed and given, and the decision problem is to select from among them.

Suggestions for Cases where Preferential Independence is Absent

Keeney [1992, p. 166] suggests that if an independence assumption is found to be inappropriate, either a fundamental objective has boon overlooked or means objectives are being used as fundamental objectives. Therefore, identification of the absence of independence should lead to greater understanding of the decision maker's fundamental objectives. Keeney gives an example involving a consulting firm with the three objectives of maximizing retained earnings (O_1), maximizing salary increases of exempt employees (O_2), and maximizing salary increases of nonexempt employees (O_3). Assessments revealed that O_2 and O_3 were both preferentially independent of O_1, but that O_1 and O_2 were not preferentially independent of O_3, and that O_1 and O_3 were not preferentially independent of O_2. Further investigation revealed that if nonexempt employees received low raises, value assessments were such that less of retained earnings should be applied to increase exempt employee salaries. It was apparent that there was a fundamental equity objective that had not been included in the hierarchy.

Keeney also presented theories to explain other difficulties encountered in value analysis. For instance, sometimes decision makers may have difficulty expressing value tradeoffs among attributes. Keeney suggests that this may be due to a poor definition of attributes or the need to clarify underlying objectives. He gave a number of examples, including analysis of the impact of acid rain on an acre of forest versus an acre of lake. Decision makers had difficulty equating these two attributes. Keeney stated that the difficulty was surmounted by identifying the missing fundamental objective of the impact on employment.

Energy Hierarchies

The decision context of energy policy has been an especially fruitful area of multiobjective analysis. Four studies in four different countries, with four different purposes, are used to describe how objectives were treated and combined into hierarchies.

Gillmor [1987] Irish Energy Policy

Gillmor reported a framework of guidance provided by the Republic of Ireland for evaluation of energy policy decisions. Here, eight broad objectives were given without subdivision at this stage. These eight objectives were:

1. Optimum **development of indigenous resources**
2. **Security of supply** by diversification of sources
3. **Stockpiling** of fuel
4. Access to the **cheapest markets** for imported energy supplies
5. Promotion of **economy in fuel use**
6. Encouraging **exploration** for hydrocarbons and uranium
7. Participation in **research** aimed at discovering and developing new sources
8. Protection of the **environment**.

Gillmor went on to evaluate in general terms how different energy forms (hydroelectricity, peat, coal, oil, and natural gas) available to Ireland rated on each of these objectives in general terms. This provides a means of developing policy guidelines, steering development of new sources to specific energy forms. But a specific decision framework was not given. For specific decisions, the hierarchy would at a minimum include specific sources available. Some of these eight objectives might be combined, such as development of indigenous resources, security of supply, and stockpiling, if the decision maker was interested in all three concepts from the standpoint of assured supplies of energy. The objectives of access to cheapest markets and economic use of fuels are uniquely different concepts, but both relate to economic matters. Therefore, they could logically be combined below a common superior element in the hierarchy. Similarly, encouraging exploration and conducting research for new forms of energy are different ways to seek a larger supply base, and could logically be combined into an overall development objective. If different concepts were intended by each of these three objectives, they would be preferentially independent and should be left as separate branches below a common superior node.

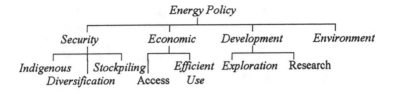

If the subobjectives of security overlapped in intent (they were not preferentially independent), the three objectives could be replaced by one branch—assured supplies.

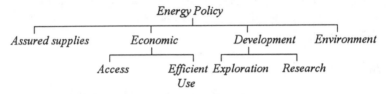

This hierarchy required top-down development, because available alternatives are not necessarily all known. This is also appropriate because of the strategic nature of the problem environment. The hierarchy could be used for an intermediate policy decision of determining which forms of energy to pursue, as well as the starting point for subsequent decision making about which specific projects for increased energy production might be appropriate.

Hämäläinen [1988] Finnish energy policy

Hämäläinen's study went a step beyond Gillmor's, in that a decision support system was developed to aid the policy issue of which source of energy to encourage. The Finnish Department of Energy conducted studies indicating that new sources of power would be required in the mid-1990s. Three general forms of energy were considered: (1) use of large nuclear plants; (2) use of large coal plants; and (3) adoption of conservation policies and small decentralized power plants. A 1983 poll indicated that fewer than 50% of the population supported nuclear power. In 1984, two power companies applied for a license to construct nuclear plants. Parliament, with the final approval authority, was split on the issue, which involved technically difficult questions and a continuous flow of new and contradictory information. Hämäläinen was asked to develop a decision aid, which he developed around an AHP model with the following hierarchy:

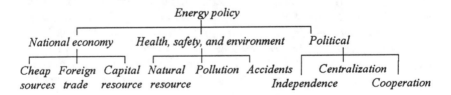

Here the nine subordinate objectives were all represented by measurable attributes. Further, the nine subordinate objectives were all independent concepts. In this case, there were three alternatives generated using a top-down approach. Alternatives generated for parliament to consider were: (1) a 1000 megawatt nuclear plant **N**; (2) two 500-megawatt coal-fired plants **C**; and (3) adoption of a philosophy of conservation with construction of small plants **S**.

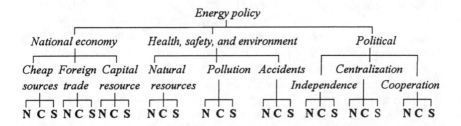

The decision aid that was developed was actually used by members of Parliament as well as representatives of interest groups. The specific decision intended was for Parliament to pass a resolution indicating what type of power sources should be pursued for future expansion. However, the vote was precluded by events at Chernobyl, USSR, in 1986.

Kok [1986] Dutch Energy Policy

Kok reported the application of multiple objective programming models to aid a similar energy policy decision, specifically a long-term planning model of the Dutch energy system. Representatives of five organizations (Federation of Netherlands Industries, Netherlands Trade Union Federation, Centre for Energy Conservation—an environmentalist body, Ministry of Housing, and Ministry of Economic Affairs) were given responsibility for energy planning. After three sessions of discussion, nine objectives were generated:

1. Minimize costs in specific monetary units
2. Minimize sulphur dioxide (SO_2) in kilotons
3. Minimize nitrous oxides (NOx) in kilotons
4. Minimize nuclear generation in megawatts
5. Maximize renewable energy in physical terms
6. Maximize profits from Dutch natural gas produced in monetary units
7. Minimize Dutch natural gas used in billion cubic meters
8. Minimize oil imports in thousand tons
9. Minimize fossil fuels used in physical terms

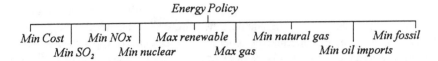

These objectives include some overlapping terms. One could argue that minimization of sulphur dioxide and nitrous oxides were important for the same reason that pollution should be reduced. They are different measures, and may not be correlated over the data set of available alternatives. But preferentially, they probably represent the same concept. On the other hand, Objective 6 involved maximization of profits from Dutch natural gas, while Objective 7 sought minimization of Dutch natural gas used. Preferentially, these are different concepts. Barring radical changes in pricing schemes, there is probably a very high negative correlation between the two objectives, so statistically they are dependent. But the hierarchy is for the preference structure of the decision maker, and these objectives could well be preferentially independent.

AHP was first applied with the group of representatives. This resulted in radically different weights for each of the five committee members. The aggregation of these weights for the group resulted in yet a sixth radically different set of weights. All six sets of weights were used in a mathematical programming model, generating six diverse energy plans.

The group decided to take a closer look at their weights. The hierarchy was trimmed because all group members had given relatively low weights to four of the objectives. This resulted in a reduced hierarchy:

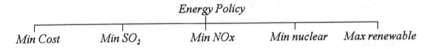

This hierarchy still contained the probably overlapping preference concepts relating to pollution, but had the advantage of simplicity. Criteria that were not relevant (because they had little weight) were eliminated. This study was not totally successful, because the groups held strongly opposing views. But the model hierarchy gave the decision makers a framework of analysis, enabling them to better understand the problem. This application demonstrates complications involved in conflict decision environments.

Keeney, Renn, and von Winterfeldt [1987] German Energy Planning

A comprehensive and politically legitimate list of criteria to evaluate energy systems was developed from interviews with representatives from a broad spectrum of West German society in the 1980s. The intention was to include a wide spectrum of views of energy systems into a value tree for energy policy evaluation. The organizations that participated were the Association of German Industries, the

German Society for Nature Protection, an electrical producer, the German Catholic and German Lutheran churches, the Society of German Engineers, a power plant producer, the Federation of German Labor Unions, and an organization of several ecological institutes. Discussions were held with small groups of one to three representatives from each of the nine organizations. In order to reduce the likelihood of omitting significant values, both top-down and bottom-up approaches were employed.

Very thorough lists of criteria for each of the nine groups were obtained, falling into a three-level value tree of general criteria, fundamental objectives, and means objectives. Criteria were eliminated that were not value relevant. Other criteria were added to fill holes in the value tree. Criteria were then aggregated into groups. As a check, Keeney, et al. employed a series of checks:

- Do criteria explain general value, or are they subordinate?
- Are any criteria in more than one superior category? (to identify interdependencies which can then be avoided)
- Is the list of criteria exhaustive?
- Are there any redundant criteria?

The general criteria corresponded to the four criteria of the government commission for which the study was designed (economics, environmental compatibility, social compatibility, and international compatibility), but expanded these top layer objectives to eight to cover the diversity of fundamental objectives given by the nine groups. There was substantial agreement among groups on general value categories. When overlap between some general criteria across groups was identified, a general criterion for each was employed, resulting in eight general criteria:

1. Financial, technical, and material requirements
2. Security of energy supplies
3. National economic impacts
4. Impacts on the natural environment
5. Health and safety
6. Social impacts
7. Political impacts
8. International impacts

There were 85 second and third level criteria that were logically fitted to these eight general criteria. A number of shifts of lower level criteria within some hierarchical elements were necessary. Once the second level elements were identified, they were clustered into logical packages, yielding 21 second level criteria. Then the remaining 64 criteria were grouped under the second level, with additional clustering.

The use of the combined value tree was to form an overall framework within which energy policy questions could be debated. There would likely continue to be conflicts between groups. But areas of agreement and disagreement could be identified, which could be used as the basis for devising compromises and seeking joint gains in the negotiation process.

Conclusions

Structuring of a value hierarchy is a relatively subjective activity, with a great deal of possible latitude. It is good to have a complete hierarchy, including everything that could be of importance to the decision maker. However, this yields unworkable analyses, a prime example of analysis paralysis. Hierarchies should focus on those criteria that are important in discriminating among available alternatives. The key to hierarchy structuring is to identify those criteria that are most important to the decision maker, and that will help the decision maker make the required choice.

Keeney's approach to this dilemma is to generate as thorough a list as possible, and then go back and weed out redundancies as well as those criteria that are unimportant for the specific decision. This is clearly the safest path. It also tends to much larger hierarchies, in part attested to by reviewing the four energy cases.

There are two ways to begin development of hierarchies. The top-down approach works well for strategic problems, where there is some freedom available to design alternatives. The bottom-up approach is more appropriate for decisions where alternatives are imposed. The bottom-up approach will have fewer efforts devoted to criteria that are equally attained by the alternatives available.

References

Buede, D.M. 1986. Helping the decision maker to choose between alternatives. *Interfaces* 16:2, 52–68.

Brownlow, S.A. and S.R. Watson. 1987. Structuring multi-attribute value hierarchies. *Journal of the Operational Research Society* 38:4, 309–317.

Dyer, J.S. and Sarin, R.K. 1979. Measurable multiattribute value functions. *Operations Research* 27:4, 810–822.

Gillmor, D.A. (August) 1987. Objectives in Irish energy policy. *Energy Policy*, 363–375.

Hämäläinen, R.P. 1988. Computer assisted energy policy analysis in the parliament of Finland. *Interfaces* 18:4, 12–25.

Keeney, R.L. 1992. *Value-focused thinking: A path to creative decisionmaking*. Cambridge, MA: Harvard University Press.

Keeney, R.L. and Raiffa, H. 1976. *Decisions with multiple objectives: Preferences and value tradeoffs*. New York: John Wiley & Sons.

Keeney, R.L., Renn, O., and von Winterfeldt, D. 1987. Structuring Germany's energy objectives. *Energy Policy* 15, 352–362.

Kok, M. 1986. The interface with decision makers and some experimental results in interactive multiple objective programming methods. *European Journal of Operational Research* 26, 96–107.

Saaty, T.L. 1988. *Decision making for leaders: The analytic hierarchy process for decisions in a complex world*, Pittsburgh: RWS Publications.

Von Winterfeldt, D. 1980. Structuring decision problems for decision analysis. *Acta Psychologica* 45, 71–93.

3
Multiattribute Utility Theory

The utility theory approach is an attempt to rigorously apply objective measurement to decision making. Also known as the decision analysis method, the principle behind utility theory is that if alternative performances on concrete, measurable attributes are compared in a rational, unbiased manner, sounder decisions will result. The value of an alternative is assumed to consist of measures over the criteria that contribute to worth, all converted to a common scale of **utils**. Each alternative's performance on each criterion is assumed known. Possible attainments on each criterion are measured by a single-measure utility function (**SUF**). These measures have the characteristic that more of a good is better than less (and conversely, less of an evil is better than more). While continuous scales of value are not required of alternatives, the measurement of their value is considered continuous. Once the single-measure utility functions are identified, the value of an alternative is measurable by an overall utility function, which weights each of the criteria of value. This weighting does not necessarily have to be linear. The following case demonstrates the kind of problem where utility analysis can be applied.

Case: Nuclear Depository Siting

Ralph Keeney   Multiobjective Conference—Bangkok—6 December 1989

The Department of Energy faced the problem of picking a site to dump nuclear wastes. This was expected to involve an investment of about $25 to $250 billion. Using their own methods, the agency selected Hanford, Washington, the site of one of the first nuclear power stations in the country.

The decision received some criticism, because the analysis treated rankings as if they were ratings. Alternatives were weighted, scored, and then ranked. This disregarded the interactions among criteria. The Government Accounting Office reviewed the decision process. The National Science Foundation severely criticized the process, and recommended the use of multiple attribute utility theory (MAUT). Subsequently, the Department of Energy commissioned a MAUT analysis, obtaining the services of Keeney and his associates.

The study was commissioned to illuminate issues with the intention of providing insights rather than making the final decision. The problem involved multiple impacts, with many uncertainties. The measures of value were crucial to determining the relative advantage of alternative sites. The commission included the charge to somehow aggregate the value of alternatives, which involved vexing tradeoffs. MAUT was considered appropriate for this application because of its ability to separate facts and values, insuring that hard data did not drive out soft data. Explicit professional judgments could be identified, making rational peer review possible. Fourteen criteria were identified and arranged in a hierarchy. Such criteria should be independent for application of MAUT, so those criteria which overlapped were condensed. Each alternative's value on each criterion were measured with a metric that made sense relative to the decision. For instance, the measure of radiation impact was in expected deaths rather than in rads.

A utility function was developed through interviewing policy makers using market basket tradeoffs. For each criterion, disfunction was measured over a range from 0 to the maximum disbenefit expected from all alternatives. The relative disfunction of public fatalities versus worker fatalities was explored. Additionally, the dollar value of fatalities was examined through market basket tradeoffs. Keeney noted that the four policy makers who conducted the tradeoff analysis tended to share organizational policy, or take on the moral judgments of the agency they worked for. The functions tended to be linear. Keeney concluded that if an issue is important, and involved the public, the function should be linear. He also commented that for important problems, there should not be any noted intransitivity. The analysis yielded a disutility formula of the type:

$$\text{disutility} = a - 1/b[\Sigma_m \, K_i \, C_i(X_i)] \text{ for m criteria, alternative } i$$

where a and b are constants, C_i = % of range

The analysis started with the easy judgments. The disutility aggregation was made the sum of component scores. Each alternative was ranked on each criterion.[1]

The method used was very appropriate for dealing with uncertainties. Many interest groups were involved. The methodology kept the analysis clear and explicit, separating means from ends, thus making it possible to explain the procedure to each interest group. The study ranked five alternative sites. Hanford was ranked fifth of the five. The Department of Energy decided to select two or three alternative sites, including Hanford. The intention was to start each project and simulate more detailed aspects of the analysis as real data became available.

Multiple Attribute Utility Theory

The basic hypothesis of MAUT is that in any decision problem, there exists a real valued function U defined on the set of feasible alternatives which the decision maker wishes, consciously or not, to maximize. This function aggregates the criteria g_1, g_2..., g_k. The role of the analyst is to determine this function. Bunn [1984] presented the following theoretical assumptions of utility.

● **Structure** The choices available to the decision maker can be sufficiently

---

[1]Merkhofer, M.W. & Keeney, R.L., A multiattribute utility analysis of alternative sites for the disposal of nuclear waste, *Risk Analysis* 7:2 [1987] 173-194.

Keeney, R.L., An analysis of the portfolio of sites to characterize for selecting a nuclear repository, *Risk Analysis* 7:2 [1987] 195-218.

Gregory, R. & Lichtenstein, S., A review of the high-level nuclear waste repository siting analysis, *Risk Analysis* 7:2 [1987] 219-223.

described by the payoff values and associated probabilities of those choices. This implies that the value of a choice consists of the choice's measures on factors of value to the decision maker.

- **Ordering** The decision maker can express preference or indifference between any pair of tradeoffs.
- **Reduction of Compound Prospects** Decision makers are indifferent between compound prospects and their equivalent simple prospects. This implies that decision makers give no value to playing the game, or gambling, or working in a business that is exciting because it is risky.
- **Continuity** Every payoff can be considered to be a certainty equivalent for the prospect of some probability **p** of the worst outcome and the inverse probability (1-**p**) of the best outcome. This assumption implies that severe outcomes would be risked at some small probability.
- **Substitutability** Any prospect can be substituted for by its certainty equivalent.
- **Transitivity of Prospects** Decision makers can express preference or indifference between all pairs of prospects. This extends the assumption of ordering of payoffs to prospects.
- **Monotonicity** For two options with the same payoffs, decision makers should prefer the option with the higher probability of the better payoff. Cases where this is not demonstrated imply that there is some other factor of value that has not been considered.

Bunn also discusses some of the caveats of utility theory. Utility theory is normative, describing how decision makers *should* behave. Many decision makers, some successful, behave in ways that are notably in violation of the above assumptions. There are also a number of other features of utility that need to be considered. Utility values are not necessarily additive. $U(A + B)$ may be $\neq U(A) + U(B)$. This means that utility functions can curve, which seems entirely reasonable. Utility theory provides a numerical scale to order preferences, not to measure their strengths. And of course, utilities are personal attributes, which do not carry over to other people.

The concept of preferential independence can be demonstrated with a simple example case. Given four choices over three measures:

	g_1	g_2	g_3	
A	45	100	70	more is better than less for g_1, g_2 and g_3
B	45	100	90	
C	50	80	70	
D	50	80	90	If $A \succ C$, then $B \succ D$ where $\succ$ indicates "is preferred to"

Preferences between actions that are only different on a subset of criteria do not depend on their values on the other criteria. If there exist K increasing functions U_n such that $U = U_1(g_1) + U_2(g_2) + \ldots + U_n(g_n)$ then for every criterion, that criterion is preferentially independent. For every efficient solution A, there is a set of weights λ_k such that for increasing functions, Max $\Sigma_k \lambda_k g(k)$ yields A if criteria are preferentially independent. The tradeoff between criteria i and j under preferential independence is expressed:

$$w_{ij} = [\partial U/\partial g_j]/[\partial U/\partial g_i]$$

Note that functions are viewed as **utility functions** when they are based upon tradeoffs identified through risk lotteries. When they are directly assessed with techniques not using risk lotteries, they are conventionally called **value functions**. Utility functions and value functions operate precisely the same way once functions are identified.

Logical Decision is a package supporting decision making by applying the concepts of utility theory. The package provides an effective means of defining the goal structure of criteria, the alternative choices available and their measures on criteria, and a means of assessing preference for individual decision makers. The operation of this software package will be described through three example problems. The first is a simple value tradeoff between salary and risk of job loss. This will be followed by a case involving site selection for a nuclear waste center, involving a set of independent criteria. The last case, selection of a house, involves interactions among criteria.

Tradeoff Analysis

Perhaps the easiest aspect of utility to understand is the tradeoff between pay and risk. Consider jobs with salaries in the $30,000 to $100,000 per year range, as well as the probability of getting canned (assuming your most prudent efforts) or the folding of your employer. Further assume a fairly difficult employment market, so that you would not have bright prospects of replacing the job that was lost.

Name	Salary	Risk of Loss
Job 1	30,000	.01
Job 2	40,000	.02
Job 3	50,000	.04
Job 4	60,000	.07
Job 5	70,000	.11
Job 6	80,000	.16
Job 7	90,000	.22
Job 8	100,000	.30

The Problem

The problem is simple, in that tradeoffs among only two criteria need to be considered. Further, we assume no interaction between these criteria (they are considered independent), implying that each salary amount has value regardless of the risk level, and that each level of lack of risk has a value regardless of the salary level. Each criterion is assumed to have a value scale that is insatiable. This implies that the utility value for any particular salary is less than the utility value of any other higher salary. However, the analysis will be limited to reasonably available (or acceptable) alternatives. This allows us to assign a value of 1.0 for a salary of 100,000, and a value of 0 to a salary of 30,000. It is also assumed here that .01 is the best risk possible (value of 1.0), while a risk of .3 is the worst reasonably available risk probability (value of 0).

The *Logical Decision* package is accessed. The initial menu you will see is the **Main Menu**, allowing the opening of an existing file. Select **Files** from the **Main**

Menu. A menu of existing *Logical Decision* files on your disk will be displayed, with the .LD filename extension. Initially, of course, there will be no existing file for a given problem. When you complete an analysis, you can save the file with any name and the .LD extension.

Defining Alternatives

The **Main Menu** allows for definition of alternatives by accessing the **Alternatives** lines on the main menu. This gives a menu including the ability to **Add an Alternative**. The name of the alternative is asked for. Any name scheme can be used. The initial alternative here could be called *Job 1*, for instance. You will then be asked for the measure levels for the alternative. Initially, you can skip entering measures, and enter these after goals are defined. You have options available to edit the alternatives as well. All eight alternative names can be entered at this stage. Return to the main menu when this task is completed.

Defining Goals

The next task is to define the goals, or objectives, of the analysis. Here we have an intentionally simple tradeoff between salary and risk. The current version of the software will give trouble if a goal is stated without a subordinate goal. Therefore, our hierarchy will consist of the overall goal (value) with the subordinate **measures**, salary and risk.

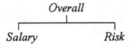

Notice that the objectives of salary and risk are entered as measures, not as goals. This is necessary in order to be able to conduct tradeoff assessments with *Logical Decision*. From the Goals Menu, **Add a Goal** is selected, and in response to the prompts the name *Overall*. The default nominal utility of 1 will be selected. **Return to Main Menu** is then selected.

Measures for Goals

The next task is to enter the measures for goals. From the main menu, the **Measures** menu is selected. From this menu, **Add a Measure** is selected. The first measure defined is *Salary*, which is given the units *Thousand dollars* with a worst measure of 30 and a best measure of 100. Cutoffs are allowed, which treat anything worse than the cutoff as 0 utility. If no such cutoff limits apply, the default can be selected. You are then asked if you wish to enter the measure values for the defined alternatives. This is how the database of alternative scores is developed. The second measure, *Risk*, is also added. When asked for units, *Probability* can be used. The best measure is 0 and the worst measure 1. The default cutoff can be used. Data values for the eight alternatives can now be entered.

Preference Sets

The next task is to enter preference sets. Preference sets are a function of individuals. *Logical Decision* allows multiple users to apply their preference function over the same problem data set. **Add a Preference Set** is a means to identify an individual user. Here we will define two users, working together, one more risk averse than the other. These users will be imaginatively named *one* (more risk averse) and *two*. Only one preference set is active at a time.

To define preference functions, **Measure Preferences** is selected from the main menu. This gives the option of **Assess SUF**. *Logical Decision* provides a very easy means of defining an individual's scale of value for any objective. The base values of 1.0 (best score) and 0 (worst score) are set based upon the entries given when goals were defined. A number of value forms are available. The simplest, a linear function, is the default function. However, a curvilinear function (using the functional form $U(x) = a + b\,e^{-cx}$) can be generated when the user simply sets the midpoint of this curve (the midpoint being the criterion measure yielding a utility of .5). If the midpoint is set left of center on the criterion measurement scale, the curve will have declining rates of return for larger values. If the midpoint is set right of center on the criterion measurement scale, the curve will have increasing rates of return for larger values. More complex curves can be generated by splitting ranges. The same functional form is used for each range segment, but the midpoint for each of these segments can be set by the user.

User One

For user *one*, we will use a midpoint for *Salary* of 60, and a midpoint for *Risk* of .1. This will give a very slight decreasing return to scale for salary, and a very steep inverse curve reflecting risk aversion. The utility contribution formulas for salary of $U(\mathbf{salary}) = 2.274 - 2.915\,e^{-.008277\mathrm{sal}}$ and $U(\mathbf{risk}) = -.0009872 + 1.001\,e^{-6.922\mathrm{risk}}$. For the alternative with a salary of 90 thousand and risk of .22, $U(\mathbf{salary}) = .8901$ and $U(\mathbf{risk}) = .2173$.

Importance of Objectives

The next task is to define the relative importance of objectives. From the main menu, the **Goal Preferences** menu is selected. The option **Assess Tradeoffs** gives a means to define the relative importances of measures and goals by asking tradeoffs questions. You are asked to select a measure or goal that has not yet been included in a tradeoff. In this simple example, there are only two measures to tradeoff. A graph with the 2 measures is presented, where the horizontal axis represents the range of the first measure, and the vertical axis represents the range of the second measure. Each point on the graph represents a simplified hypothetical alternative with the corresponding attainment levels indicated. Crosses represent the attainments of the alternatives defined in the database of alternatives. A hypothetical alternative with the most preferred level of attainment on the first measure and the least preferred attainment on the second measure is labeled *Alternative A*. The opposite situation is labeled *Alternative B*. You are asked which of these alternatives is preferred. If equal preference is indicated, the criterion measures are weighted equally. If one or the other alternative is preferred, you are asked to improve the attainment on one of the criteria for the alternative not selected until the preference between alternatives is equal.

User One

For demonstration purposes, assume decision maker one preferred the salary of 100 thousand with associated risk of 1.0 over the option with a salary of 30 thousand and a risk of 0 [*Salary* = 100, *Risk* = 1] > [*Salary* = 30, *Risk* = 0]. The system now asks the decision maker to increase the salary of the second option (with a risk of 0) until it is equally attractive with the first option. In this case, assume the decision maker set the second salary at 45 thousand [*Salary* = 100, *Risk* = 1] ≈ [*Salary* = 45, *Risk* = 0]. The system now takes this value and adjusts the relative weights of the measures salary and risk by solving the following:

The user states that w_{salary} U(45 thousand) + w_{risk} U(0.0) = w_{salary} U(100 thousand) + w_{risk} U(1.0). This equates to .2655 w_{salary} + 1 w_{risk} = 1 w_{salary} + 0 w_{risk}, which simplifies to w_{salary} = 1.3615 w_{risk} It is also known that w_{salary} + w_{risk} = 1 (if we assume value does not depend on interactions between salary and risk). Solving these simultaneously, w_{salary} = .5765 and w_{risk} = .4235.

Therefore, for the alternative with a salary of 90 thousand and risk of .22, the overall utility calculation is

$$.5765 \times (.8901) + .4235 \times (.2173) = .6052.$$

Apply Formula—User One

The last step is to apply the utility formula over the entire set of alternatives. This is accomplished by accessing the **Results** menu from the main menu, and selecting **Rank Alternatives**. This quickly gives the following table of scores:

Alternative	Salary	Risk	Utility
Job 8	100	.30	.6293
Job 7	90	.22	.6052
Job 6	80	.16	.5839
Job 5	70	.11	.5671
Job 4	60	.07	.5490
Job 3	50	.04	.5210
Job 2	40	.02	.4728
Job 1	30	.01	.3951

Note that these results are explained solely by the ranking of salary (or the inverse of the risk ranking).

User Two

Assume a second user of the system with different inputs for assessing single measure utility functions as well as a different input for the multiple measure value function.

The second user is defined by accessing the **Preference Set** option from the main menu, and **Add a Preference Set**. This user will be defined as *two*. Returning to the main menu, **Measure Preferences** is selected, followed by **Assess SUFs**. For *Salary*, the utility midpoint is set at 40 thousand, yielding the SUF $U(\textbf{salary}) = 1.008 - 7.87\ e^{-.06849sal}$. For *Risk*, the utility midpoint is set at .4, yielding the SUF $U(\textbf{risk}) = -.784 + 1.784\ e^{-.8222rlsk}$. Next the combined effect of **salary** and **risk** need to be assessed by accessing the **Goal Preferences** option from the main menu, from which the **Assess Tradeoffs** option is selected. User two prefers the hypothetical option with salary of 30 thousand and risk of 0.0 over the option with salary 100 thousand and risk 1.0 [30 0] > [100 1], and is asked to increase the risk of the first option until the utility of the two options are the same. User two settles on a salary level of 100 thousand and risk 0.2 as equal in value to the salary of 30 thousand and risk of 0.0 [100 .2] ≈ [30 0]. Given that $w_{\textbf{salary}} + w_{\textbf{rlsk}} = 1$ and that $u_{risk}(.2) = .7295$, this yields scaling constants of $w_{\textbf{salary}} = .2129$ and $w_{\textbf{risk}} = .7871$. Accessing **Results** from the main menu, the following utility scores are obtained:

Alternative	Salary	Risk	Utility
Job 3	50	.04	.9018
Job 4	60	.07	.8957
Job 2	40	.02	.8706
Job 5	70	.11	.8665
Job 6	80	.16	.8217
Job 1	30	.01	.7756
Job 7	90	.22	.7659
Job 8	100	.30	.6931

Note that this decision maker is much more risk averse than the first decision maker.

Nuclear Dump Site Selection

The next example involves categorical criteria. The scenario is to select a nuclear dump site. Criteria considered include cost, expected lives lost, risk of catastrophe, and civic improvement. Expected lives lost reflects workers as well as expected local (civilian bystander) lives lost. The hierarchy of objectives is:

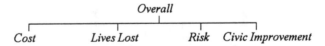

The alternatives available, with measures on each criterion (including two categorical measures) are:

	Cost (billions)	Expected Lives Lost	Risk	Civic Improvement
Nome, AK	40	60	very high	low
Newark, NJ	100	140	very low	very high
Rock Springs, WY	60	40	low	high
Duquesne, PA	60	40	medium	medium
Gary, IN	70	80	low	very high

The alternatives, goals, and measures can be entered as in the prior example. *Cost*, *Lives Lost*, *Risk*, and *Civic Improvement* are entered as measures. The assessment of preferences would be the next step. The SUFs for the continuous scale measures (*Cost* and *Lives Lost*) are entered by selecting the midpoint. In the example, the midpoints selected were 85 billion dollars for *Cost*, and 35 expected *Lives Lost*.

Entering categorical utilities is easiest by determining the utility of each category before going to the system, and entering these values as data for the categorical measure. For instance, the *Risk* categories for the five alternatives include very high, medium, low, and very low risk assessments. The most favorable category is very low risk. This can be assigned a utility of 1. The worst case is very high risk, which can be assigned a utility of 0. Medium risk can be assigned any value between 0 and 1 (.5 would indicate exactly in the middle of the value scale). The same is true for low risk, although care should be taken that the utility for this category remains between that of medium and very low risk. We will use a linear scale for *Risk* (you can always reflect the value of discrete outcomes in a linear fashion). *Logical Decision* develops a curve for whatever scale is used. The same process applies to the category of *Civic Improvement*. Here we can assume utility of 1.0 for very high civic improvement, .75 for high improvement, .5 for medium, .25 for low, and 0 utility for very low improvement.

The next step is to assess tradeoffs among measures and goals. *Logical Decision* asks you to select a base measure for comparison. *Cost* seems an appropriate base, because it demonstrates well the concept of utility that requires identification of commonality. Utility could be viewed as putting all measures on a common scale. The same idea is true when one states that everything has its price. The default in *Logical Decision* is linear tradeoff. An important consideration to remember, however, is that the tradeoffs in utility are not required to be linear.

Cost can be compared to the other measures, such as *Risk* and *Civic Improvement*. When compared with *Risk*, the pair [*Cost* = 100, *Risk* = 0] was selected over the pair [*Cost* = 0, *Risk* = 1]. The system then asked how much risk in the second pair would have to be lowered to equal the utility of the pair [*Cost* = 100, *Risk* = 1]. A risk of .4 was entered, implying $U([100,0]) \approx U([0,.4])$.

For the cost/civic improvement tradeoff, the pair [*Cost* = 0, *Civic Improvement* = 0] was selected over the pair [*Cost* = 100, *Civic Improvement* = 1]. When asked how much cost needed to be lowered to equal the value of the first pair, the response was 30, implying $U([0,0]) \approx U([30,1])$.

The system now can apply the implied formulas to the available alternatives. Since the criteria in this case are assumed independent, there is no need to explore the contingent interactions, yielding an additive multiattribute utility function. The system yielded the following parameters:

Measure	a	b	c	Weight
Cost	1.011	−.01067	−.04551	.1333
Lives Lost	−.09575	1.096	.01741	.5293
Risk	1	−1	0	.3333
Civic Improvement	0	1	0	.0041

Applied to the data set of criteria attainment, the following utilities were obtained.

The *Logical Decision* system has the ability to express everything in terms of a specific measure, such as cost, which is also given.

Alternative	Utility	Equivalent Cost
Rock Springs	.6043	123.753 billion
Duquesne	.5200	127.985 "
Gary	.4478	131.055 "
Newark	.3374	135.050 "
Nome	.2803	136.861 "

An additional feature of *Logical Decision* is sensitivity analysis. For instance, by looking at the sensitivity of the solution to *Cost*, a graph is provided demonstrating the relative positions of all five alternatives for various weights on *Cost*. In this case, one could see that the Nome option would improve its relative position as *Cost* received heavier weight, but that Rock Springs would still be the preferred choice until a very heavy weight was given to *Cost*. When *Lives Lost* weights were varied, Rock Springs continued to be the first choice until the maximum possible weight was given to *Lives Lost*, and Duquesne's score equalled that of Rock Springs. When the weight for *Risk* was varied to very high levels, Newark became the first choice. When *Civic Improvement* was given very high weights, Gary became the first choice.

House Selection

The last example we will present involves contingent tradeoffs. The context is purchase of a house. Criteria considered include monetary considerations (*Fiscal*—consisting of *Payment* as well as *Investment*), *Appearance*, and *Convenience* (consisting of distance to *School* and distance to *Work*). There are two contingent tradeoffs, acting in different ways. The first tradeoff is for the *Fiscal* goal. The decision maker would like the monthly *Payment* to be as low as possible. On the other hand, purchase of the house as an *Investment*, anticipating increase in the value of the house over time, has an opposing effect. As the value of the house goes up, *Investment* becomes more attractive. The hierarchy of goals and measures is:

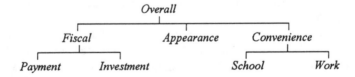

There are five alternatives under consideration. Alternatives and measures are:

Alternative (units)	Payment (dollars)	Investment (thousand dollars)	Appearance (categorical)	School (blocks)	Work (miles)
Ramshackle	400	50	0	1	10
Baltic Avenue	500	55	.2	8	3
Tennessee Avenue	650	70	.5	7	15
Illinois Avenue	800	90	.6	15	25
Park Place	1000	120	.9	12	45

Assume that the single-attribute utility functions are based upon setting midpoint utility levels as follows:

Attribute	Minimum	Maximum	Midpoint	a	b	c	
Payment	1	1000	400	-.7768	1.778	.000828	dollars
Investment	0	120	80	-.309	.309	-.01203	1000 dollars
Appearance	0	1	.5	linear	—	—	categorical
School	1	15	4	-.05184	1.304	.215	blocks
Work	0	50	20	1.784	-1.784	.01644	miles

This approach applies the same procedure as was used in the nuclear siting example. The goal assessment tradeoffs used were:

1. *Payment—Investment* extreme selection was [1000 120] preferred over [1 0].(a) In the second vector, *Investment* was increased to 30 thousand [1 30] to be equivalent to the first vector.

2. Comparing *Appearance* and *Payment*, the vector [1 1000] was preferred over the vector [0 1]. *Appearance* was increased in the second vector to .4 [.4 1] to be equivalent to the preferred vector.

3. Comparing *Work* and *Payment*, the vector [0 1] was preferred to the vector [50 1000]. *Payment* in the second vector was decreased to 800 [50 800] to gain equivalent value with the vector [0 1].

4. In comparing *School* and *Work*, the vector [1 0] was preferred over the vector [15 50]. In the second vector, blocks were lowered from 15 to 6 [6 50] to gain equivalent value with [1 0].

The utility rankings for the alternatives are:

Alternative (Weight)	Payment .1688	Investment .1951	Appearance .2814	School .2096	Work .1452	Overall 1.0
Park Place	0	1	.9	.0470	.9328	.5936
Illinois Avenue	.1399	.6034	.6	0	.6014	.3975
Ramshackle	.5	.2549	0	1	.2705	.3830
Tennessee Avenue	.2612	.4083	.5	.2377	.39	.3709
Baltic Avenue	.3985	.2899	.2	.1817	.0859	.2306

Use of Interactions

The goal *Fiscal* can have a dependent curvature. A decision maker could view either a very low *Payment* or a very high *Investment* as preferable to intermediate values on both. This leads to **constructive** curvature (with a ∪ shape) of the value function.

The opposite effect is demonstrated by the *Convenience* goal. The decision maker wants the distance to school to be small, and the distance to work to be far (within reason). Here the two objectives are independent over alternatives (an alternative could have high values on both scales, or low values on both scales). But the overall value would be **destructive** (with a ∩ shape), in that a poor value on either measure would yield a low *Convenience* utility.

These concepts can be modeled using a multiplicative utility form. The standard form for multiplicative utility involves two types of parameters: K (**big K**) and k_j (**small ks**, one for each criterion). The functional form is:

$$U(x_j) = 1/K\{[\Pi_i\,(1 + Kk_iU(x_i)] - 1\}$$

This form has $n + 1$ parameters (n for each of the k_i, plus K). Available equations to allow determination of parameters are of three types.

I: for each of the tradeoffs between measures (and/or goals), MUF tradeoff information can be used. There is a slight difference from what we did in the linear case, because the interaction terms yield nonlinear relationships.

$$U = k_{pay}U(\text{pay}) + k_{inv}U(\text{inv}) + K \times k_{pay} \times U(\text{pay}) \times k_{inv} \times U(\text{inv})$$

When comparing the tradeoff between *Payment* and *Investment*, we stated that the value of [*Payment* = 1000, *Investment* = 120] was equal to the value of [*Payment* = 1, *Investment* = 30]. Given that the value of an investment of 30 thousand is .1343 (from the SUF):

$$U[1,30] = 1 \times k_{pay} + .1343 \times k_{inv} + K \times (1) \times k_{pay} \times (.1343) \times k_{inv};$$
$$\text{while } U[1000,120] = 0 \times k_{pay} + 1 \times k_{inv} + K \times 0 \times k_{pay} \times 1 \times k_{inv}.$$

These values are equal. Therefore, $k_{pay} -.8657\,k_{inv} + .1343K \times k_{pay} \times k_{inv} = 0$

II: *Payment* and *Investment* interactions are assessed by presenting a probabilistic tradeoff between a .5/.5 chance between the best of one factor and the worst of the other against a probability to be set by the decision maker for the best of both factors as opposed to 1 minus this probability chance of the worst on both factors. In this case the decision maker determined that a .85 probability of attaining the best on both factors was necessary to balance the value of a .5 probability of the extreme cases. This yields:

$$.5\ [Payment = 1, Investment = 0] + .5\ [Payment = 1000, Investment = 120]$$
$$= \textbf{prob .85} \times\ [Payment = 1, Investment = 120] +$$
$$(1 - .85) \times [Payment = 1000, Investment = 0].$$

This summarizes to: $.5\ (k_{pay}) + .5\ (k_{inv}) = .85$
III: Our last equation is:

$$1 + K = (1 + K \times k_{pay})(1 + K \times k_{inv}).$$

In this case, these three equations yield the parameters:

$$k_{pay} = .8392 \qquad k_{inv} = .8608 \qquad K = -.9690$$

U_x	U_y	$U_{overall}$	U_x	U_y	$U_{overall}$	U_x	U_y	$U_{overall}$
0	0	0	.4	0	.335	.8	0	.671
0	.2	.172	.4	.2	.452	.8	.2	.731
0	.4	.344	.4	.4	.568	.8	.4	.791
0	.6	.516	.4	.6	.684	.8	.6	.851
0	.8	.688	.4	.8	.800	.8	.8	.911
0	1	.860	.4	1	.916	.8	1	.972
.2	0	.168	.6	0	.503	1	0	.839
.2	.2	.312	.6	.2	.591	1	.2	.871
.2	.4	.456	.6	.4	.679	1	.4	.903
.2	.6	.600	.6	.6	.768	1	.6	.935
.2	.8	.744	.6	.8	.856	1	.8	.967
.2	1	.888	.6	1	.944	1	1	1.0

For the *Convenience* goal, the following assessments were made:

I: Value of [*School* = 1, *Work* = 0] = value of [*School* = 6, *Work* = 50] $1 \times k_{sch} + 0 \times k_{work} + K \times 1 \times k_{sch} \times 0 \times k_{work} = .3071 \times k_{sch} + 1 \times k_{work} + K \times .3071 \times k_{sch} \times 1 \times k_{work}$

II: Assume the decision maker weighs the probabilistic tradeoff between distance to school and work, and states:

.5[*School* = 1, *Work* = 0] + .5[*School* = 15, *Work* = 50] = **.30**[*School* = 1,*Work* = 50] + (1 − .30)[*School* = 15, *Work* = 0].

III: $1 + K = (1 + K \times k_{sch})(1 + K \times k_{work})$.

These equations yield:

$$k_{sch} = .427 \qquad k_{work} = .173 \qquad K = 5.41479$$

U_x	U_y	$U_{overall}$	U_x	U_y	$U_{overall}$	U_x	U_y	$U_{overall}$
0	0	0	.4	0	.171	.8	0	.342
0	.2	.035	.4	.2	.237	.8	.2	.440
0	.4	.069	.4	.4	.304	.8	.4	.539
0	.6	.104	.4	.6	.371	.8	.6	.637
0	.8	.138	.4	.8	.437	.8	.8	.736
0	1	.173	.4	1	.504	.8	1	.835
.2	0	.085	.6	0	.256	1	0	.427
.2	.2	.136	.6	.2	.338	1	.2	.542
.2	.4	.187	.6	.4	.421	1	.4	.656
.2	.6	.237	.6	.6	.504	1	.6	.771
.2	.8	.288	.6	.8	.587	1	.8	.885
.2	1	.338	.6	1	.669	1	1	1.0

In comparing these two sets of generated numbers, note that in the constructive case, the values of $U_{overall}$ are about twice as high as those for the destructive set. This higher value is even more pronounced for the case of $U_x = 0$. The values of the two sets converge when higher U values appear.

These interactions yielded the following:

Overall goal = $.6940 \times \{[(1 - .9690 \times .8392\ U_{pay})(1 - .9690 \times .8608\ U_{inv}) - 1]/(-.9690)\} + .1610\ U_{app} + .1450 \times \{[(1 + 5.4148 \times .427\ U_{sch})(1 + 5.4148 \times .173\ U_{work}) - 1]/5.4148\}$

For the available alternatives, this gives the following utilities:

Alternative	Overall Utility
Park Place	.7711
Illinois Avenue	.5126
Ramshackle	.4660
Tennessee Avenue	.4546
Baltic Avenue	.3956

Conclusions

Utility theory provides an accepted method to normatively analyze choice problems. The first focus is on identifying criteria of interest. This is much the same as in Analytic Hierarchy Process. A caveat is that care should be taken to select goals (and measures) which are as independent as possible. The analysis of a set of independent goals is much easier than for dependent goal sets. Interactions between goals (or measures) can be modeled.

A small sample of the theory of multiattribute utility theory is provided by Keeney and Raiffa [1976], Dyer and Sarin [1979], and Keeney [1992]. There have been many reported applications of multiattribute utility theory, many of which extend beyond risk to consideration of multiple criteria. Bodily [1977] presented a very useful description of an application, which can serve as a practical guide for implementation. Corner and Kirkwood [1991] give a very thorough review of applications through 1989. The entire issue of *Interfaces* **22**:6, November–December 1992, is devoted to decision and risk analysis, including a report of DuPont's experiences applying risk analysis (Krumm and Rolle [1992]), and an interesting group decision in Hungary (Vári and Vecsenyi [1992]).

Once the goal hierarchy is developed, the next step is to identify the relative utilities of each measure. A standard functional form of the type $U(x) = a + b\,e^{-cx}$ has proven to fit commonly encountered risk averse human decision makers. *Logical Decision* software makes fitting such a curve very easy, requiring that the decision maker only identify the x value yielding the midpoint of utility value. More complex curves can also be developed using *Logical Decision*.

The last step of developing the utility formula is to identify the relative contribution to value of goals and measures. The conventional means of developing these tradeoffs is through probabilistic lotteries. The first lottery is the sum of a .5 probability of [best on measure 1, worst on measure 2] + a .5 probability of [worst on measure 1, best on measure 2]. The second lottery is some probability **p** of [best on measure 1, best on measure 2] + (1 – **p**)[worst on measure 1, worst on measure 2]. If there are no interactions among goals and measures, a linear form results. If there are interactions, a multiplicative form can be developed, allowing reflection of contingent tradeoffs.

Once the utility function is developed, the idea is that any alternative, objectively measured, can be compared with any other alternative. It is necessary to carefully verify that the assessments and tradeoffs obtained from decision makers are consistent.

This presents some of the basic concepts of multiattribute utility theory, as well as introducing the package *Logical Decision*. Note that *Logical Decision* includes a number of excellent graphical features, giving the user the ability to conduct sensitivity analysis. From the **Results Menu**, besides ranking alternatives on any part of the goal/measure hierarchy, the formula parameters can be obtained. The relative importance of measures can be viewed graphically. Graphing alternatives gives the ability to see what weights for a specific measure would yield any of the alternatives in the data set. Measure Equivalents Ranking gives the ability to express relative advantages/disadvantages in terms of any of the measures in the system.

References

Bodily, S. 1977. A multiattribute decision analysis for the level of frozen blood utilization. *IEEE Transactions on Systems, Man, and Cybernetics* **SMC-7**:10, 683–694.

Bunn, D. W. 1984. *Applied decision analysis*. New York: McGraw Hill.

Corner, J.L. and Kirkwood, C.W. 1991. Decision analysis applications in the operations research literature, 1970–1989, *Operations Research* **39**:2, 206–219.

Dyer, J.S. and Sarin, R.K. 1979. Measurable multiattribute value functions, *Operations Research* **27**, 810–822.

Keeney, R.L. 1992. *Value-focused thinking: A path to creative decisionmaking*. Cambridge, MA: Harvard University Press.

Keeney, R.L. and Raiffa, H. 1976. *Decisions with multiple objectives: Preferences and value tradeoffs*, New York: Wiley.

Krumm, F. C. and Rolle, V. F. 1992. Management and application of decision and risk analysis in Du Pont, *Interfaces* **22**:6, 84–93.

Vári, A. and Vecsenyi, J. 1992. Experiences with Decision Conferencing in Hungary. *Interfaces* **22**:6, 72–83.

4
SMART

SMART (Simple Multi-Attribute Rating Technique, [Edwards, 1971, 1977]) provides a simple way to implement the principles of multiattribute utility theory (MAUT). Edwards [1977] argued that decisions depend on values and probabilities, both subjective quantities. Error can arise in modeling, and can also arise from elicitation. Modeling error is due to applying a model with simplifying assumptions. Elicitation error arises when measures obtained do not accurately reflect subject preference. The more complicated the questions, the more elicitation error there will be. *SMART* requires no judgments of preference or indifference among hypothetical alternatives, as is required with *Logical Decision* and most MAUT methods. Edwards argued [1977, p. 327] that hypothetical judgments were unreliable and unrepresentative of real preferences, and bore untutored decision makers into rejection of the elicitation process or acceptance of any response that would most quickly terminate questioning.

The basic idea of multiattribute utility measurement is that every outcome of an action may have value on a number of different dimensions. MAUT seeks to measure these values one dimension at a time, followed by aggregation of these values across dimensions through a weighting procedure. The simplest and most widely used aggregation rule is to take a weighted linear average. Value $= \Sigma_k w_k s_{jk}$, where w_k is the weight of the kth dimension and s_{jk} is the measure of alternative j on dimension k. Edwards [1977, p. 328] contended that theory, simulation, and experience all suggested to him that weighted linear averages yielded extremely close approximations to value as measured by more complicated nonlinear utility functions.

Note that in the discussion to follow, we are dealing with the case of decisions under certainty. Other approaches are available for the broader case of decision making under uncertainty.

The *SMART* Technique

Edwards proposed a ten step technique. Some of these steps include the process of identifying objectives and organization of these objectives into a hierarchy.

Guidelines concerning the pruning of these objectives to a reasonable number were provided.

Step 1: *Identify the person or organization whose utilities are to be maximized.* Edwards [1977] argued that MAUT could be applied to public decisions in the same manner as was proposed for individual decision making.

Step 2: *Identify the issue or issues.* Utility depends on the context and purpose of the decision.

Step 3: *Identify the alternatives to be evaluated.* This step would identify the outcomes of possible actions, a data gathering process.

Step 4: *Identify the relevant dimensions of value for evaluation of the alternatives.* It is important to limit the dimensions of value. This can be accomplished by restating and combining goals, or by omitting less important goals. Edwards argued that it was not necessary to have a complete list of goals. Fifteen were considered too many, and eight was considered sufficiently large. If the weight for a particular goal is quite low, that goal need not be included. There is no precise range of the number of goals appropriate for decisions.

Step 5: *Rank the dimensions in order of importance.* For decisions made by one person, this step is fairly straightforward. Ranking is a decision task that is easier than developing weights, for instance. This task is usually more difficult in group environments. However, groups including diverse opinions can result in a more thorough analysis of relative importance, as all sides of the issue are more likely to be voiced. An initial discussion could provide all group members with a common information base. This could be followed by identification of individual judgments of relative ranking.

Step 6: *Rate dimensions in importance, preserving ratios.* The least important dimension would be assigned an importance of 10. The next-least-important dimension is assigned a number reflecting the ratio of relative importance to the least important dimension. This process is continued, checking implied ratios as each new judgment is made. Since this requires a growing number of comparisons, there is a very practical need to limit the number of dimensions (objectives). Edwards expected that different individuals in the group would have different relative ratings.

Step 7: *Sum the importance weights, and divide each by the sum.* This step allows normalization of the relative importances into weights summing to 1.0.

Step 8: *Measure the location of each alternative being evaluated on each dimension.* Dimensions were classified into the groups subjective, partly subjective, and purely objective. For subjective dimensions, an expert in this field would estimate the value of an alternative on a 0–100 scale, with 0 as the minimum plausible value and 100 the maximum plausible value. For partly subjective dimensions, objective measures exist, but attainment values for specific alternatives must be estimated. Purely objective dimensions can be measured. Raiffa [1968] advocated identification of utility curves by dimension. Edwards [1971] proposed the simpler expedient of connecting the maximum plausible and minimum plausible values with a straight line. It was argued that the straight line approach would provide an acceptably accurate approximation.

Step 9: *Calculate utilities for alternatives.* $U_j = \Sigma_k w_k u_{jk}$ where U_j is the utility value for alternative j, w_k is the normalized weight for objective k, and u_{jk} is the scaled value for alternative j on dimension k. $\Sigma_k w_k = 1$. The w_k values were obtained from Step 7 and the u_{jk} values were generated in Step 8.

Step 10: *Decide.* If a single alternative is to be selected, select the alternative with maximum U_j. If a budget constraint existed, rank order alternatives in the order of U_j/C_j where C_j is the cost of alternative j. Then alternatives are selected in order of highest ratio first until the budget is exhausted.

Independence

The additive or multiplicative version of the aggregation rule both assume value independence. Value independence implies that the extent of preference for one alternative over another on a particular dimension is unaffected by relative attainment values. Edwards [1977, p. 330] argued that while value independence is a strong assumption, quite substantial amounts of deviation from value independence will make little difference to an alternative's U_j, and even less difference to ranking of alternatives. A condition that often is present is conditional monotonicity, where more of a good is preferable to less of that good, throughout the range of plausible dimension values. When conditional monotonicity is present, value independence was contended to not be likely to cause inaccurate results.

Environmental independence refers to relationships likely to exist over two dimensions that are value-independent. Traffic congestion is likely to increase as population served increases. Environmental dependence can lead to double counting. If environmental dependence exists [dimensions are highly correlated), only one of these correlated dimensions should be included in the analysis. If both were included, care must be taken to assure that aggregate importance weights properly capture joint importance.

Nuclear Dump Site Example

We can apply *SMART* to the nuclear dump site problem used in Chapter 3.

Step 1: The decision maker here is someone or some group responsible for dealing with a public issue.

Step 2: The issues involved could include a number of cost categories, such as the cost of construction, cost of operation, and cost of incorporating adequate safety policies. Expected lives lost could come in a variety of subsets, such as the cost of lives in terms of construction workers, operators of the system once it is built, and of the public who are not directly employed in any aspect of the facility. Catastrophic risk could include risk of earthquake, risk of flood, or other major traumatic incidents. Civic improvement provides an encompassing objective as well. There could be other objectives considered, such as providing public works to a particular area.

Step 3: Alternatives are generated, along with data measuring (or if necessary, evaluating) how well each alternative would perform on each dimension considered. At this stage in Step 2, we were considering more objectives. Therefore, the following table would have been expended to include cost subitems, expected lives lost subcategories, and risk subcategories. However, the point can be demonstrated with the following table as presented on page 26 in Chapter 3.

	Cost (billions)	Expected Lives Lost	Risk	Civic Improvement
Nome, AK	40	60	very high	low
Newark, NJ	100	140	very low	very high
Rock Springs, WY	60	40	low	high
Duquesne, PA	60	40	medium	medium
Gary, IN	70	80	low	very high

Step 4: The number of objectives considered in Step 2 includes a number of objectives that can be combined (*Cost* objectives, *Lives Lost* objective, catastrophic risk categories). There also could be objectives that are considered too unimportant to the matter at hand (providing public works to a particular constituency). Here we end up with four objectives as outlined. This step concludes by organizing the objectives retained for analysis into a hierarchy:

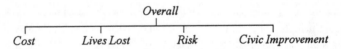

Overall

Cost   Lives Lost   Risk   Civic Improvement

Step 5: Those objectives finally selected for analysis would be rank ordered by importance. In this case, we might rank them in the order:

Lives > Risk > Cost > Improvement

Step 6: This step provides an opportunity for the decision makers to carefully weigh the relative importance of objectives. The least important objective (*Improvement*) is given a value of 10.

Then *Cost* is compared with *Improvement* to determine the ratio of relative importance. Initial rating might give *Cost* a score of 60 compared to *Improvement*'s 10.

Risk is compared to *Improvement*, and given a relative weighting of 150. *Risk* is compared with *Cost* and given a rating 3 times *Cost*, or 180. These ratings are slightly different, and need to be reconciled. Upon additional consideration, the score for *Cost* is reduced to 50, providing consistency between the three pairs of ratings.

Lives is initially considered about 25 times as important as *Improvement*, 7 times as important as *Cost*, and 2 times as important as *Risk*. This set of ratings provides three implied relative scores for *Lives*: 350, 250, and 100. After deliberation, the relative score for *Cost* to *Improvement* is reduced to 4 to 1. Further, the relative ratio of *Lives* to *Risk* is reduced a bit, settling on *Lives* being 25 times *Improvement*, and *Risk* having a score 15 times *Improvement*. This yields relative scores of *Lives* = 250, *Risk* = 150, *Cost* = 40, and *Improvement* = 10.

Step 7: These relative scores are normalized to produce a set of weights with the property that the sum of weights = 1.0. Dividing each score obtained in Step 6 by the sum (450), the following weights are obtained:

$$Lives = 55.6, Risk = 33.3, Cost = 8.9, Improvement = 2.2$$

Step 8: Scores for each of the alternatives on each objective are developed. The minimum plausible attainment on each objective is given a score of 0. The best plausible attainment level is given a score of 100. For continuous variables, a straight line function can be developed. For qualitatively rated measures, scores can be assigned reflecting relative performance.

Cost is measured on a continuous scale, based on cost estimates. While cost estimates on long-range projects are by their nature somewhat uncertain, they can be viewed as providing an objective "best-guess" of relative cost. The least plausible cost might be considered to be $40 billion in net present terms. The maximum plausible cost could be $100 million. A formula converting the cost of project j into a 0–100 scale would be:

$$score_{j,cost} = 100(100 - Cost_j)/(100 - 40) = 100(100 - Cost_j)/60$$

Lives is also measured on a continuous scale, based on estimates. As with *Cost*, this estimate is highly uncertain, but also should be the best estimate available. The least plausible number of lives expected to be lost might be 30, and the greatest number plausibly expected to be lost to be 140. The formula converting the expected number of lives lost for any plausible project j is:

$$score_{j,lives} = 100(140 - Lives_j)/(140 - 30) = 100(140 - Lives_j)/110$$

Risk is a categorical variable, measured on a qualitative scale. The best possible category is given a score of 100, and the worst possible a score of 0, with all other categories given intermediate scores considered appropriate. In this case, a "very high" rating is assigned a $score_{j,risk} = 0$, "high" = 25, "medium" = 50, "low" = 75, and "very high" = 100.

Improvement is treated the same as *Risk*, only in this case high is better than low. Therefore, for the "very low" civic improvement category, $score_{j,improve} = 0$, "low" = 25, "medium" = 50, "high" = 75, and "very high" = 100.

Step 9: Utilities are calculated by the formula: $U_j = \Sigma_k w_k u_{jk}$

	Cost (billions)	Expected Lives Lost	Risk	Civic Improvement
Weight	.089	.556	.333	.022
Nome, AK	100	36.4	0	25
Newark, NJ	0	0	100	100
Rock Springs, WY	66.7	90.9	75	75
Duquesne, PA	66.7	90.9	50	50
Gary, IN	50	54.5	75	100

The resultants are the products of weights time scores (W × S).

Nome	.089(100)	+	.556(36.4)	+	.333(0)	+	.022(25)	=	29.7
Newark	.089(0)	+	.556(0)	+	.333(100)	+	.022(100)	=	35.5
Rock Springs	.089(66.7)	+	556(90.9)	+	.333(75)	+	.022(75)	=	83.1
Duquesne	.089(66.7)	+	.556(90.9)	+	.333(50)	+	.022(50)	=	74.2
Gary	.089(50)	+	.556(54.5)	+	.333(75)	+	022(100)	=	61.9

Step 10: The system recommends locating the nuclear dump site in Rock Springs. As with any method, humans should retain the right of veto. Those who view objective measurement as a good in itself would want very convincing arguments as to why Rock Springs should not be awarded the site.

House Selection Example

In chapter 3, we discussed a problem of selecting a house. This problem will also be used to demonstrate *SMART*.

Step 1: Decision makers are identified. In buying a house, there usually are two decision makers, often with conflicting objectives.

Step 2: Issues relative to the decision are identified. A large number of house features could be of importance. As outlined in Chapter 3, keeping payments down is important. However, the house is also an investment, and if the value of real estate is expected to increase, more is better than less. The appearance of the house, inside and out, is of importance, as are features that the house may have, such as swimming pools, kiosks, landscape gardening, view, and a myriad of other things. Convenience in terms of access to transportation, distance to schools, distance to work, and other facilities can also be important.

Step 3: In the case of purchasing a house, there are probably going to be hundreds of feasible alternatives available. This is too many to consider, so the real estate purchasing process has developed a number of aids to focus on those houses likely to be of interest to the prospective buyer. These can consist of pruning devices such as the listings carried by the realtor who is helping the prospective buyers, the price considered feasible by the purchasers' banker, and those houses considered minimally acceptable by the more sensitive of the purchasers. The joint set of houses satisfying these practical constraints often yields a surprisingly small set of alternatives. Here we will repeat the five alternatives used in Chapter 3.

Alternative (units)	Payment (dollars)	Investment (thousand dollars)	Appearance (categorical)	School (blocks)	Work (miles)
Ramshackle	400	50	0	1	10
Baltic Avenue	500	55	0.2	8	3
Tennessee Avenue	650	70	0.5	7	15
Illinois Avenue	800	90	0.6	15	25
Park Place	1000	120	0.9	12	45

Step 4: The number of objectives considered for analysis are reduced to a feasible number. Note that *Payment* and *Investment* are totally different concepts. Further, the convenience of access to school is furthered by getting reasonably close to school (but not across the street), while the decision maker ideally wants to be some distance from work. Therefore, these measures are indeed quite different. We follow the analysis of Chapter 3, resulting in the hierarchy:

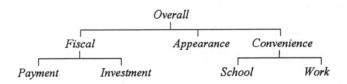

Step 5: Rank order objectives. In this case, there are five objectives to consider, those without subordinate objectives in the hierarchy from Step 4. We assume the rank order:

Appearance > School > Invest > Payment > Work

Step 6: The least important objective (*Work*) is given a score of 10.

Payment is compared with *Work*. We will initially rate *Payment* as 1.2 times as important as *Work*, yielding a score for *Payment* of 12.

Invest is compared with *Work*, and rated as 1.4 times as important. *Invest* is considered about 1.2 times as important as *Payment*. This yields alternative scores of 14 and 15, practically identical. Therefore, at this stage we will keep these ratings.

School is rated as 1.4 times as important as *Work*, 1.25 times as important as *Payment*, and 1.1 times as important as *Invest*. The implied scores for *School* are therefore 14, 15, and 15.4. Relative scores are agreed upon of *School* 16, *Invest* 15, *Payment* 12, and *Work* 10.

The most important objective, *Appearance*, is compared to each of the other four objectives. *Appearance* is considered twice as important as *Work*, 1.7 times as important as *Payment*, 1.4 times as important as *Invest*, and 1.3 times as important as *School*. This yields implied scores for *Appearance* of 20, 20.4, 21, 20.8. These are all very close. After consideration, a score for *Appearance* of 20.5 is selected.

Step 7: These scores are normalized by dividing each by the sum of 73.5, yielding: *Appearance* = .279, *School* = .218, *Invest* = .204, *Payment* = .163, and *Work* .136.

Step 8: Scores for possible objective attainments are identified. *Payment* is measurable on a continuous scale, with the plausible minimum of $400 per month and the bank's view of a plausible maximum of $1000. The formula converting any plausible monthly payment into a score ranging from 0 to 100 is:

$$score_{j,pay} = 100(1000 - pay_j)/(1000 - 400) = 100(1000 = pay_j)/600$$

Since investments return more the more that's invested, the best available house value is considered the most attractive. The plausible maximum is considered to be $120,000, while the plausible minimum is 0 in the minds of the decision makers. The formula would therefore be:

$$score_{j,invest} = 100(Invest_j)/(120,000 - 0) = 100(Invest_j)/120,000$$

Appearance is subjectively measured (in the eye of the beholder). The decision makers could agree on a joint assessment on a scale of 0 to 100 directly.

Distance to school is measurable for any given house. However, the decision maker preference might prefer to be a short distance away from school, but not too far. The decision makers could again assign a score between 0 and 100 for each of the available alternatives, with 100 representing the ideal state and 0 the worst conceivable.

The decision maker might desire to maximize distance to work. This would then be an objective measure. There are limits, but up to 45 miles away might be considered entirely feasible, and even desirable. Therefore, scores for distance to work would be:

$$score_{j,work} = 100(Distance_j)/45$$

The resulting scores for the available alternatives are:

Alternative	Payment	Investment	Appearance	School	Work
Weights	.163	.204	.279	.218	.136
Ramshackle	100	41.7	0	75	22.22
Baltic Avenue	83.3	45.8	20	20	6.7
Tennessee Avenue	58.3	58.3	50	25	33.3
Illinois Avenue	33.3	75	60	5	55.6
Park Place	0	100	90	10	100

Step 9: Calculation of alternative utilities.

Ramshackle	.163(100)	+ .204(41.7)	+ .279(0)	+ .218(75)	+ .136(22.2) = 44.2
Baltic	.163(83.3)	+ .204(45.8)	+ .279(20)	+ .218(20)	+ .136(6.7) = 33.8
Tennessee	.163(58.3)	+ .204(58.3)	+ .279(50)	+ .218(25)	+ .136(33.3) = 45.3
Illinois	.163(33.3)	+ .204(75)	+ .279(60)	+ .218(5)	+ .136(55.6) = 46.1
Park Place	.163(0)	+ .204(100)	+ .279(90)	+ .218(10)	+ .136(100) = 61.3

Step 10: The decision makers would make their selection. In most house purchasing decisions, group processes are involved. If such groups used totally objective and accurate analysis, in this case they would select Park Place. Note that in Chapter 3, distance to school was to be minimized, and Ramshackle received a relatively higher score on that dimension. Here we used a more subjective score assignment, penalizing that location for being too close to school. Ramshackle therefore lost a position in relative rankings to Tennessee.

SMARTS

A problem identified in *SMART* was that the values of weights w_k are related to the values of the single-dimension utilities s_{jk}. The weights could be used to select the range of the objective measure being weighted as well as its importance. *SMART* was therefore modified by the addition of swing weights (*SMARTS*). Swing weights change the score of some object of evaluation on some dimension to insure that the full range of plausible values are represented.

The steps involved in SMARTS were outlined in Edwards and Barron [1994] as follows:

Step 1: *Identify decision purpose and decision makers*. This matches Steps 1 and 2 of *SMART*.

Step 2: *Elicit objectives and hierarchy*. Keeney and Raiffa [1976] and von Winterfeldt and Edwards [1986] were cited as sources for elicitation procedures. Edwards and Barron argued that all participants in the decision should agree on the structure and composition of objectives. One approach would be to include all suggested objectives initially, and then have the participants meet to eliminate duplicate objectives. It was suggested that the number of objectives be reduced to no more than 12, through combining related objectives, and eliminating those objectives that would receive very low relative weights.

Step 3: *Identify alternatives*. If real alternatives were not available, hypothetical alternatives that covered the range of expected alternatives to be encountered should be included. Scoring rules must be well defined at this stage to assure objectivity.

Step 4: *Develop dimensions by attributes matrix*. The matrix would consist of measures of how well each alternative considered performed on each objective. Physical measures should be used if available. Other subjective measures could be used if physical measures are not available. All that is necessary is some number such that a higher number is preferable to a lower one.

Step 5: *Eliminate dominated alternatives.* Ordinal dominance can be identified by inspection. Cardinal dominance is more difficult to detect, but if it is identified, dominated alternatives could be eliminated. This reduces the number of alternatives. Should the range of measure on an objective be reduced, two possible actions were suggested. If it was important to keep the objective for future analyses, the dominated alternative might be retained to represent the reasonable range of objective performance. If no alternatives with low performance on this objective are anticipated, the objective could be eliminated from the analysis, thus simplifying computations.

Step 6: *Develop single-dimension utilities.* This step converts the measures of attainment on each objective into a value score, with 0 representing the worst possible (plausible) score, and 1.0 the best possible (plausible) score. If physical measures were available, a straight-line single-dimension utility function as used in *SMART* was suggested. If that was not appropriate, other methods as discussed in MAUT could be used. If no physical measure was available, elicitation of utility is necessary. The subjects for this process could be experts on the particular objective dimension, or could be the decision maker(s). In *Logical Decision,* this step is accomplished graphically by identifying the measure that provides 0.5 relative value, and a curve is fit through three points (0 value, 0.5 value, and the best value). A final task is to test for conditional monotonicity. If present, an additive model was suggested. If not, nonlinear models as in *Logical Decision* could be used.

Step 7: *Swing weighting.* This step obtains the rank order of weights. Edwards describes swing weighting as requiring two judgmental steps, one easy (Step 7) and one hard (Step 8). This is accomplished by asking the decision maker: "Imagine a new alternative that had the worst possible performance on all objectives, the worst possible alternative that could exist. You can improve one objective dimension from its current worst value to its best possible attainment level. Which of the k dimensions would you improve?" The decision maker would then select one of the k objectives. The next question would ask the decision maker which objective other than the one selected before would be preferred to be changed from the worst possible level to the best possible level. This continues, with the outcome that a rank ordering of objectives is obtained. The most important objective was the first selected in the swing operation, the last selected the least important.

Step 8: *Swing weight calculation.* This step yields the weights w_k for each of the k objectives. From Step 7, the order of objective importances has been identified, including identification of the most important and least important objectives. The weight of the most important of the k objectives is given a value of 100. Some other objective of absolutely no importance is given a value of 0. Then the second most important objective is considered. The decision maker is asked to place the value of the second most important objective on this 0–100 point scale, when compared with a swing from a score of 0 to 100 on the most important objective.

Once this is accomplished, each of the other objectives is considered in turn and given a value on this 0–100 scale. When all objectives have been scored, these scores are normalized.

An alternative approach applies indifference judgments. The decision maker is asked to consider an alternative with the worst performance on all criteria, with the objective being considered improved from the worst possible attainment level to the best possible. Then the decision maker is asked for the level of improvement required on a more important objective in order to equal the preference value of the 100 point improvement on the less important objective.

Step 9: *Decision*. $U_j = \Sigma_k w_k u_{jk}$ as before, with that alternative with the highest U_j selected.

Nuclear Site Selection with SMARTS

Step 1: The decision is for some group to select a nuclear dump site.

Step 2: The objectives to be considered are identified, as in Step 2 of *SMART*. In *SMART*, Step 4 was used to prune the number of objectives and place them in a hierarchy. In *SMARTS*, these actions are collapsed into one step. We assume the same hierarchy as presented previously in *SMART*.

Step 3: The alternatives identified would be the same as with Step 3 of *SMART*. Unlike *SMART*, data collection is covered in Step 5 in *SMARTS*.

Step 4: A matrix of attribute performances over each objective is developed, as in Step 3 of *SMART*.

Step 5: This step was not used in *SMART*. Dominated alternatives are eliminated in *SMARTS*. The step has the feature of simplifying the problem by not wasting time on alternatives that are never superior to some other alternative on any objective, while being inferior on at least one objective. If all objectives of importance are considered, then there would be no logical reason to select the dominated alternatives, and the time wasted analyzing them can be saved. In this case, alternative Rock Springs dominates Duquesne. Therefore, there are only four alternatives to consider (Nome, Newark, Rock Springs, and Gary). This reduces the range of objective attainments considered.

Step 6: Single dimension utilities are calculated for each alternative on each objective. These could be identical to those obtained in Step 8 of *SMART*.

Step 7: The application of swing weighting is the primary difference between *SMARTS* and *SMART*. In this step, the relative rank order of objectives is the result of a more careful process than the direct ranking used previously in *SMART*. The decision maker is asked to imagine an alternative with a cost of 100 billion, 140 expected lives lost, very high risk of catastrophe, and very low civic improvement. The decision maker is then given the choice of one objective to improve. Let us assume that the decision maker selected *Lives* as the one objective most attractive to improve. The same question is then asked, barring *Lives* as an option. The decision maker might select *Risk*. Then the decision maker is asked to select between *Cost* and *Improvement*, given that all four objectives are at their worst plausible levels. Our decision maker might select *Cost*. This would yield the ranking:

$$Lives > Risk > Cost > Improvement$$

This ranking matches the ranking obtained in Step 5 of *SMART*.

Step 8: The relative weights of the four objectives are obtained in a different manner than they were with *SMART*. The most important objective (*Lives*) is given a value of 100. A hypothetical objective of absolutely no importance is given a value of 0. The second most important objective (*Risk*) is then considered, with the decision maker placing it on the 0–100 scale reflecting its relative importance. In our case, *Risk* might be placed at 60, *Cost* at 25, and *Improvement* at 5. Normalizing these scores (dividing by the sum of 190) yields weights of:

$$Lives\ .526, Risk\ .316, Cost\ .132, \text{and } Improvement\ .026.$$

Step 9: The recommended decision is obtained by applying the formula $U_j = \Sigma_k w_k u_{jk}$. Here that would yield:

	Cost (billions)	Expected Lives Lost	Risk	Civic Improvement
Weight	0.132	0.526	0.316	.026
Nome, AK	100	36.4	0	25
Newark, NJ	0	0	100	100
Rock Springs, WY	66.7	90.9	75	75
Duquesne, PA	66.7	90.9	50	50
Gary, IN	50	54.5	75	100

The resultants are the products of weights time scores ($w \times s$).

Nome	.132(100) +	.526(36.4) +	.316(0) +	.026(25) = 33.0
Newark	.132(0) +	.526(0) +	.316(100) +	.026(100) = 34.2
Rock Springs	.132(66.7) +	.526(90.9) +	.316(75) +	.026(75) = 82.3
Gary	.132(50) +	.526(54.5) +	.316(75) +	.026(100) = 61.6

In this case, the recommended site is Rock Springs.

SMARTER

SMARTER (*SMART* Exploiting Ranks) uses Barron and Barrett's [1995] rank weights to eliminate the most difficult judgmental step in *SMARTS*. The relative importance of objectives is based on the order of objectives, using the centroid

(Kmietowicz and Pearman, 1984; Olson and Dorai, 1992; and others) method, which uses rank order to estimate the set of weights, minimizing maximum error by identifying the centroid of all possible weights maintaining the rank order of objective importance.

The steps in *SMARTER* are the same as those in *SMARTS*, except that while *SMARTS* requires the hard second step of obtaining judgmental weights, *SMARTER* replaces this difficult operation with a calculation based on the output of the first step. An additional difference is that a different method is used to calculate relative weights in Step 8. The centroid method assigns weights as follows: w_1 is the weight of the most important objective, w_2 the weight of the second most important objective, and so on. For k objectives:

$$w_1 = (1 + 1/2 + 1/3 +...+ 1/k)/k$$
$$w_2 = (0 + 1/2 + 1/3 +...+ 1/k)/k$$
$$w_k = (0 + 0 +...+ 0 + 1/k)/k$$

The sum of these weights will equal 1.0. The more objectives that exist, the less error this approximation involves. For two objectives, $w_1 = (1 + 1/2)/2 = 0.75$, and $w_2 = (0 + 1/2)/2 = 0.25$. While this would minimize the maximum error (weight extremes would be $w_1 = 1$ and $w_2 = 0$, $w_1 = 0.5$ and $w_2 = 0.5$), with only two objectives the error could be substantial. With more objectives, the error for ranked objectives will be much less.

House Selection Example Using SMARTER

The house selection example presented with *SMART* can also be analyzed with *SMARTER*. The steps would differ slightly, as follows:

Step 1: The decision purpose and decision makers would be identified.

Step 2: Elicit objectives and hierarchy. This step would combine Step 2 and Step 4 of *SMART*, and place them in a hierarchy. It would be the same as given in Step 4 for the house selection example.

Step 3: Identify alternatives. This step would be exactly the same as Step 3 in *SMART*.

Step 4: Develop dimensions by attributes matrix. This data development step is the same as Step 3 in *SMART*.

Step 5: Eliminate dominated alternatives. Of the five houses considered, none are dominated by any other alternative. Therefore, there are five alternatives to compare, as in the *SMART* analysis presented (Ramshackle, Baltic Avenue, Tennessee Avenue, Illinois Avenue, and Park Place).

Step 6: Development of single-dimension utilities. This would be the same as in the *SMART* analysis given.

Step 7: Swing weighting. This would be the same as in Step 7 of the *SMARTS* analysis. In that analysis, the relative order of objectives was:

$$Appearance > School > Invest > Payment > Work$$

Step 8: Multiattribute utility elicitation. This is the step where *SMARTER* provides a much quicker way to generate relative objective weights. Here there are five objectives. The weights are:

w_1 (*Appearance*)	(1	+	1/2	+	1/3	+	1/4	+	1/5)/5	= .457
w_2 (*School*)	(0	+	1/2	+	1/3	+	1/4	+	1/5)/5	= .257
w_3 (*Invest*)	(0	+	0	+	1/3	+	1/4	+	1/5)/5	= .157
w_2 (*Payment*)	(0	+	0	+	0	+	1/4	+	1/5)/5	= .090
w_2 (*Work*)	(0	+	0	+	0	+	0	+	1/5)/5	= .040

Step 9: The recommended decision is obtained by applying the formula $U_j = \Sigma_k \, w_k u_{jk}$. Here that would yield:

Alternative	Payment	Investment	Appearance	School	Work
Weights	.09	.157	.457	.257	.040
Ramshackle	100	41.7	0	75	22.2
Baltic Avenue	83.3	45.8	20	20	6.7
Tennessee Avenue	58.3	58.3	50	25	33.3
Illinois Avenue	33.3	75	60	5	55.6
Park Place	0	100	90	10	100

Ramshackle	.090(100)	+ .157(41.7)	+ .457(0)	+ .257(75)	+ .040(22.2)	= 35.7
Baltic	.090(83.3)	+ .157(45.8)	+ .457(20)	+ .257(20)	+ .040(6.7)	= 29.2
Tennessee	.090(58.3)	+ .157(58.3)	+ .457(50)	+ .257(25)	+ .040(33.3)	= 45.0
Illinois	.090(33.3)	+ .157(75)	+ .457(60)	+ .257(5)	+ .040(55.6)	= 45.7
Park Place	.090(0)	+ .157(100)	+ .457(90)	+ .257(10	+ .040(100)	= 63.4

The method would again recommend Park Place. Here the relative weights differed quite a bit from those obtained using *SMART*, but the order of the alternatives turned out the same. If there are a small number of objectives, SMARTER involves more approximation error than if there are a larger number of objectives. Also, there is more approximation error if the relative weights are very close to each other, as is the case in this example using *SMART*. Still, SMARTER is quite robust, and as happened here, the same relative order can sometimes be obtained.

Summary

SMART provides a means to apply the principles of multiattribute utility theory without the need for complex software or lottery tradeoff analysis. The method has

48   4. SMART

been applied many times. A few examples are Brooks and Kirkwood [1988], Jones, et al. [1990], Quaddas, et al. [1992], and Watson and Buede [1987]. Edwards and Barron [1994] argued that *SMART* had a flaw in that the values of objectives w_k were related to the scores of alternatives on objectives u_{jk}. For instance, halving the value of u_{jk} could be adjusted for by doubling w_k and then renormalizing. Therefore, weights reflected both the range of objective attainment as well as objective importance. *SMARTS* provides swing weights to reflect the full range of possible objective scores. *SMARTER* uses the *SMARTS* technique, with the exception that the most difficult elicitation step (for w_k) is replaced by an ordinal approximation.

References

Barron, F.H. and Barrett, B.E. 1995. Working paper. Decision quality using ranked and partially ranked attribute weights.

Brooks, D.G. and Kirkwood, C.W. 1988. Decision analysis to select a microcomputer networking strategy: A procedure and a case study. *Journal of the Operational Research Society* **39**, 23–32.

Edwards, W. 1971. Social utilities. *The Engineering Economist* Summer Symposium Series **6**, 119–129.

Edwards, W. 1977. How to use multiattribute utility measurement for social decisionmaking. *IEEE Transactions on Systems, Man, and Cybernetics* **SMC-7**:5, 326–340.

Edwards, W. and Barron, F. H. 1994. SMARTS and SMARTER: Improved simple methods for multiattribute utility measurement. *Organizational Behavior and Human Decision Processes* **60**, 306–325.

Jones, M., Hope, C. and Hughes, R. 1990. A multi-attribute value model for the study of UK energy policy. *Journal of the Operational Research Society* **41**:10, 919–929.

Keeney, R.L. and Raiffa, H. 1976. *Decisions with multiple objectives: Preferences and value tradeoffs.* New York: Wiley.

Kmietowicz, A.W. and Pearman, A.D. 1984. Decision theory, linear partial information and statistical dominance. *Omega* **12**, 391–399.

Olson, D.L. and Dorai, V.K. 1992. Implementation of the centroid method of Solymosi and Dombi. *European Journal of Operational Research* **60**:1, 117–129.

Quaddus, M.A., Atkinson, D.J. and Levy, M. 1992. An application of decision conferencing to strategic planning for a voluntary organization. *Interfaces* **22**:6, 61–71.

Raiffa, H. 1968. *Decision analysis: Introductory lectures on choices under uncertainty.* Reading, MA: Addison-Wesley.

von Winterfeldt, D. and Edwards, W. 1986. *Decision analysis and behavioral research.* New York: Cambridge University Press.

Watson, S.R. and Buede, D.M. 1987. *Decision synthesis: The principles and practice of decision analysis.* New York: Cambridge University Press.

5
The Analytic Hierarchy Process

The Analytic Hierarchy Process (AHP) T. Saaty [1977, 1982]; R.W. Saaty [1987] is a technique for converting subjective assessments of relative importance into a set of weights. It has proven to be very useful in assisting selection from a finite set of alternatives (see Zahedi, 1986 and Shim, 1989 for surveys). AHP has also been used to develop linear utility functions reflecting the relative importance of decision objectives or problem features that have been used for mathematical programming, as well as for ranking things (such as seeding tennis tournaments or selecting the best cities to live in).

Description of AHP

AHP is a means of developing measures in physical or social environments when physical or statistical measures are unavailable. In the social environment, AHP is a means of converting subjective assessments into relative values. Three principles are applied in AHP: (1) problems are decomposed by identifying those factors that are important, (2) comparative judgments are made on the decomposed elements of the problem, and (3) measures of relative importance are obtained through pairwise comparison matrices which are finally recombined into an overall rating of available choices.

To demonstrate the features of AHP, a simple multiple objective selection decision is assumed. An educational institution has a lot of students, and parking is a major problem. Currently, parking is assigned to a series of small asphalt lots spread throughout campus. This is relatively inexpensive, but land is becoming scarce, and building programs are not only encroaching upon the parking lots, but adding to the demand for parking space. While specified parking areas are assigned, with the diminishment of convenient lot space, many people are parking where they are not authorized. This has the result that those who have paid for a specific lot often cannot find a vacant space. Complaints have led to an increased security policy of issuing tickets, as well as towing vehicles. This in turn leads to a very short-tempered attitude on the part of all concerned.

The need to change the system has been recognized, although available solutions each have some deficiencies. Three alternative systems are under consideration:

1. *Lot*: Expansion of the current system of asphalt lots to wherever lots will fit
2. *Garage*: Construction of a mammoth parking garage near facilities run by Premier Parking Inc.
3. *Shuttle*: A shuttle bus system which would utilize asphalt lots at some distance from facilities

Five objectives in the decision have been identified as:

1. *Service*: The ideal system would provide close parking facilities for at least 2000 customers.
2. *Control*: There should be some way of alleviating behavioral problems by adequately enforcing order.
3. *Convenience*: Building the system should minimize disruption of activities.
4. *Investment*: Cost for the system should be minimized.
5. *Cost*: Cost for customers should be minimized.

The three alternatives have the following measured or rated characteristics:

	Service	Control	Convenience	Investment	Cost
Lot	800	very poor	medium	$2,000,000	$100/yr
Garage	2000	excellent	high	$6,000,000	$150/yr
Shuttle	1200	poor	low	$500,000	$50/yr

A hierarchy of these objectives is developed, grouping those objectives relating to customer service, convenience, and cost.

Hierarchy Development

Analytic hierarchy process provides a means of quantifying otherwise subjective decision problems. Those factors important in the decision have been identified. The next step is to organize these factors into a hierarchy. At the top of the hierarchy is the *Goal*, which is to select the appropriate parking alternative. The AHP hierarchy consists of **branches**, which identify those elements contributing to attaining the *Goal*. Here, the branches are features providing *Customer* satisfaction, ability to *Control* the system, and *Investment* required. Branches can have subbranches. For instance, *Customer* consists of three measures: the number of customers provided *Service*, *Convenience* to customers, and *Cost* to customers. Hierarchies can consist of any number of layers of goal branches and subgoals. As a rule of thumb, it may be best to keep the number of branches from any one node limited to a maximum of seven, because it is difficult for humans to concentrate on more than seven things at one time. And, it would be best that each branch from a given node be as independent of the other branches as possible. Finally, the bottom level of the hierarchy usually consists of the available choices (here L = lot, G = garage, and S = perimeter lots and shuttle buses). The hierarchy for this problem is:

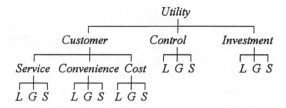

Subjective Pairwise Comparisons

The next phase in the AHP analysis is to obtain the relative importance of factors within each hierarchical level for each factor. This is accomplished through a pairwise comparison of all elements in that section of the hierarchy. One pairwise comparison would be required for overall utility, comparing *Customer*, *Control*, and *Investment* factors. Assuming they are ranked in order of greatest preference first, the upper right triangular portion of the following matrix would be completed with the strength of preference given according to the scale in Table 5-1. Even (or fractional) numbers can be used for ratings between the other ratings.

Pairwise comparisons are needed at each node of the hierarchy (node meaning any place where branches extend below). Some think it is best to start at the bottom of the hierarchy, and work up. It might not matter, but we will do that. At the bottom of the hierarchy, we have to compare how well each parking alternative does on each of the five criteria one level up from the bottom. The pairwise comparisons are meant to state how many times the row factor is more preferable than the column factor. Given accurate measures, the pairwise comparisons are simply algebra.

At the bottom of the hierarchy, each alternative (L = lots, G = garage, S = shuttle) need to be evaluated for the relative accomplishment of each alternative on each objective. For instance, each of the alternatives evaluated on *Control* could be as given on the left. The parking garage is rated as having a *Control* performance 7 times that of the current lot system (and thus L is $1/7$th as effective as G), and 5 times as effective as the proposed shuttle bus system. In turn, the shuttle bus system is rated as 3 times as effective relative to *Control* than the current lot system. Only the upper right triangle of pairwise comparisons are obtained. The full matrix, on the right, is developed by inverting corresponding elements.

	Control				Control		
	L	G	S		L	G	S
L	1	1/7	1/3	L	1	1/7	1/3
G	—	1	5	G	7	1	5
S	—	—	1	S	3	1/5	1

These reflect the decision maker's estimation of relative attainment of each alternative relative to the criterion *Control*. The next step is to convert these ratio comparisons into relative scores.

TABLE 5.1 Subjective AHP scale

1 — base factor **roughly equivalent** in importance to other factor
3 — base factor **moderately** more important than other factor
5 — base factor **essentially** more important than other factor
7 — base factor relative importance **very strong**
9 — base factor **overwhelmingly** more important than other factor

Calculation of Implied Weights

There is no one correct way to calculate relative scores or weights. The relative scale of importance can be obtained by normalizing any column. Here we encounter some estimation error. The question is whether or not this error is serious (due to inconsistent ratings such as saying alternative A is better than alternative B, alternative B is better than alternative C, and alternative C is better than alternative A), or just different estimates of a rough relative ratio.

The ways to calculate relative scores or weights include simply averaging the three weights given above, which is probably the simplest method, but relatively unstable. Another approach would be obtaining the geometric mean (see Chapter 6), which has theoretical advantages (see Chapter 6), as well as being relatively easy computationally. The eigenvector provides a robust estimator, and is justified by Saaty [1977]. As we will show, the eigenvector method provides a means of assessing the relative consistency of a matrix as well. If you are interested in the mathematics involved, the Appendix to this chapter enlarges upon the eigen value calculations given here.

To demonstrate, the arithmetic mean of each normalized column is a source of relative performance for each of the three alternatives on criterion *Control*. Each column can be normalized by dividing each element by the column total. That yields:

	Control			*Control*			
	L	G	S	L	G	S	Average
L	1	1/7	1/3	.09091	.10638	.05263	.08331
G	7	1	5	.63636	.74468	.78947	.72350
S	3	1/5	1	.27273	.14894	.15789	.19319
Totals	13	47/35	19/3				

Note that if each of the ratio pairwise comparisons given by the decision maker were precisely accurate, each of the normalized columns would yield identical values. However, when obtaining subjective estimates of relative value, one would expect some variance. That is one reason that multiple estimates of the ratios are obtained (by filling in the entire upper right triangle of pairwise comparisons). The example we have just reviewed involves a little variance in the estimates of relative performance. It appears that the parking garage (G) would provide about nine times as much control as would the current lot system (.72/.08). However, based upon the

TABLE 5.2 AHP Consistency limits

Factors	Mean Random	Limit
2	0	0
3	.58	.06
4	.90	.09
5	1.12	.11
6	1.24	.12
7	1.32	.13

pairwise comparisons, this could vary from 7 times (.63/.09) to about 15 (.79/.05). The next question we will address is how much inconsistency we will tolerate in the pairwise comparisons.

Consistency Measure

The maximum eigen value provides a measure of inconsistency, which can be used to validate whether the differences in the resulting weights were greater than expected at random. The consistency index (C.I.) is a function of the maximum eigen value and the number of elements (n) in the pairwise comparison:

$$I.I. = (\lambda_{max} - n)/(n-1)$$

where λ_{max} is the maximum eigen value for the pairwise comparison matrix and n is the number of objectives compared. This consistency index can be compared with values expected from a random distribution. Saaty [1977] has proposed a cutoff limit of .10 of this random index. If there were five factors, and $CI > .112$, the decision maker should be asked to revise his pairwise comparisons.

The eigenvector for the *Control* pairwise comparison matrix is:

$$.08096 \; \mathbf{L} + .73065 \; \mathbf{G} + .18839 \; \mathbf{S}$$

with a consistency index of .032. This consistency index is well below the table limit of .06 for three compared elements, and the conclusion is that this set of pairwise comparisons is adequately consistent. Note that the limits for inconsistency vary by the number of elements in the pairwise comparison matrix. This requires looking up different limits for different sized matrices. Both *Expert Choice* and *Criterium*, another well known commercial package, adjust the inconsistency index calculation so that the user only needs to worry about keeping the index below .10. The calculation is adjusted for pairwise comparison matrix size.

The pairwise comparisons for the bottom level of the hierarchy are:

Service			Cost			Convenience			Control			Investment		
L	G	S	L	G	S	L	G	S	L	G	S	L	G	S
L 1	—	—	L 1	1.5	—	L 1	—	5	L 1	—	—	L —	3	—
G 2.5	1	1.67	G —	1	—	G 7	1	9	G 7	1	5	G —	1	—
S 1.5	—	1	S 2	3	1	S —	—	1	S 3	—	1	S 4	12	1

The resulting eigenvectors:

	Service	Cost	Convenience	Control	Investment
L	.20000	.27273	.17342	.08096	.18750
G	.50000	.18182	.77204	.73065	.06250
S	.30000	.54545	.05455	.18839	.75000
C.I.	.00	.00	.104**	.032	.00

Note that the consistency index for *Convenience* exceeds .058. This indicates that the pairwise comparison matrix relative to *Convenience* has relatively high inconsistency. It would be recommended that the decision makers reconsider their pairwise comparisons for this matrix.

Convenience	L	G	S	Eigenvector
L	1	—	5	.31805
G	2	1	9	.61361 C.I. .020**
S	—	—	1	.06835

The upper level of the hierarchy involve two nodes. *Customer* related criterion include *Service, Cost,* and *Convenience.* The top node of the hierarchy consists of *Customer* related criteria, *Control,* and *Investment.* The two pairwise comparisons could be:

Utility	Customer	Control	Investment
Customer	1	3	5
Control		1	3
Investment			1

That is, of course, assuming that ample resources were available, and customer service was given a high relative emphasis. This matrix involved three pairwise comparisons, rating *Customer* as moderately more important than *Control,* and essentially more important than Investment. *Control* in turn was rated as moderately more important than *Investment.* The eigenvector in this case would yield:

$$Utility = .63698 \ Customer + .25829 \ Control + .10473 \ Investment$$

The consistency index (C.I.) for this matrix is .01926, which is well below the cutoff of .058, indicating an acceptable degree of consistency.

While we have the final weights for *Control* and *Investment* at this stage, we still need to allocate the .63698 weight for *Customer* over its components of *Service, Cost,* and *Convenience.* This can be accomplished with another pairwise comparison matrix.

Customer	Service	Cost	Convenience
Service	1	2	5
Cost		1	3
Convenience			1

The resulting eigenvector yields:

Customer = .58155 *Service* + .30900 *Cost* + .10945 *Convenience*.

The C.I. for this matrix is .00185, which is extremely consistent.
    The weights obtained imply an overall formula of:

$$\begin{aligned} Utility = \quad &.37043 \; Service \\ +&.19683 \; Cost \\ +&.06972 \; Convenience \\ +&.25829 \; Control \\ +&.10473 \; Investment \end{aligned}$$

The final step in the process is now to obtain the relative performance of each alternative choice on overall value as measured by AHP. This is done through synthesis

Synthesis

Synthesis simply implies multiplying down the hierarchy and adding the products for each alternative. Multiplying down through level 3 provides a linear approximation of value.

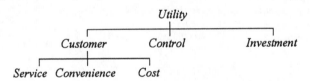

	Lot		Garage		Shuttle	
.37043 Service	×.2	=.07409	×.5	=.18522	×.3	=.11113
+.19683 Cost	×.27273	=.05368	×.18182	=.03579	×.54545	=.10736
+.06972 Convenience	×.31805	=.02217	×.61361	=.04278	×.06836	=.00477
+.25829 Control	×.08096	=.02091	×.73065	=.18872	×.18839	=.04866
+.10473 Investment	×.18750	=.01964	×.06250	=.00655	×.75000	=.07855
Score		.19049		.45905		.35046

With this method, there is a check available. The sum of weights over all alternatives will add to one. The *Garage* would be recommended. Since the scores are all ratios of relative importance, the *Garage* can be interpreted as literally 1.3 times as valuable as the *Shuttle* system (.46/.35), and 2.6 times as valuable as the current *Lot* system (.46/.19).

AHP has also been used in developing a weighted, combined objective function reflecting a number of objectives in mathematical programming applications (Mitchell and Bingham, 1986; Bard, 1986; Olson, et al., 1986). While this approach is widely used in applications of AHP, T. Saaty [1987] and Harker and Vargas [1987] have pointed out that AHP is more robust as a ranking device than as a formula (utility) generator.

To rank the preference of each alternative, or to obtain a formula which could be applied to current and future alternatives, the only difference would be obtaining the estimates of how well each available alternative does on each criterion and would be based on a 0–1 scale rather than pairwise comparisons. This method is preferred by some researchers (for instance, Belton and Gear [1985]), as an anchored scale is considered by them to be more accurate. Using the formula approach, each rating is normalized to a 0–1 scale, with 1 the preferred rating and 0 the worst.

	Service	Control	Convenience	Investment	Cost
Lot	0	0	.5	.364	.5
Garage	1	1	1	0	0
Shuttle	.333	0	0	1	1

We can apply the formula for each alternative:

	Lot		Garage		Shuttle	
.37043 Service	×0	= 0	×1 =	.37043	× .333 =	.12348
+.19683 Cost	× .5	= .09842	×0 = 0		×1	= .19683
+.06972 Convenience	× .5	= .03486	×1 =	.06972	×0	= 0
+.25829 Control	×0	= 0	×1 =	.25829	×0	= 0
+.10473 Investment		.364 = .03812	×0 = 0		×1	= .10473
Score		.17140		.69844		.42504

The alternative with the highest score would be recommended. In this case, the *Garage* is selected, primarily because of the low relative importance of *Cost*.

Calculations for the Nuclear Waste Disposal Siting Problem

In the MAUT chapter (Chapter 3), a nuclear waste disposal problem was used to demonstrate how that selection technique worked. The same problem can be solved with AHP. The hierarchy for the problem was:

Overall

Cost   Lives Lost   Risk   Civic Improvement

Data for the problem was as follows:

	Cost (bill)	Expected Lives Lost (transport–local)	Risk	Civic Improvement
Nome, AK	40	60	very high	low
Newark, NJ	100	140	very low	very high
Rock Springs, WY	60	40	low	high
Duquesne, PA	60	40	medium	medium
Gary, IN	70	80	low	very high
Yakima Flats, WA	70	80	high	medium
Turkey, TX	60	70	high	high
Wells, NE	50	30	medium	medium
Anaheim, CA	90	130	very high	very low
Epcot Center, FL	80	120	very low	very low
Duckwater, NV	80	70	medium	low
Santa Cruz, CA	90	100	very high	very low

Pairwise comparisons relatively compatible with the MAUT analysis comparing the five criteria would be:

	Cost	Lives	Risk	Improve
Cost	1	1/9	1/3	9
Lives		1	6	9
Risk			1	9
Improve				1
Weights	.11082	.66536	.19428	.02954

Overall weights:		
	Cost	.11082
	Live	.66536
	Risk	.19428
	Improve	..02954

These pairwise comparisons reflect a very strong advantage for all other criteria over civic improvement (*Improve*). Note that this relative advantage was greater than 9 times for the MAUT analysis, a source of some difference in results. We could match the numbers obtained with MAUT by allowing higher ratios than 9. But we will follow through the demonstration limiting the maximum relative ratio to 9, as is forced by *Expert Choice* and *Criterium*.

AHP is meant for comparison of a short list of alternatives (seven or less). We select the same five alternatives evaluated in the MAUT chapter. The pairwise comparisons reflecting relative performance of each alternative on each criteria follow. Note that for *Cost* and *Lives*, numbers were available, making precise estimates of relative value (with no inconsistency). Subjective pairwise comparisons were used for the categorical data given for *Risk* and civic *Improvement*.

Cost	Nome	Newa	Rock	Duqu	Gary	Weights	Consistency index
Nome	1	2.5	1.5	1.5	1.75	.30259	0.0
Newark		1	.6	.6	.7	.12104	
Rock Springs			1	1	7/6	.20173	
Duquesne				1	7/6	.20173	
Gary					1	.17291	

Lives	Nome	Newa	Rock	Duqu	Gary	Weights	Consistency index
Nome	1	7/3	2/3	2/3	4/3	.19310	0.0
Newark		1	2/7	2/7	4/7	.08276	
Rock Springs			1	1	2	.28966	
Duquesne				1	2	.28966	
Gary					1	.14483	

Risk	Nome	Newa	Rock	Duqu	Gary	Weights	Consistency index
Nome	1	1/9	1/7	1/5	1/5	.03083	.0444
Newark		1	3	5	3	.46936	
Rock Springs			1	3	1	.20394	
Duquesne				1	1/3	.09192	
Gary					1	.20394	

Improve	Nome	Newa	Rock	Duqu	Gary	Weights	Consistency index
Nome	1	1/7	1/5	1/3	1/7	.03892	.0340
Newark		1	3	5	1	.36209	
Rock Springs			1	3	1/3	.16069	
Duquesne				1	1/5	.07620	
Gary					1	.36209	

The synthesis of these matrices yields final weights for the five alternatives of:

Rock Springs	.25945
Duquesne	.23519
Newark	.17036
Nome	.16915
Gary	.16584

AHP could also be used as a means to develop a utility formula, which could then be applied to as many alternatives as there was data for. This data on the alternatives would have to be scored on some common interval, such as 0–1, in order to avoid warping the relative importance weights.

	Cost		Lives		Risk		Improve	
Nome	40	0.9	60	0.25	very high	0.0	low	0.25
Newark	100	0.0	140	0.0	very low	1.0	very high	1.0
Rock Springs	60	0.7	40	0.4	low	0.75	high	0.75
Duquesne	60	0.7	40	0.4	medium	0.50	medium	0.5
Gary	70	0.6	80	0.15	low	0.75	very high	1.0
Yakima Flats	70	0.6	80	0.15	high	0.25	medium	0.50
Turkey	60	0.7	50	0.3	high	0.25	high	0.75

Wells	50	0.8	30	0.6	*medium*	0.50	*medium*	0.50
Anaheim	90	0.4	130	0.05	*very high*	0.0	*very low*	0.0
Epcot Center	80	0.55	120	0.1	*very low*	1.0	*very low*	0.0
Duckwater	80	0.55	70	0.2	*medium*	0.50	*low*	0.25
Santa Cruz	90	0.4	100	0.2	*very high*	0.0	*very low*	0.0

Multiplying these weights times the weights of relative importance, each alternative receives an overall score that can be rank-ordered just as the full pairwise comparison scores. This approach is expected to be less precise than full pairwise comparison, but has the advantage that it can be applied to a database of alternatives, as in an expert system. On the other hand, this is the approach used in *SMART* (von Winterfeldt and Edwards [1986]), which has been argued as having superior accuracy in some conditions as stated before. The scores for the twelve alternatives given are:

Criterion	*Cost*	*Lives*	*Risk*	*Improve*	Total
Weight	.11082	.66536	.19428	.02954	
Wells	0.8	0.6	0.50	0.50	.59978
Rock Springs	0.7	0.4	0.75	0.75	.51158
Duquesne	0.7	0.4	0.50	0.5	.45563
Turkey	0.7	0.3	0.25	0.75	.34791
Gary	0.6	0.15	0.75	1.0	.34155
Epcot Center	0.55	0.1	1.0	0.0	.32177
Duckwater	0.55	0.2	0.50	0.25	.29855
Nome	0.9	0.25	0.0	0.25	.27436
Yakima Flats	0.6	0.15	0.25	0.50	.22964
Newark	0.0	0.0	1.0	1.0	.22382
Santa Cruz	0.4	0.2	0.0	0.0	.17740
Anaheim	0.4	0.05	0.0	0.0	.07760

Note that the two approaches yielded quite different rankings of the five alternatives considered in the full pairwise comparison method. In fact, these orders were both different than the order obtained using MAUT.

MAUT		*Formula AHP*		*Full AHP*	
Rock Springs	.6043	Rock Springs	.51158	Rock Springs	.25945
Duquesne	.5200	Duquesne	.45563	Duquesne	.23519
Gary	.4478	Gary	.34155	Newark	.17036
Newark	.3374	Nome	.27346	Nome	.16915
Nome	.2803	Newark	.22382	Gary	.16584

All three methods obtained the same top two rankings. The last three rankings are somewhat jumbled. MAUT had a more nonlinear relationship using precise measures. That does not necessarily make it more appropriate, especially if the error tolerance of the measures was not that great (MAUT may be taking into account minor differences in measures that have no real meaning).

Calculations for the Housing Selection Decision

In the MAUT chapter, a selection problem involving the purchase of a house was considered. The hierarchy for that decision was:

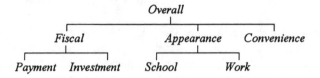

The alternatives available, and their measures on the criteria given in the hierarchy were:

Alternative (units)	Payment (dollars)	Investment (thousand dollars)	Appearance (categorical)	School (blocks)	Work (miles)
Ramshackle	400	50	very poor	1	10
Baltic Avenue	500	55	poor	8	3
Tennessee Avenue	650	70	medium	7	15
Illinois Avenue	800	90	good	15	25
Park Place	1000	120	very good	12	45

A set of pairwise comparison matrices compatible with the inputs used in the prior chapter are:

	Fiscal	Appear	Conven		Payment	Invest		School	Work
Fiscal	1	2	1	Payment	1	1/2	School	1	2
Appear		1	1/2	Invest		1	Work		1
Conven			1						
Weights	.400	.200	.400		.333	.667		.667	.333
II		0.0				0.0			0.0

This yields an overall weighting of criteria:

.13333 *Payment* + .26667 *Invest* + .20000 *Appear* + .26667 *School* + .13333 *Work*

The pairwise comparisons of alternatives evaluated with respect to each criterion:

Payment	R	B	T	I	P	Weights	II
R	1	5/4	6.5/4	2	2.5	.30162	0.0
B		1	1.3	1.6	2	.24130	
T			1	8/6.5	10/6.5	.18561	
I				1	5/4	.15081	
P					1	.12065	

Invest	R	B	T	I	P		
R	1	10/11	5/7	5/9	5/12	.12987	0.0
B		1	11/14	11/18	11/24	.14286	

	R	B	T	I	P	
T			1	7/9	7/12	.18182
I				1	3/4	.23377
P					1	.31169

Appear	R	B	T	I	P		
R	1	1/3	1/5	1/6	1/9	.03536	.0447
B		1	1/3	1/4	1/7	.06839	
T			1	1/2	1/5	.14371	
I				1	1/3	.22694	
P					1	.52559	

School	R	B	T	I	P		
R	1	3	3	7	5	.47168	.0207
B		1	1	5	3	.20192	
T			1	5	3	.20192	
I				1	1/2	.04591	
P					1	.07857	

Work	R	B	T	I	P		
R	1	2	1/2	1/5	1/7	.06529	.0212
B		1	1/5	1/7	1/9	.03744	
T			1	1/2	1/5	.13497	
I				1	1/2	.27036	
P					1	.49194	

The synthesis of these matrices is:

Park Place	.29087
Ramshackle	.21641
Illinois Avenue	.17612
Tennessee Avenue	.17382
Baltic Avenue	.14278

Real-World Applications of AHP

There are a tremendously large number of AHP applications that have been published. The references to Zahedi [1986] and Shim [1989] list just some of the many analyses where AHP has been applied. A major reason for this popularity is that AHP is relatively easy to understand, and the overall process provides a rational means of approaching a decision that is very easy to explain to others as well. A side benefit of this ease of presentation is that AHP has been incorporated in group decision environments a number of times.

Example 1

Two example applications involving public policy questions are presented. In the first of these, AHP provided a means for the U.S. Air Force to reach a specific decision.

The ability to explain what precisely was assumed and what precisely went into the analysis was a major positive feature.

Air Force Project Evaluation

In 1984, the U.S. Congress passed the Competition in Contracting Act, requiring competitive sources for systems the government buys. For those cases where it is economically infeasible to develop multiple sources, subsystem and component items are to be competitively obtained by the primary contractor. If the government feels that a prime contractor has not sufficiently developed competitive sources, the government can buy the subsystem or component separately and provide it to the prime contractor. This procedure is referred to as "breaking out."[1]

A program director, assisted by staff functional experts, is in charge of systems procurement for everything related to that system (an example system being a specific airplane). Because of the complexity of decisions facing the director, decisions are frequently delegated to middle managers, with final approval authority remaining with the director. Middle managers are expected to follow a rational, optimizing approach in recommending a course of action.

The program director for the F-15 fighter aircraft system is responsible for development, production, deployment, and initial operational support of F-15 aircraft. The subcontractor supplying a major radar system had a history of late deliveries, contributing to late deliveries of the aircraft from the prime contractor to the Air Force. A common method of motivating suppliers is to solicit or develop alternative supply sources (break out the component). The decision alternatives included breaking out the radar system, finding other means of motivating improved performance, or readjusting the expected delivery times. The decision involved many criteria and alternatives. Some of these involved quantitative data, but others required qualitative judgments by functional experts. The decision group included engineers, a contracting officer, logisticians, manufacturing engineers, cost analysts, and a project manager.

The analysis began with identification of criteria and synthesis of the quantitative and qualitative inputs from group members. Time was of the essence. The analytic hierarchy process was selected to support this decision. The package *Expert Choice* was used. The hierarchy developed included top level objectives of cost, management visibility, impact on integration, impact on management effort, and impact on delivery schedule. Each of these 5 objectives had at least three subobjectives at the next level of the hierarchy. The bottom level of the hierarchy consisted of the two options (to break out the project or not to break out the project).

Once the hierarchy was constructed, the group developed weights for each of the criteria and subcriteria. *Expert Choice* allows verbal, numerical, and graphical means

---

[1]C.R. Cook. 1989. Decision support for the U.S. Air Force: Component breakout — A case history. in *DSS-89: Transactions of the Ninth International Conference on Decision Support Systems*, G.R. Widmeyer, ed. Providence RI: The Institute of Management Sciences 259–264.

of developing these weights. The verbal mode was preferred by the group over direct numerical scales.

The next step was to compare the alternatives with respect to each of the subcriteria. The same verbal comparison routine was used. In this case, the recommended alternative was not to break out (.576 to .424) the radar system from the prime F-15 contract. An overall inconsistency index of .04 was obtained.

The users felt that this system was useful, because an unstructured decision was transformed into one with more structure. This decision support system increased group and management confidence in the decision-making process, and therefore the recommendation was adopted with greater confidence. AHP provided precise definition of factors that were considered in a manner understood by all participants. Cook felt that this was valuable in building consensus. In the group's opinion, the process took less time than would have been required with an alternative methodology.

In order to present the group's case to higher bureaucratic elements, a word processor (part of the software) was used to explain the rationale at each node of the hierarchy. The final decision of not breaking out the radar system was approved.

This example included a group decision, applying AHP across two levels. Those with decision authority provided the subjective information for the relative weights given to various policy elements, whereas technicians provided assessments of alternative performance on each of these policies. In this group decision environment, many of the policy opinions were shared, a necessary condition for this approach to work.

Example 2

The next example application of AHP is less structured, but also highly interesting. Here AHP was not used to make a decision, but was used rather as a framework for a number of individuals (legislators in this case) to learn more about the ramifications of a problem, and to see the impact of various degrees of emphasis on the criteria considered.

Finnish Electrical Generation Policy

Evaluation of energy generation alternatives is highly important because of the extremely high cost involved, its long range impact (power plants may last fifty years or more), and the dynamic environment in the industry (fuel prices fluctuate drastically, and new technologies are regularly developed). Nuclear power has advantages relative to pollution generation and renewable resource depletion, but involves additional risk which many perceive as unacceptable, making it a highly controversial source of power.

Because it is so cold and because it has a high density of heavy industry, Finland has a high per-capita consumption of energy. Four nuclear power plants provide 17% of Finland's energy. The Finnish Parliament has final authority to accept or reject licenses for nuclear power plants. The Finnish Department of Energy conducted studies indicating that new sources of power would be needed by the mid-1990s at current growth rates. If the economy stagnated, this demand for new capacity would be delayed until the year 2000. Other studies indicated large nuclear and coal-fired plants to be the most economical sources of new power. There was an additional policy option requiring no new large plants, but rather a mix of conservation measures and decentralization of small and medium sized plants. Nuclear plants require eight to ten years to construct.

A 1983 poll indicated fewer than 50% of the population supported nuclear power. In 1984, two power companies announced an interest in applying for a license to construct nuclear plants. Parliament was split on this issue. The issue was also considered technically difficult, with a continuous flow of new and often contradictory information. Both Parliament and the electrical utilities wanted to identify the outcome before the fact, because a negative vote would impact future proposals.

A project was funded by the Academy of Finland to develop a micro-computer decision aid. The project developers had no involvement with the decision.[2] This made the analysis independent of any of the different stakeholders in the issue. The aim of the project was to help structure the Parliamentary energy debate through the use of the decision aid. Each political party was contacted, explaining the project, principles, and goals. Each party was asked to select one or two members of Parliament to participate. All parties except one participated, and twelve members worked with the decision aid, one at a time. Each participant completed the decision analysis session in less than two hours.

An analytic hierarchy process model was developed based upon the factors identified in this phase of the analysis. Top level factors were **national economy**, **health safety and environment**, and **political** factors, each with subelements exhibited below.

Energy Policy

National economy	Health, safety & environment	Political
Cheap electricity	Natural resources	Independence
Foreign trade	Unavoidable pollution	Centralization
Capital resources	Accidents	Cooperation

The alternatives were for Parliament to approve a 1000 MW nuclear plant, two 500 MW coal fired plants, or adopt the philosophy of conservation and no large plants. The hierarchical weightings of Parliament members and energy experts were analyzed, and a comprehensive report on the results was prepared and published in the fall of 1984.

The second phase of the project was to use the framework of the decision aid to structure the debate in Parliament and in the Finnish media. Top-level experts from government, power companies, and research institutions were invited to evaluate the model. The major anti-nuclear group in Finland was invited as well, but chose not to participate.

---

[2]R.P. Hämäläinen. 1990. A Decision Aid in the Public Debate on Nuclear Power. *European Journal of Operational Research* **48**:1 66–76.

Four widely divergent views among Parliamentary members were identified. It was noted that these same four classes of emphasis were shared by technical experts, indicating that additional knowledge was not required. The debate therefore centered on differences in values among Parliamentary members.

The decision analysis indicated that the nuclear power and no large plant options emerged as the primary alternatives to be discussed. It turned out that no decision was ever required. The power companies delayed their formal application until early 1986, shortly before the Chernobyl accident. After that incident, the application was withdrawn. Measures were taken to increase imports, and begin construction of medium scale peat and coal plants. Hydroelectric possibilities are being explored.

The politicians who worked with the model were impressed positively with the analysis. The consensus was that the decision aid helped clarify the issue for individual decision makers, and provided deeper understanding of alternatives. The public was given an overall framework for the energy problem. The analytic hierarchy process technique was originally chosen because it was easy to understand, and lived up to this expectation. AHP was found to present the issue with such clarity and simplicity that all participants, regardless of computer or mathematical background, felt at ease when using it.

Computer Support for AHP

There are a number of very effective packages available to support AHP. *Expert Choice*, produced by Decision Support Software Inc. of Pittsburgh, PA is a well established package making it very easy and natural to go through the entire AHP process, including building the hierarchy. *Criterium* is a newer product, produced by Sygenex [1989] of Redmond, WA. *Criterium* allows users to use a more spreadsheet oriented approach, which can be effective as well. Both of these packages have been noted to be quite easy to use, even for large AHP models.[3]

One could develop a spreadsheet model to solve AHP problems. The most difficult element is to solve the pairwise comparison matrices, but it can be done as a challenging mathematical exercise.

There are other approaches to AHP that have been implemented in software products. *HIPRE 3+*, produced by Scandinavian Softline Technology, Espoo, Finland, incorporates the idea of interval pairwise comparisons. With this approach, decision makers are not asked for a precise ratio of the relative value of one element over another, but rather are asked for a range of relative advantage. If the system is able to prove that the final score of the leading alternative could be no worse than the best all other alternatives could be, it concludes with a recommendation. The benefit of this approach is that ranges of preference might be more accurate representations of decision maker preferences than some precise value. The problem is that the

---

[3]D.M. Buede. 1992. Software review: Three packages for AHP: Criterium, Expert Choice and HIPRE 3+. *Journal of Multi-Criteria Decision Analysis* 1:2, 119–121.

analysis may take considerable time if the first two alternatives are very close in worth.

Yet another approach is espoused by F.A. Lootsma. *REMBRANDT* is a system which uses geometric means rather than eigen values to calculate weights, uses a logarithmic scale rather than the 1–9 verbal scale used in AHP, and aggregates scores by weighted products rather than by arithmetic means as is used in this chapter. *REMBRANDT* also provides the option of assessing relative advantage by standardized scoring rather than by pairwise comparisons. This package provides computer support to those who have questioned some of the approaches incorporated into AHP, and is covered in Chapter 6.

Summary

Analytic hierarchy process (AHP) is a very popular technique to support selection decisions. It is very easy to understand (except possibly for the part about how eigen values are generated), which makes it easy to use and explain to others. This ability to explain to others is a very important factor, because there are not many important decisions which are made by individuals any more. It is necessary to consider the preferences of a lot of people, which usually means that there will be more than one objective to consider. AHP is very good for this type of problem, and has in fact been used in many applications.

There are a number of optional features in AHP that could be applied. Software for these options exist.

Appendix: Calculation of Maximum Eigen Value and Eigenvector

For the matrix

$$
\begin{array}{c c c c}
 & X & Y & Z \\
X & 1 & 5 & 9 \\
Y & .2 & 1 & 3 \\
Z & .111 & .333 & 1
\end{array}
$$

The eigenvector technique would require solution of:

$$
\begin{bmatrix} 1 & 5 & 9 \\ .2 & 1 & 3 \\ .111 & .333 & 1 \end{bmatrix} - \lambda \begin{bmatrix} 1 & 0 & 0 \\ 0 & 1 & 0 \\ 0 & 0 & 1 \end{bmatrix} = 0 \text{ yielding } \begin{bmatrix} 1-\lambda & 5 & 9 \\ .2 & 1-\lambda & 3 \\ .111 & .333 & 1-\lambda \end{bmatrix} = 0
$$

This can be solved by determinants, yielding the formulation:

$$(1-\lambda)^3 + 5/3 + .6 - 3(1-\lambda) = 0$$

which simplifies to $\lambda^2(3-\lambda) = -.266667$

This is a cubic form, meaning that there are three solutions for λ. Not all of these solutions have to be real numbers, but Saaty established that the **maximum** value for λ (λ_{max}) will be a real number, and will also be $\geq n$. For perfectly consistent matrices, $\lambda_{max} = n$. For this problem, a search will yield $\lambda_{max} = 3.02906$. The consistency index is $(\lambda_{max} - n)/(n-1)$. For this matrix, that would yield .015, a very consistent matrix. The other two solutions for λ in this problem are complex numbers: $-.014532 + .29635\sqrt{-1}$ and $-.014532 - .29635\sqrt{-1}$.

Once λ_{max} is determined, the eigenvector of weights can be obtained by solution of set of n simultaneous equations. For each row of the pairwise comparison matrix A, $Aw = \lambda_{max}w$.

$$1 \; w_1 + \; 5 \; w_2 + 9 \; w_3 = 3.02906 \; w_1$$
$$.2 \; w_1 + \; 1 \; w_2 + 3 \; w_3 = 3.02906 \; w_2$$
$$1/9 \; w_1 + 1/3 \; w_2 + 1 \; w_3 = 3.02906 \; w_3$$

An additional requirement is that $w_1 + w_2 + w_3 = 1$. Because any two of the first three equations (in general, n equations) contain all the necessary information, one of them can be deleted, and replaced with the additional requirement, thus yielding a system of n equations in n unknowns, which can be solved many ways, including linear programming. In this case, the eigenvector of weights is: $w_1 = .751405$, $w_2 = .178178$ and $w_3 = .070417$.

References

Bard, J. F. 1986. A multiobjective methodology for selecting subsystem automation options. *Management Science* 32, 1628–1641.

Belton, V. and Gear, T. 1985. A series of experiments into the use of pairwise comparison techniques to evaluate criteria weights. In *Decision Making with Multiple Objectives: Proceedings VI—Cleveland, OH, Jun 1984*, Y.Y. Haimes and V. Chankong, eds., 375–387.

Harker, P. T. and Vargas, L. G. 1987. The theory of ratio scale estimation: Saaty's analytic hierarchy process. *Management Science* 33:110, 1383–1403.

Mitchell, K. H. and G. Bingham. 1986. Maximizing the benefits of Canadian Forces equipment overhaul programs using multi-objective optimization. *INFOR* 24, 251–264.

Olson, D. L., M. Venkataramanan and J. Mote. 1986. A technique using analytic hierarchy process in multiobjective planning models. *Socio-Economic Planning Sciences* 20, 361–368.

Saaty, R. W. 1987. The analytic hierarchy process: What it is and how it is used. *Mathematical Modelling* 9, 3–5, 161–176.

Saaty, T. L. 1977. A scaling method for priorities in hierarchical structures. *Journal of Mathematical Psychology* 15, 234–281.

Saaty, T. L. 1982. *Decision Making for Leaders*. New York: Van Nostrand Reinhold.

Saaty, T. L. 1987. Rank generation, preservation, and reversal in the Analytic Hierarchy Process. *Decision Sciences* 18:2, 157–177.

Saaty, T. L. 1988. *The analytic hierarchy process*, 2nd ed. New York: McGraw-Hill.

Shim, J.P. 1989. Bibliographical research on the analytic hierarchy process (AHP). *Socio-Economic Planning Sciences* 23:3, 161–167.

Sygenex, Inc. 1989. *CRITERIUM User's Guide*.

Von Winterfeldt, D. and Edwards, W. 1986. *Decision analysis and behavioral research*. Cambridge, UK: Cambridge University Press.

Zahedi, F. 1986. The analytic hierarchy process: A survey of the method and its applications. *Interfaces* **16**:4, 96–108.

6
Geometric Mean Technique

The geometric mean is another way to solve pairwise comparison matrices. Barzilai, et al. [1987] identified three desired properties of a solution technique:

1. For perfectly consistent matrices, the weights obtained by standardizing any column should be obtained (the average of the weights). The estimator $w_i = 1/[(\Pi_{j=1,n}\, a_{ij})^{1/n}]$ (where a_{i1} is the pairwise comparison matrix element for factor i in Column 1) does not have this property (and gives the opposite order of the other techniques). This estimator does satisfy the other two properties below.
2. The solution should be stable for all permutations of the ways to measure preference. For instance, the estimator $w_i = a_{i1}/[(\Pi_{j=1,n}\, a_{ij})^{1/n}]$ does not have this property. It does satisfy properties 1 and 3.
3. When levels of the hierarchy are combined, the same solution should be obtained if matrices with multiple levels are combined into one judgment matrix. The eigen vector technique does not have this property, although it does have properties 1 and 2.

Barzilai, et al. [1987] noted that only the geometric mean, where $w_i = (\Pi_{j=1,n}\, a_{ij})^{1/n}$, satisfies all three properties.

Geometric Mean Solution

Barzilai, et al. [1990a; 1990b] discussed the solution of three mathematical problems. The first problem is solution of a pairwise comparison matrix in order to obtain relative importances of the elements being compared. Saaty [1977] proposed the eigen vector for solution of this problem. Lootsma [1980, 1991], Belton and Gear [1983, 1985a, 1985b], Barzilai, et al. [1987] and Schoner and Wedley [1989] argued that the geometric mean is more appropriate. The second problem is synthesis of individual matrix scores over the hierarchy. Saaty used the arithmetic mean for this problem. Barzilai, et al., again argue for use of the geometric mean. The third problem is aggregation of scores of individual group members into a consensus. Both Saaty and Barzilai, et al. propose the geometric mean for this third problem.

The parking system problem will be used to demonstrate Barzilai, et al.'s approach. A problem arises when there are multiple hierarchical levels. Barzilai, et al. propose normalizing each bottom level matrix (containing the decision alternatives) multiplicatively ($\prod^i w_i = 1$ for i alternatives compared on each criterion), while all higher level matrices are normalized additively ($\Sigma_i w_i = 1$ for i elements). The bottom level of the hierarchy is synthesized by $w_i = \prod_j w_{ij}^{o(j)}$ where $i = 1$ to the number of criteria. The product of $w_i = 1$. Lootsma [1992] applied the geometric mean approach and solved the problem of synthesizing the hierarchy by allowing only one level superior to the decision alternatives. We will demonstrate that approach.

The first modification we will make to the parking system problem discussed in the AHP chapter (Chapter 5) is to convert the hierarchy to have one criterion level over one alternative level.

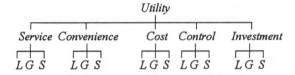

The pairwise comparisons for the bottom level alternatives over each of the criterion are the same as with AHP:

Service				Cost				Convenience				Control				Investment		
	L	G	S		L	G	S		L	G	S		L	G	S		L	G	S
L	1			L	1	1.5		L	1		5	L	1			L		3	
G	2.5	1	1.67	G		1		G	7	1	9	G	7	1	5	G		1	
S	1.5		1	S	2	3	1	S			1	S	3		1	S	4	12	1

There is a need for a combined pairwise comparison matrix for the criteria. Based upon least absolute value regression, and rounding to integer values, the following matrix is fairly close to the two pairwise comparison matrices used in the AHP analysis:

	Service	Cost	Convenience	Control	Investment
Service	1	2	5	2	3
Cost	1/2	1	2	1	2
Convenience	1/5	1/2	1	1/3	1/2
Control	1/2	1	3	1	2
Investment	1/3	1/2	2	1/2	1

The geometric means can then be calculated as the pth root of the product of p elements. For instance, the geometric mean for service is $(1 \times 2 \times 5 \times 2 \times 3)^{.2}$. The geometric means of the criterion level are normalized additively by dividing each geometric mean by the total of the geometric means, yielding a set of weights for each criterion:

	Service	Cost	Convenience	Control	Investment	Geometric Mean	Additively Normalized
Service	1	2	5	2	3	2.26793	.39088
Cost	1/2	1	2	1	2	1.14870	.19798
Convenience	1/5	1/2	1	1/3	1/2	.44093	.07599
Control	1/2	1	3	1	2	1.24573	.21470
Investment	1/3	1/2	2	1/2	1	.69883	.12044
						5.80212	

The matrices comparing relative alternative performance on each criterion are obtained by geometric mean.

	Service	Cost	Convenience	Control	Investment
L	.64366	.90856	.89390	.36246	.90856
G	1.60915	.60571	3.97906	3.27107	.30285
S	.96549	1.81712	.28114	.84343	3.63424

Synthesis is obtained by calculating a weight for each alternative i:

$$w_i \prod_{j-1}^{J} w_{ij}^{o_j}$$

For the current lot system (L), the calculation is:

$.64366^{.39088} \times .90856^{.19798} \times .89390^{.07599} \times .36246^{.21470} \times .90856^{.12044} = .65106.$

For the parking garage (G) the resulting calculation is 1.35284, and for expanding lots (S) the result is 1.13536. Note that these are multiplicatively normal (their product equals 1). Final weights can be obtained by additively normalizing these values (dividing each by the sum), yielding weights for each alternative of:

L	.20739
G	.43094
S	.36166

REMBRANDT

This approach has been developed into a software package by Lootsma and Rog called *REMBRANDT* (Ratio Estimation in Magnitudes or deci-Bells to Rate Alternatives which are Non-DominaTed: Lootsma, Mensch and Vos, 1990; Lootsma, 1992). This system is intended to adjust for three contended flaws in AHP. First, direct rating is on a logarithmic scale (Lootsma, 1988), which replaces the fundamental 1–9 scale presented by Saaty. Second, the Perron-Frobenius eigenvector method of calculating weights is replaced by the geometric mean, which avoids potential rank reversal (Barzilai, Cook and Golanyi, 1987). And third, aggregation of scores by arithmetic mean is replaced by the product of alternative relative scores weighted by the power of weights obtained from analysis of hierarchical elements above the alternatives.

TABLE 6.1 Verbal description

Verbal description	Saaty ratio w/w_k	REMBRANDT δ_{jk}
very strong preference for object k	1/9	−8
strong preference for object k	1/7	−6
definite preference for object k	1/5	−4
weak preference for object k	1/3	−2
indifference	1	0
weak preference for object j	3	+2
definite preference for object j	5	+4
strong preference for object j	7	+6
very strong preference for object j	9	+8

The first issue addressed by Lootsma is the numerical scale for verbal comparative judgment. Lootsma feels that relative advantage is more naturally concave, and presents a number of cases where a more nearly logarithmic scale would be appropriate, such as planning horizons, loudness of sounds, and brightness of light. Therefore, Lootsma presents a geometric scale where the gradations of decision maker judgment are reflected by the scale as follows:

- 1/16   **strict preference** for object 2 over base object
- 1/4   **weak preference** for object 2 over the base object
- 1   **indifference**
- 4   **weak preference** for the base object over object 2
- 16   **strict preference** for the base object over object 2

The ratio of value r_{jk} on the geometric scale is expressed as an exponential function of the difference between the echelons of value on the geometric scale δ_{jk}, as well as a scale parameter γ. Lootsma considers two alternative scales γ to express preferences. For calculating the weight of criteria, $\gamma = \ln \sqrt{2} \approx .347$ is used. In REMBRANDT, only one hierarchical level (no matter how many criteria) is used, superior to the level of alternatives. For calculating the weight of alternatives on each criterion, $\gamma = \ln 2 \approx .693$ is used. The difference in echelons of value δ_{jk} is graded as in Table 6.1, which compares Saaty's ratio scale with the REMBRANDT scale.

The second suggested improvement is the calculation of impact scores. The arithmetic mean is subject to rank reversal of alternatives. The geometric mean is not subject to rank reversal, nor is logrithmic regression. Barzilai, Cook and Golany [1987] argued that the geometric mean was more appropriate for calculation of relative value (through weights) than the arithmetic mean used by Saaty.

Lootsma proposes logarithmic regression, minimizing:

$$\Sigma_{j<k} (\ln r_{jk} - \ln v_j + \ln v_k)^2$$

where r_{jk} are the ratio comparisons made by the decision maker for base object j and compared object k, and the weight for j (w_j) is represented by $\ln v_j$. Ratio r_{jk} is the ratio of w_j/w_k. The analysis is to calculate these weights. Since $r_{jk} = w_j/w_k$, error is represented by $r_{jk} - w_j/w_k$. The ratio comparisons made by the decision maker are observations, and regression minimizing the squared error yields the set of weights w_i which best fit the decision maker expressed preferences. Solving this is complicated by the fact that the resulting data set is singular. However, a series of normal equations can be solved to yield the desired weights.

To demonstrate, assume a pairwise comparison ratio comparing three factors {A, B & C}, where A is definitely preferred over B, A is strongly preferred over C, while B is weakly preferred over C. This yields the matrix $\delta(jk)$ of preferences, transformed into $r_{jk} - e^{347\delta(jk)}$. Weights are desired that minimize the function $\Sigma_{j=1,n} \Sigma_{k=1,n} (\ln a_{jk} - \ln w_j + \ln w_k)^2$. The ratio matrix in *REMBRANDT* for criteria is transformed through the operator $e^{347r(jk)}$ to generate the set of values transformed to the logarithmic scale. Křovác [1987] notes that the geometric means of row elements of such a matrix yields the solution minimizing the sum of squared errors of the form $\Sigma_{j=1,n} \Sigma_{k=1,n} (\ln r_{jk} - \ln w_j + \ln w_k)$. This yields:

$\delta(jk)$	$e^{347\,\delta(jk)}$	Geometric means
$\begin{bmatrix} 0 & +4 & +6 \\ -4 & 0 & +2 \\ -6 & -2 & 0 \end{bmatrix}$	$\begin{bmatrix} 1 & 4 & 8 \\ .25 & 1 & 2 \\ .125 & .5 & 1 \end{bmatrix}$	3.175 .794 .397

This solution is normalized by product. It is a simple matter to normalize by sum, simply dividing each element by the total. *REMBRANDT* includes a consistency check, in that cases where alternative j is preferred to alternative k on some criteria implies that the resulting score w_j on this criteria should be greater than score w_k. If not, the user is informed.

The third improvement proposed by Lootsma is aggregation of scores. *REMBRANDT* uses one hierarchical level (allowing 25 criteria), with the alternative level (allowing 25 alternatives) subordinate to it. This lowest level is normalized multiplicatively, so that the product of components equals 1 for each of the k factors over which the alternatives are compared. Therefore, each alternative has an estimated relative performance w_k for each of the k factors. The components of the hierarchical level immediately superior to this lowest level are normalized additively, so that they add to 1, yielding weights $O(j)$. The aggregation rule for each alternative j is:

$$w_j = \Pi_{i=1,k} \, w_i^{O(i)}$$

Nuclear Disposal Site Selection Problem.

We will demonstrate *REMBRANDT* using the nuclear disposal site selection problem used in prior chapters. The following hierarchy combines types of lives lost into one criterion, because *REMBRANDT* uses only one criterion level.

Overall

```
        ┌──────────┬──────────┬──────────┐
      Cost    Lives Lost     Risk    Civic Improvement
```

The pairwise comparisons for this hierarchy are assumed to be:

	Cost (bill)	Expected Lives Lost	Risk	Civic Improvement
Nome, AK	40	60	very high	low
Newark, NJ	100	140	very low	very high
Rock Springs, WY	60	40	low	high
Duquesne, PA	60	40	medium	medium
Gary, IN	70	80	low	very high

REMBRANDT allows two modes of input: a multiplicative scale and an anchored scale as used in *SMART*. *REMBRANDT* is also designed to accomodate groups of decision makers, aggregating their inputs using geometric means. We will use two decision makers, called Tom and James. Tom will use the multiplicative scale and James will use the *SMART* scale.

The first requirement is for Tom to input his preferences, first comparing the criteria, and then evaluating the alternatives on each criterion. The scale used for the multiplicative input is the δ_{jk}, where +8 represents a very strong preference for object j over object k, 0 represents indifference, and −8 represents a very strong preference for object k over object j. The input screen for the multiplicative input is:

Pairwise Comparison of the Criteria

( ) +8 first much more important
( ) +7 —
( ) +6 first something more important
( ) +5 —
( ) +4 first more important
( ) +3 —
( ) +2 first somewhat more important
( ) +1 —
( ) =0 both criteria have equal importance
( ) −1 —
( ) −2 second somewhat more important
( ) −3 —
( ) −4 second more important
( ) −5 —
( ) −6 second something more important
( ) −7 —
( ) −8 second much more important

Thinking of the criterion, express most accurately your comparative judgement between the two named criteria.

Intermediate grades may be used when hesitating between two named gradations. When you are finished, press "OK". If you have no opinion, select "No opinion".

No opinion   OK

Tom's input:

| | Criteria | | | |
	Cost	Lives	Risk	Impr
Cost		−8	−2	+8
Lives			+5	+8
Risk				+8
Impr				

Cost	Nome	Newa	Rock	Duqu	Gary	Lives	Nome	Newa	Rock	Duqu	Gary
Nome		+2	+1	+1	+1	Nome		+2	−1	−1	+1
Newa			−1	−1	−1	Newa			−3	−3	−1
Rock				0	0	Rock				0	+1
Duqu					0	Duqu					+1

Risk	Nome	Newa	Rock	Duqu	Gary	Impro	Nome	Newa	Rock	Duqu	Gary
Nome		−8	−6	−4	−4	Nome		−6	−4	−2	−6
Newa			+2	+4	+2	Newa			+2	+4	0
Rock				+2	0	Rock				+2	−2
Duqu					−2	Duqu					−4

This input yields relative scores for Tom of:

Criterion	Weight	Nome	Newark	Rock Springs	Duquesne	Gary
Cost	.097	.364	.091	.182	.182	.182
Lives	.711	.185	.046	.323	.323	.122
Risk	.178	.003	.664	.166	.041	.126
Improve	.014	.007	.430	.107	.027	.430
Total scores		.106	.120	.344	.263	.168

James prefers to use the anchored scale. A rating of 10 would be assigned to an ideal alternative as evaluated on this criterion. A rating of 4 is assigned to as poor a rating as could be reasonably considered.

Comparison of the Criteria Using Grades

( ) 10.0 Excellent   Thinking of criterion, express
( ) 9.5 -   most accurately your
( ) 9.0 =   judgement of criterion one.
( ) 8.5 -   Intermediate grades may
( ) 8.0 Good   be used when hesitating
( ) 7.5 -   between two named
( ) 7.0 =   gradations. When you are
( ) 6.5 -   finished, press "Ok'. If
( ) 6.0 Fair   you have no opinion,
( ) 5.5 -   select "No opinion".
( ) 5.0 =
( ) 4.5 -
( ) 4.0 Poor
       No opinion   Ok

The ratings on this scale for James (reasonably compatible with Tom's relative opinions) are:

	Criteria			
	Cost	Lives	Risk	Impr
	6	10	8	4
Nome	9	7	4	5
Newark	4	4	10	10
Rock Springs	6	9	8	8
Duquesne	6	9	6	6
Gary	5	5	8	10

This input yields relative scores for James of:

Criterion	Weight	Nome	Newark	Rock Spring	Duquesne	Gary
Cost	.133	.744	.023	.093	.093	.047
Lives	.533	.107	.013	.427	.427	.027
Risk	.267	.010	.634	.158	.040	.158
Improve	.067	.013	.427	.107	.027	.427
Total scores		.112	.089	.430	.271	.098

The anchored scale has scores slightly more dispersed, although both results have the same relative order. The group score is calculated using geometric means of individual ratings (before logarithmic regression), yielding:

Criterion	Weight	Nome	Newark	Rock Spring	Duquesne	Gary
Cost	.116	.567	.050	.142	.142	.100
Lives	.630	.146	.026	.385	.385	.059
Risk	.223	.006	.650	.162	.041	.141
Improve	.032	.009	.428	.107	.027	.428
Total socres		.112	.091	.398	.280	.119

This compares as follows with other technique results:

MAUT		Formula AHP		Full AHP		REMBRANDT	
Rock Springs	.6043	Rock Springs	.51158	Rock Springs	.25945	Rock Springs	.398
Duquesne	.5200	Duquesne	.45563	Duquesne	.23519	Duquesne	.280
Gary	.4478	Gary	.34155	Newark	.17036	Gary	.119
Newark	.3374	Nome	.27346	Nome	.16915	Nome	.112
Nome	.2803	Newark	.22382	Gary	.16584	Newark	.091

Note that *REMBRANDT* provides a relative ranking quite similar to the other techniques. All of them would provide precisely the same relative scoring given input precisely the same. As in AHP, the input was somewhat subjective, although basically the same. *REMBRANDT* has more dispersed scores than full AHP, because of the wider scale used in *REMBRANDT*.

REMBRANDT provides some feedback relative to inconsistent input. There is no index for every matrix, but if the relative preference of two objects is reversed relative to prior input, the user is informed.

House Selection Calculations

We will finally demonstrate *REMBRANDT* using the house selection problem dealt with in prior chapters. Here we can easily accomodate the realism of a group decision. Assume a family making this decision. The husband and wife both have a weight of 9, and the kid has a weight of 1. Each of these three people have different perspectives about the relative importance of criteria, as well as how well each available house accomplishes attainment of each criterion. *REMBRANDT* is designed to reflect all of these differences. Further, each decision maker can use either input form (multiplicative or anchored) for any element of the hierarchy. The hierarchy is:

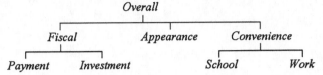

Available alternatives are:

Alternative (units)	Payment (dollars)	Investment (thousand dolllars)	Appearance (categorical)	School (blocks)	Work (miles)
Ramshackle	400	50	very poor	1	10
Baltic Avenue	500	55	poor	8	3
Tennessee Avenue	650	70	average	7	15
Illinois Avenue	800	90	good	15	25
Park Place	1000	120	very good	12	45

The husband's input reflects a fairly high emphasis upon financial matters, and a higher emphasis on the distance to work than is shared by his family:

Husband	Criteria Payment	Investment	Appearance	School	Work
Payment		−2	+3	+7	+5
Investment			+5	+8	+7
Appearance				−4 −2	
School					−2

Payment	Ram	Bal	Ten	Ill	PPl
Ramshackle		+1	+2	+4	+6
Baltic			+1	+3	+5
Tennessee				+2	+4
Park Place					+2

Investment	Ram	Bal	Ten	Ill	PPl
Ramshackle		0	−2	−4	−7
Baltic			−2	−4	−6
Tennessee				−2	−4
Park Place					−2

Appearance	Ram	Bal	Ten	Ill	PPl
Ramshackle		−1	−4	−6	−8
Baltic			−3	−5	−7
Tennessee				−2	−4
Park Place					−2

School	Ram	Bal	Ten	Ill	PPl
Ramshackle		+2	+2	+4	+3
Baltic			0	+2	+1
Tennessee				+2	+1
Park Place					−1

Work	Ram	Bal	Ten	Ill	PPl
Ramshackle		+2	−2	−4	−6
Baltic			−4	−6	−8
Tennessee				−2	−4
Park Place					−2

This input yields relative scores for husband of:

Criterion	Weight	Ramshackle	Baltic	Tennessee	Illinois	Park Place
Payment	.293	.547	.274	.137	.034	.009
Investment	.546	.009	.010	.042	.168	.771
Appearance	.045	.003	.006	.047	.189	.755
School	.048	.593	.148	.148	.037	.074
Work	.068	.012	.003	.047	.188	.751
Total score		.087	.067	.155	.242	.448

The husband clearly prefers Park Place. The wife's inputs and results:

Wife	Criteria Payment	Investment	Appearance	School	Work
Payment		+3	−4	−2	+6
Investment			−7	−5	+3
Appearance				+2	+7
School					+8

Payment	Ram	Bal	Ten	Ill	PPl
Ramshackle		+1	+4	+6	+8
Baltic			+3	+5	+7
Tennessee				+2	+4
Park Place					+2

Investment	Ram	Bal	Ten	Ill	PPl
Ramshackle		−1	−2	−4	−5
Baltic			−1	−3	−4
Tennessee				−2	−3
Park Place					−1

Appearance	Ram	Bal	Ten	Ill	PPl
Ramshackle		−2	−6	−7	−8
Baltic			−4	−5	−6
Tennessee				−1	−2
Park Place					−1

School	Ram	Bal	Ten	Ill	PPl
Ramshackle		+1	+1	+6	+4
Baltic			0	+5	+3
Tennessee				+5	+3
Park Place					−2

Work	Ram	Bal	Ten	Ill	PPl
Ramshackle		+2	0	+2	+4
Baltic			−2	0	+2
Tennessee				+2	+4
Park Place					+2

Note that the wife has different views about what has value with respect to distance to work. Her input yields relative scores of:

Criterion	Weight	Ramshackle	Baltic	Tennessee	Illinois	Park Place
Payment	.148	.632	.316	.040	.010	.002
Investment	.052	.018	.036	.073	.291	.582
Appearance	.481	.002	.009	.141	.283	.565
School	.296	.481	.241	.241	.008	.030
Work	.023	.390	.098	.390	.098	.024
Total score		.086	.123	.367	.156	.268

Based on the heavier weight given to *School* and the lower weights given to *Investment* and *Work*, the wife has a different preferred house than the husband. The kid is yet to be heard from.

Kid	Criteria Payment	Investment	Appearance	School	Work
Payment		+1	−4	−8	+2
Investment			−3	−7	+1
Appearance				−4	+6
School					+8

Payment	Ram	Bal	Ten	Ill	PPl
Ramshackle	0	+1	+2	+3	
Baltic		0	+1	+2	
Tennessee			0	+1	
Park Place				0	

Investment	Ram	Bal	Ten	ll	PPl
Ramshackle	0	0	0	0	
Baltic		0	0	0	
Tennessee			0	0	
Park Place				0	

Appearance	Ram	Bal	Ten	Ill	PPl
Ramshackle	0	−4	−7	−8	
Baltic		−4	−7	−8	
Tennessee			−3	−4	
Park Place				−1	

School	Ram	Bal	Ten	Ill	PPl
Ramshackle	−2	−2	+4	+2	
Baltic		0	+6	+4	
Tennessee			+6	+4	
Park Place				−2	

Work	Ram	Bal	Ten	Ill	PPl
Ramshackle	+2	0	0	0	
Baltic		−2	−2	−2	
Tennessee			0	0	
Park Place				0	

The kid doesn't see any difference in *Investment*. He also has different views of relative value of the distance to *School*. The kid's input yields relative scores of:

Criterion	Weight	Ramshackle	Baltic	Tennessee	Illinois	Park Place
Payment	.055	.389	.257	.169	.112	.074
Investment	.052	.200	.200	.200	.200	.200
Appearance	.192	.002	.002	.040	.318	.637
School	.669	.107	.430	.430	.007	.027
Work	.032	.235	.059	.235	.235	.235
Total score		.112	.266	.463	.042	.118

This all aggregates to:

Criterion	Weight	Ramshackle	Baltic	Tennessee	Illinois	Park Place
Payment	.289	.593	.301	.079	.021	.005
Investment	.236	.016	.023	.063	.233	.666
Appearance	.222	.003	.007	.081	.241	.669
School	.195	.518	.208	.208	.017	.048
Work	.058	.142	.036	.274	.274	.274
Total score		.174	.151	.250	.181	.244

REMBRANDT will calculate an aggregate score reflecting whatever weights of group member importance are included. Here, there were different outcomes preferred, with the wife and kid both preferring the house on Tennessee Avenue, while the husband preferred Park Place. As in all such family compromises, *REMBRANDT* can see the writing on the wall, and recommends the house on Tennessee Avenue.

	Husband	Wife	Kid	Aggregate
Ramshackle	.087	.086	.112	.174
Baltic Avenue	.067	.123	266	.151
Tennessee Avenue	.155	.367*	.463*	.250*
Illinois Avenue	.242	.156	.042	.181
Park Place	.448*	.268	.118	.244

References

Barzilai, J., Cook, W. and Golany, B. 1987. Consistent weights for judgements matrices of the relative importance for alternatives. *Operations Research Letters* **6**:3, 131–134.

Barzilai, J., Cook, W. and Golany, B. 1990. The analytic hierarchy process: Structure of the problem and its solutions. In *Extremal Methods and Systems Analysis II*, A. Ben-Israel, A. Ben-Tal, B. Golany, K.O. Kortanek and J.J. Rosseau, eds., Westport, CT: Greenwood Press.

Barzilai, J. and Golany, B. 1990. Deriving weights from pairwise comparison matrices: The additive case. *Operations Research Letters* **9**:6, 407–410.

Belton, V. and Gear, A.E. 1983. On a shortcoming of Saaty's method of analytical hierarchies. *Omega* **11**:3, 227–230.

Belton, V. and Gear, A.E. 1985a. The legitimacy of rank reversal—A comment. *Omega* **13**:3, 143–144.

Belton, V. and Gear, T. 1985b. A series of experiments into the use of pairwise comparison techniques to evaluate criteria weights. In *Decision Making with Multiple Objectives: Proceedings VI — Cleveland, OH, Jun 1984*, Y.Y. Haimes and V. Chankong, eds., 375–387.

Křováč, J. 1987. Ranking alternatives: Comparison of different methods based on binary comparison matrices. *European Journal of Operational Research* **32**, 86–95.

Lootsma, F.A. 1980. Saaty's priority theory and the nomination of a senior professor in operations research. *European Journal of Operational Research* **4**, 380–388.

Lootsma, F.A. 1988. Numerical scaling of human judgement in pairwise-comparison methods for fuzzy multi-criteria decision analysis, in: G. Mitra (ed.), *Mathematical Models for Decision Support*. Berlin: Springer-Verlag, 57–88.

Lootsma, F.A., Mensch, T.C.A. and Vos, F.A. 1990. Multi-criteria analysis and budget reallocation in long-term research planning. *European Journal of Operational Research* **47**, 293–305.

Lootsma, F.A. 1991. Scale sensitivity and rank preservation in a multiplicative variant of the AHP and SMART. Report 91-67, Faculty of Technical Mathematics and Informatics, Delft University of Technology, Delft, The Netherlands.

Lootsma, F.A. 1992. The REMBRANDT system for multi-criteria decision analysis via pairwise comparisons or direct rating. Report 92-05, Faculty of Technical Mathematics and Informatics, Delft University of Technology, Delft, The Netherlands.

Saaty, T.L. 1977. A scaling method for priorities in hierarchical structures. *Journal of Mathematical Psychology* **15**, 234–281.

Schoner, B. and Wedley, W.C. 1989. Ambiguous criteria weights in AHP: Consequences and solutions. *Decision Sciences* **20**, 462–475.

7
Preference Cones

Multiple objective approaches generally seek to identify the set of nondominated solutions to a decision model. A solution is defined as nondominated if no other solution exists which would improve one or more objectives without detriment to some other objective. One complication in mathematical programming models is that there may be an extremely large nondominated set. Nondominated theory can limit the decision maker selection to a smaller set of theoretically rational alternatives (more of a good is always better than less) This approach is valid if decision makers have expressed all objectives. The next evolutionary problem is how to select from among the nondominated set. If there are seven or fewer choices, decision maker judgement should be adequate. Quite often, however, there are more than seven nondominated alternatives to select from. Simple pairwise comparisons among alternatives will identify the preferred solution without too much difficulty, but the prevailing consensus is that this would only work for 12–15 alternatives. When there are likely to be more alternatives, the weights obtained in Chapter 6 could be used to score each alternative being considered. If those approaches are not considered attractive for some reason, there are other approaches. This chapter reviews preference cone techniques. Preference cones use information from decision maker pairwise comparisons to logically eliminate alternatives which would require intransitivity to be selected.

Combination of multiple objectives is complicated by the nonlinear nature of utility. From Debreu [1959], rational decision maker utility should be at least quasi-concave, with more of a good being preferred to less of that good, *ceteris parebis*, but at a diminishing rate. But most decision makers are not expected to apply this nonlinear function of utility. Interactive multiobjective techniques, however, provide a means to allow decision makers to express nonlinear utility without its expression. Steuer [1977] presents theory based upon the preference cone established by decision maker pairwise comparisons assuming linear utility. A linear form of utility would be expressed by a set of weights. For a utility function of k objectives,

$$Utility = \Sigma_k W_k Z_k$$

where Z_k is the attainment on each objective, while W_k represents the weight on each objective. Korhonen, et al. [1984] established the necessary theory to apply the concept of cones inferred from decision maker pairwise comparisons, given a quasi-concave utility function.

An additional complication is that the relative scales of measurement of each of the k objective functions need to be considered. It does little good to develop relative weights for each objective and then distort them by different scales of measurement. Relative attainments can be reflected by standardizing each objective function (for instance, to a 0–1 scale, or alternatively, by modifying the weights).

Procedure

Given a set of solution alternatives, preference cones can be used to reduce the nondominated set, as well as direct the search to the decision maker's preferred solution.

Step 1: *Eliminate dominated solutions.* A comparison algorithm evaluates feasible solutions, retaining for consideration nondominated alternatives. This weeding process is very rapid by computer. However, it is very difficult to predict how many alternatives will be eliminated. For problems involving more objectives, fewer eliminations by this step are expected.

Step 2: *Generate a set (two to seven) of nondominated solutions for decision maker preference.*
    Two phases are recommended in this step.
    Phase 1: The first phase would be to eliminate the impact of different scales for each criterion measure by developing a standardized 0–1 metric of relative attainment. This would place the attainment of each alternative on each objective on a common 0–1 scale, where 0 is the worst identified attainment among the nondominated set, and 1 is the best attainment in that set. (This concept was presented by Benayoun, et al. [1971] in their presentation of the Step Method). For an objective to be maximized, given that Z_k^* = optimal attainment for objective k over all alternatives

$$Z_k^- = \text{least attractive nondominated attainment for objective } k$$

the relative score for an arbitrary alternative i on objective k would be:

$$\frac{Z_k^* - Z_k}{Z_k^* - Z_k^-}$$

For an objective to be minimized, the formula would be:

$$\frac{Z_k - Z_k^*}{Z_k^- - Z_k^*}$$

Phase 2: Generate alternatives for decision maker consideration. Two closely related (adjacent) solutions are used in pairwise comparison of alternatives to obtain decision maker preference. This approach follows the concept of Korhonen et al. [1984], extended to nonlinear functions by Köksalan and Taner [1992]. Malakooti [1988] presented a similar approach. The benefit would be that nonlinear utility could more accurately be reflected. The concept would be to use the preference information as gradients of the decision maker's utility function. A potential deficiency is that identification of the preferred solution may be much slower than with Steuer's approach. Köksalan and Taner [1992], however, report very attractive results.

Step 3: *Develop the cone of decision maker utility and generate a new set of alternatives.* As presented in Korhonen, et al., knowledge of decision maker preference can easily be formulated into a small linear programming model, which can establish if the attainment of other alternatives must be dominated by the alternative selected by the decision maker. Note that there are a number of alternative means of calculation. The straightforward way, basing the objective function on the best current solution, won't guarantee that the true best alternative will not be eliminated by the preference cone (Ramesh, et al. 1988, p. 1095). Guarantee of not eliminating alternatives that are dominated by convex combinations of other alternatives requires basing the objective function coefficients on the *worst* alternative considered to date (Korhonen, et al., 1984). However, this yields a weaker cone, which results in more pairwise comparisons. Köksalan and coresearchers have developed more efficient methods. Here we will discuss more basic versions of preference cones.

Basing Objective on Current Best Choice

For a set of alternatives involving K criteria, given that alternative A is preferred to alternative B, in order to evaluate a third alternative C the LP model is:

$$\text{variables} = \lambda_k \text{ representing each of the } K \text{ objectives.} \qquad [7\text{-}1]$$

Let A_k, B_k, and C_k represent the attainment of each alternative on objective k.

- Max $\Sigma_k (C_k - A_k)\lambda_k$ move in direction indicated by preference
- st$(B_k - A_k)\lambda_k \leq 0$ stay within preference cone
- $\lambda_k \geq 0$ for all k

If there is not a solution with a positive objective function value to this LP, then alternative C is dominated by alternative A (moving in the direction of the candidate solution would require leaving the preference cone).

Step 4: *Decision maker selection until convergence (the preference cone eliminates all candidate solutions other than the preferred solution).*

Basing Objective on Worst Choice to Date

The formulation would be very similar to [7-1], with the exception being the calculation of the objective function coefficients:

$$\text{variables} = \lambda_k \text{ representing each of the } K \text{ objectives} \qquad [7\text{-}2]$$

Let A_k, B_k, and C_k represent the attainment of each alternative on objective k.

- Max $\Sigma_k (C_k - B_k)\lambda_k$ move in direction indicated by weaker preference cone
- st $(B_k - A_k)\lambda_k \leq 0$ stay within preference cone
- $\lambda_k \geq 0$ for all k

This formulation will require more pairwise comparisons of alternatives by the decision maker, and will also require the decision maker to keep track of the *worst* alternative considered to date. But it guarantees identification of the preferred alternative when value tradeoff functions are nonlinear (and quasiconcave).

To demonstrate preference cones, consider alternatives {A}, {B}, {C} and {D} with attainments as given:

	Z_1	Z_2
{A}	104	50
{B}	96	69
{C}	69	96
{D}	50	104

Assume the decision maker selected {A} over {B}

Preference Cone:
$$(96-104) Z_1 + (69-50) Z_2 \leq 0$$

Then any other alternative {X} can be evaluated by maximizing the function:

$$(c_{1x}-104) Z_1 + (c_{2x}-50) Z_2$$

For the remaining alternatives:

$$\{C\}: \text{ Max } (69-104) Z_1 + (96-50) Z_2$$
$$\text{st} \qquad -8 Z_1 + \qquad 19 Z_2 \leq 0$$

Here the objective function is $-35 Z_1 + 46 Z_2$ subject to $Z_2 \leq 8/19 Z_1$. As the ratio 35/46 is greater than the ratio 8/19, it is impossible for the objective function to be nonnegative. This implies that {C} is dominated by the preference cone.

$$\{D\}: \text{ Max } (50-104) Z_1 + (104-50) Z_2$$
$$\text{st} \qquad -8 Z_1 + \qquad 19 Z_2 \leq 0$$

Here the objective function is $-54 Z_1 + 54 Z_2$ subject to $Z_2 \leq 8/19 Z_1$. Thus it is impossible for the objective function to be anything but negative, and {D} is dominated by the preference cone.

Adjacency Formulation

A tool sometimes used is to determine adjacency of alternatives relative to a base (current) solution. For instance, to determine the adjacency of alternative {B} to current solution {A}, the formulation would be to maximize {B} attainments for each objective minus {A} attainments, subject to constraints for each of the other actively considered alternatives.

$$\text{Max } (96-104) Z_1 + (69-50) Z_2$$
$$\text{st} \quad (69-104) Z_1 + (96-50) Z_2 \le 0 \qquad \text{for } \{C\}$$
$$(50-104) Z_1 + (104-50) Z_2 \le 0 \qquad \text{for } \{D\}$$
$$Z_1, Z_2 \ge 0$$

If the solution to this model is unbounded, the alternative being evaluated ({B} in this case) is adjacent to the base alternative ({A} in this case). If the solution to this model is negative or zero, the alternative being evaluated is not adjacent to the base alternative. In this example, the solution is unbounded, indicating that {B} is adjacent to {A}.

Cellular Manufacturing Example

We will apply the proposed technique to a cell-machine assignment problem. Assume a problem with 4 cells, 24 machines, and 50 parts to be assigned. Generated solutions are processed by a nondominated solution routine, resulting in the following 10 nondominated solutions:

Alternative	Z_1	Z_2	Z_3	Z_4
	Cost	Utilization Imbalance	% Shop Utilization	Exceptional Parts
#56	−738	−5.3	33.8	−15
#96	−702	−15.8	32.4	−15
#132	−815	−14.9	35.8	−15
#149	−612	−17.2	34.5	−13
#166	−752	−9.7	34.0	−14
#167	−698	−21.4	35.7	−16
#183	−686	−16.5	33.8	−14
#192	−914	−4.3	30.5	−20
#253	−878	−3.1	29.3	−16
#287	−633	−39.7	34.6	−14

These solutions can be transformed into their standardized scores, yielding:

| Alternative | S_1 | S_2 | S_3 | S_4 | |
	Cost	Utilization Imbalance	% Shop Utilization	Exceptional Parts	Sum
#56	.5828	.9399	.6923	.7143	2.9293
#96	.7020	.6530	.4769	.7143	2.5462
#132	.3278	.6776	1.0000	.7143	2.7197
#149	1.0000	.6148	.8000	1.0000	3.4148
#166	.5364	.8197	.7231	.8571	2.9363
#167	.7152	.5000	.9846	.5714	2.7713
#183	.7550	.6339	.6923	.8571	2.9383
#192	.0000	.9672	.1846	.0000	1.1518
#253	.1192	1.0000	.0000	.5714	1.6906
#287	.9305	.0000	.8154	.8571	2.6030

The formula for decision maker utility is assumed unknown. However, to act as a decision maker, we will assume the function:

$$U = -\Sigma_k (1-S_k)^2$$

This function has the feature that for each of the four objectives, more attainment is always preferred to less, but at a declining rate. This function will act as a surrogate for the decision maker. The utilities for the 10 nondominated solutions are:

	Alternative	$U = -\Sigma_k (1-S_k)^2$	Rank
1	#56	−0.3540	4
2	#96	−0.5645	6
3	#132	−0.6374	7
4	#149	−0.1884	1
5	#166	−0.3445	3
6	#167	−0.5150	5
7	#183	−0.3092	2
8	#192	−2.6660	10
9	#253	−1.9595	9
10	#287	−1.0593	8

We will present the procedure relying upon the gradient cone, based upon the procedure presented in Korhonen, Wallenius, and Zionts. This procedure involves pairwise comparison of two alternatives at one time. This should be safer than the other approach, based upon comparing up to seven alternatives at one time (based upon Steuer's [1977] mathematical programming approach), although more steps will be involved.

Basing Objective on Current Best Choice

The first step is to identify a starting solution, identify adjacent solutions, and present to the decision maker. The sum of the standardized weights yields alternative #149. Limiting the comparisons to adjacent solutions should provide added assurance that cones will not eliminate nondominated solutions under conditions of nonlinear utility. Adjacent solutions (following Korhonen et al. [1984]) are alternatives #56, #132, #166, and #167. The highest sum of standardized scores among these three candidate solutions is that of alternative #166. The U score indicates alternative #149 is preferred to alternative #166. The preference cone is developed, and each of the other nondominated alternatives are tested to see if this cone eliminates them from consideration.

$$\text{Max} \ \Sigma_k \ [Z_k(\text{tested alternative}) - Z_k(\#149)]V_k$$
$$\text{st} \quad \Sigma_k \ [Z_k(\#166) - Z_k(\#149)]V_k \le 0$$
$$\Sigma_k V = 1 \quad \text{all} \ V_k \ge 0$$

For instance, to test alternative #56,

$$\text{Max} -126 \ V_1 + 11.9 \ V_2 - 0.7 \ V_3 - 2 \ V_4$$
$$\text{st} \quad -140 \ V_1 + 7.5 \ V_2 - 0.5 \ V_3 - 1 \ V_4 \le 0$$
$$V_1 + V_2 + V_3 + V_4 = 1$$

The solution to this LP is $V_1 = .0508$, $V_3 = .9492$, with an objective function value of 4.8881. Since the objective function is positive, this indicates that the gradient of change from alternative #149 to alternative #56 is within the preference cone implied by the preference of #149 over #166. This implies that there is a feasible set of weights, given the preference information, which could yield alternative #56 rather than alternative #149. At this stage, after all alternatives are evaluated, alternatives #96, #183, #192 and #253 are eliminated by the preference cone. This leaves alternatives #56, #132, #167, and #287 in addition to the current solution #149.

Given the current solutions, an adjacency test is conducted. Alternatives #56, #132, and #167 are adjacent to #149. Of these, the highest sum of weights is associated with #56. The decision maker is asked to compare #149 and #56. By the utility function, #149 is preferred. This yields another cone. Since both alternatives #166 and #56 were compared with #149, the preference cone constrained by both comparisons can be used. Conducting the same test as above, no other alternatives are eliminated by this new cone.

The adjacency test is conducted again, on the smaller set of remaining solutions. Alternatives #132 and #167 are adjacent to #149. Of these, #167 has the highest sum of standard scores. Alternative #149 is preferred to alternative #167 by the utility function. The implied cone of preferences #149 > #56, #149 > #166 and #149 > #167 eliminates alternative # 287 but not #132. The last pairwise comparison finds alternative #149 preferred to #132. Thus, four pairwise comparisons were needed with this approach.

Alternative Methods

In this example, using the preference ranking of the seven alternatives with the highest sum of standardized scores (based upon Steuer's method), the preference cone eliminated all alternatives except for **#149** in one step. The preference cone used was **#149 > #183, #149 > #166, 149 > #56, #149 > #167, #149 > #132**, and **#149 > #287**. The other three nondominated alternatives were tested against this cone, and all three eliminated.

An approach compromising these two ideas is to compare all adjacent solutions to the base solution. In this case, the preference cone was **#149 > #56, #149 > #132**, and **#149 > #167**. This cone eliminated all of the other six alternative solutions. Of course, in this example, we started with the ultimately preferred solution (as is often reported by others: Korhonen, Wallenius, and Zionts as well as Malakooti).

Basing Objective on Worst Choice to Date

Here the same procedure would be followed, with the change in the calculation of the objective function coefficients.

$$\text{Max } \Sigma_k \, [Z_k(\text{tested alternative})-Z_k(\#166)]V_k$$
$$\text{st} \quad \Sigma_k \, [Z_k(\#166)-Z_k(\#149)]V_k \leq 0$$
$$\Sigma_k \, V = 1 \quad \text{all } V_k \geq 0$$

For instance, to test alternative **#56**,

$$\text{Max } 14 \, V_1 + 4.4 \, V_2 - 0.2 \, V_3 - 1 \, V_4$$
$$\text{st} \quad -140 \, V_1 + 7.5 \, V_2 - 0.5 \, V_3 - 1 \, V_4 \leq 0$$
$$V_1 + V_2 + V_3 + V_4 = 1$$

The solution to this LP is $V_1 = 1.0$ with an objective function value of 14. Since the objective function is positive, this indicates that the gradient of change from alternative **#149** to alternative **#56** is within the preference cone implied by the preference of **#149** over **#166**. This implies that there is a feasible set of weights, given the preference information, which could yield alternative **#56** rather than alternative **#149**. At this stage, after all alternatives are evaluated, alternatives **#192** and **#253** are eliminated by the preference cone. Note that alternative **#96** and **#183** are not eliminated as was the case with the formulation of objective coefficients based upon the best choice to date. A comparison of the sequence of alternatives for the two methods is:

	base C_j on best			base C_j on worst	
		Preference	Cone		Preference	Cone
P1	#149>#166	#166	#96,#183,#192,#253	#149>#166	#166	#192,#253
P2	#149>#56	#56	—	#149>#56	#56	#96
P3	#149>#167	#167	#287	#149>#167	#167	—
P4	#149>#132	#132		#149>#132	#132	—
P5				#149>#183	#183	—
P6				#149>#287	#287	

In this case, basing the calculation on the best choice (heuristic) yielded the correct solution in four pairwise comparisons, as opposed to six with the other method (guaranteed optimal).

Automation Example

The following example is taken from Wymore and Duckstein [1989]. It concerns prioritizing factory automation investments involving eight criteria. Note that the Wymore and Duckstein article applied the multicriterion-Q technique, similar to *ELECTRE*.

Eleven automation investment alternatives are available.

#1 PWB photo-processing to automate material handling and photo-processing of printed wiring boards, using conveyors and robots

#2 PWB plating bath control to automate maintenance and control of the volume and chemical content of plating baths for printed wiring boards, using sensors and actuators driven by a distributed computer network

#3 PWB optical inspection to automate inspection of printed wiring boards with multiple inner layers, involving purchase of a computerized optical inspection system

#4 PWB identification using robot and laser technology to inscribe an ID number on printed wiring boards

#5 Component preparation to automate pre-tinning component wires, using a robotic material handling system

#6 Component kitting to sort components into individual packages for circuit card assembly, using a computer driven sorting and material handling system

#7 Component insertion to place components on printed wiring boards and clench component leads

#8 Masking using a robot with a vision system to mask holes and sensitive components prior to wave solder

#9 Pre-solder inspection using a vision system to verify placement of circuit board components

#10 Point solder using a robot to hand solder components sensitive to wave solder

#11 Solder joint inspection using an X-ray system to determine validity of solder joints on circuit boards

The eight criteria were:

IRR internal rate of return based upon initial investment and labor savings

RISK investment risk — the probability a project will not succeed (qualitative)

EDGE competitive edge — competitive advantage gained by project, including perceived increase in market share and technological prowess gained over competitors (qualitative)

QUAL quality improvement — increase in product quality (qualitative)

FLEX flexibility improvement — increase in production flexibility in terms of product mix, production rate, and scheduling (qualitative — engineering analysis)

CROS   cross applicability — extent to which technology can be transferred to other areas (qualitative — engineering analysis)

LC   learning curve — amount of time necessary to complete transition from manual to automated — expressed in months (*minimize*)

MGMT management commitment (qualitative)

Project/criteria ratings are:

	IRR	RISK	EDGE	QUAL	FLEX	CROS	LC	MGMT
#1	.71	M	M	L	H	M	6	M
#2	.73	H	H	M	VH	H	8	M
#3	.73	L	M	H	M	L	6	H
#4	.22	M	M	L	M	H	3	M
#5	1.34	M	M	M	M	H	6	L
#6	.63	M	H	M	VH	VH	6	L
#7	1.51	M	H	M	VH	L	6	H
#8	.67	M	M	M	M	H	3	M
#9	.42	H	H	VH	H	H	6	M
#10	.54	M	M	M	M	H	6	M
#11	.45	H	H	H	H	L	12	H

VH = *very high*; H = *high*; M = *medium*; L = *low*; VL = *very low*

Because **LC** is to be minimized, Wymore and Duckstein used the inverse of the months of estimated transition. A nondominated analysis would reveal that #4 and #10 are dominated by #8. After elimination of these alternatives, the standardized scores are:

	IRR	RISK	EDGE	QUAL	FLEX	CROS	LC	MGMT
#1	.2661	.5000	0	0	.5000	.3333	.3600	.5000
#2	.2844	0	1	.3333	1	.6667	.1200	.5000
#3	.2844	1	0	.6667	0	0	.3600	1
#5	.8440	.5000	0	.3333	0	.6667	.3600	0
#6	.1927	.5000	1	.3333	1	1	.3600	.5000
#7	1	.5000	1	.3333	1	0	.3600	1
#8	.2294	.5000	0	.3333	0	.6667	1	.5000
#9	0	0	1	1	.5000	.6667	.3600	.5000
#11	.0275	0	1	.6667	.5000	0	0	1
W_k	3	2	2	2	1	2	1	2

Here we will use the simulated utility function: $U = -\Sigma_k W_k (1-S_k)^2$. W_k presented by Wymore and Duckstein is listed above. Sums of weights, rank on this sum, and utility are:

Alternative	Sum of S_k	Rank	U
#1	2.495	9	−7.750
#2	3.904	3	−5.523
#3	3.311	6	−6.747

#5	2.704	7	−7.115
#6	4.886	1	−3.734
#7	5.193	2	−3.847
#8	3.229	5	−6.383
#9	4.027	4	−5.534
#11	3.194	8	−7.485

Initial Comparison: The greatest sum of weights is for **#7**. Adjacent alternatives to **#7** are **#3**, **#5**, **#6**, **#8**, **#9** and **#11**. The highest score of adjacent alternatives is for **#6**. Therefore, the first pairwise comparison is made between **#7** and **#6**. By the utility functions above, **#6** is preferred to **#7**.

Preference Cone: The preference cone for this case would eliminate **#1** and **#2**. Since a new base solution has been found, adjacent alternatives to **#6** are calculated, yielding all five remaining alternatives {**#3**, **#5**, **#8**, **#9** and **#11**}. Of these five alternatives, the highest weighted sum is for **#9**.

Decision Maker Comparison: Given the simulated utility function, **#6** is preferred to **#9**.

Preference Cone: The cone constrained by **#7** ≤ **#6** and **#9** ≤ **#6** eliminates none of the remaining four alternatives. Of the remaining four, **#3** has the highest weighted sum.

Decision Maker Comparison: The simulated utility function prefers **#6** to **#3**.

Preference Cone: The constraint **#3** ≤ **#6** is added to the set of bounds, but no additional alternatives are eliminated by this contracted cone. Of the remaining alternatives, **#8** has the highest weighted sum.

Decision Maker Comparison: The simulated utility function finds **#6** preferable to **#8**.

Preference Cone: The constraint **#8** ≤ **#6** is added, but again no remaining alternatives are eliminated by the contracted cone. The highest weighted sum of the remaining alternatives is **#11**.

Decision Maker Comparison: The simulated utility function finds **#6** preferable to **#11**.

Preference Cone: Adding the constraint **#11** ≤ **#6** does not eliminate **#5**. Since only **#5** is left, a last pairwise comparison is automatic.

Decision Maker Comparison: **#6** is preferred to **#5**.

This process took six pairwise comparisons on the part of the decision maker. There was a significant amount of computation required on the part of the analyst, but with computer code, this too is relatively minimal. Note that for a perfectly consistent decision maker, this method, exhausting available alternatives, will yield the preferred solution. A complication in real life is that decision makers may have difficulty with ties among alternatives. Here, a simulated utility function can discriminate to as many decimal places as required. But decision makers may have trouble selecting the preferred solution from two very attractive alternatives.

The following compares the heuristic procedure just outlined with the preference cone method, guaranteeing identification of the best solution given quasi-concave value tradeoff:

	base C_j on best				**base C_j on worst**		
		Preference	Cone			Preference	Cone
P1	#6>#7	#7	#1,#2		#6>#7	#7	—
P2	#6>#9	#9	—		#6>#9	#9	—
P3	#6>#3	#3	—		#6>#2	#2	—
P4	#6>#8	#8	—		#6>#3	#3	—
P5	#6>#11	#11	—		#6>#8	#8	—
P6	#6>#5	#5	—		#6>#11	#11	—
P7					#6>#5	#5	—
P8					#6>#1		

Note that in this case, there were a large number of objectives (criteria) relative to the number of alternatives. The larger the number of criteria, the less effective preference cones will be. Further, the weaker (but optimal) cone again took more decision maker pairwise comparisons. In fact, in this case, the weaker cone procedure eliminated no alternatives.

Nuclear Dump Site Selection

The problem used in prior chapters involved the following hierarchy and alternatives.

	Cost (bill)	Expected Lives Lost	Risk	Civic Improvement
Nome, AK	40	60	very high	low
Newark, NJ	100	140	very low	very high
Rock Springs, WY	60	40	low	high
Duquesne, PA	60	40	medium	medium
Gary, IN	70	80	low	very high
Yakima Flats, WA	70	80	high	medium
Turkey, TX	60	50	high	high
Wells, NE	50	30	medium	medium
Anaheim, CA	90	130	very high	very low
Epcot Center, FL	80	120	very low	very low
Duckwater, NV	80	70	medium	low
Santa Cruz, CA	90	100	very high	very low

Quantifying the categorical criteria of RISK and IMPROVE, the following database is obtained. Standardized scores (on a 0–1 scale) are given for all four criteria.

	Cost		Lives		Risk		Improve		Std	
Nome	40	0.9	60	0.25	very high	0.0	low	0.25	1.40	
Newark	100	0.0	140	0.0	very low	1.0	very high	1.0	2.00	

Rock Springs	60	0.7	40	0.4	*low*	0.75	*high*	0.75	2.60
Duquesne	60	0.7	40	0.4	*medium*	0.50	*medium*	0.5	2.10
Gary	70	0.6	80	0.15	*low*	0.75	*very high*	1.0	2.50
Yakima Flats	70	0.6	80	0.15	*high*	0.25	*medium*	0.50	1.50
Turkey	60	0.7	50	0.3	*high*	0.25	*high*	0.75	2.00
Wells	50	0.8	30	0.6	*medium*	0.50	*medium*	0.50	2.40
Anaheim	90	0.4	130	0.05	*very high*	0.0	*very low*	0.0	0.45
Epcot Center	80	0.55	120	0.1	*very low*	1.0	*very low*	0.0	1.65
Duckwater	80	0.55	70	0.2	*medium*	0.50	*low*	0.25	1.50
Santa Cruz	90	0.4	100	0.2	*very high*	0.0	*very low*	0.0	0.60

The first step is to select an initial base solution. A logical method that often yields a good starting solution is to add the standardized (on a 0–1 scale) scores over the criteria. Here that would lead to Rock Springs as an initial solution (standardized scores given in the Std column).

The second step is to determine those solutions adjacent to the site at Wells. Nome, Newark, Gary, Wells, and Epcot Center are identified as adjacent solutions to Rock Springs. Among these five adjacent solutions, the highest standardized score is for Wells. So the decision maker's first preference choice is between Rock Springs and Wells. Arbitrarily selecting Rock Springs, preference cone analysis indicates elimination of:

Rock Springs > Wells   cone eliminates   Nome
                                             Duquesne
                                             Yakima Flats
                                             Anaheim
                                             Duckwater
                                             Santa Cruz

This leaves Newark, Gary, Turkey, and Epcot Center to be evaluated. Given the new smaller set of available alternatives, Newark, Gary, and Epcot Center are identified as adjacent to Rock Springs. Among these three sites, the highest standard score is for Gary. If the decision maker selected Rock Springs over Gary, the cone including constraints for both preferences to date would not eliminate any additional alternatives.

Rock Springs > Gary

Adjacent alternatives for the new smaller set of three unevaluated alternatives indicates that Newark and Epcot Center are adjacent to Rock Springs. Newark has the higher standardized score. The third decision maker choice is between Rock Springs and Newark. Assume Rock Springs was selected. The resulting cone would not eliminate any additional alternatives.

Rock Springs > Newark

Epcot Center is identified as the only adjacent alternative. Assume the decision maker selects Rock Springs over Epcot Center.

Rock Springs > Epcot Center

The cone does not eliminate Turkey, the remaining alternative. Therefore, the final pairwise comparison is made:

$$\text{Rock Springs} > \text{Turkey}$$

In this case, five pairwise comparisons were made in order to select the preferred solution from an original list of twelve alternatives. There is no way of knowing how many choices are going to be needed ahead of time. When there are a lot of dominated alternatives (in this case roughly half of the alternatives are dominated), the method will eliminate such dominated alternatives in the first cone. Typically, once these alternatives are eliminated, the cone does not eliminate many more alternatives.

To see an alternative path of pairwise comparisons, assume that Wells was selected over Rock Springs in the first decision maker choice:

Wells > Rock Springs   cone eliminates   Newark
                                           Duquesne
                                           Gary
                                           Yakima Flats
                                           Turkey
                                           Anaheim
                                           Duckwater
                                           Santa Cruz

The remaining two alternatives are Nome and Epcot Center. Epcot Center is adjacent to Wells.

$$\text{Wells} > \text{Epcot Center}$$

The resulting cone does not eliminate Nome. The final pairwise comparison is:

$$\text{Wells} > \text{Nome}$$

In this case, three pairwise comparisons were all that were required to reach the preferred solution.

Conclusions

The development of the preference cone technique arises from Zionts and Wallenius [1976]. Köksalen and his fellow researchers [1984, 1988, 1989, 1992; Taner and Köksalen, 1991] have developed the theory of preference cones for selection problems. Malakooti [1988, 1989] and Frazier, et al. [1990] address applications.

Preference cone methods provide viable means of supporting selection from a finite set of alternatives. Preference cones could theoretically be used for very large numbers of alternatives, with the hope that preference cones can eliminate large numbers of nondominated solutions. A possible concern is that when the decision maker is uncertain about which choice is preferred, the impact of selecting one or the other alternative can be quite drastic, with the cone possibly eliminating a number of remaining alternatives based on an uncertain choice. Wallenius (in personal conversation) has suggested not including those pairwise comparisons where decision makers are indifferent or nearly indifferent among alternatives.

References

Benayoun, R., deMontgolfier, J., Tergny, J., and Laridear, O. 1971. Linear programming with multiple objective functions: STEP method (STEM). *Mathematical Programming* 1:3, 366–375.

Debreu, G. 1959. *Theory of value: An axiomatic analysis of economic equilibrium* New Haven: Yale University Press.

Frazier, G.V., Gaither, N., and Olson, D.L. 1990. A procedure for dealing with multiple objectives in cell formation decisions. *Journal of Operations Management* 9:4, 465–480.

Köksalan, M.M. 1989. Identifying and ranking a most preferred subset of alternatives in the presence of multiple criteria. *Naval Research Logistics* 36, 359–372.

Köksalan, M.M., Karwan, M.H., and Zionts, S. 1984. An improved method for solving multiple criteria problems involving discrete alternatives. *IEEE Transactions on Systems, Man, and Cybernetics* SMC-14, 24–34.

Köksalan, M.M., Karwan, M.H., and Zionts, S. 1988. An approach for solving discrete alternative multiple criteria problems involving ordinal criteria. *Naval Research Logistics* 35, 625–641.

Köksalan, M.M. and Taner, O.V. 1992. An approach for finding the most preferred alternative in the presence of multiple criteria. *European Journal of Operational Research* 60, 52–60.

Korhonen, P., Wallenius, J., and Zionts, S. 1984. Solving the discrete multiple criteria problem using convex cones, *Management Science* 30:11, 1336–1345.

Malakooti, B. 1988. A decision support system and a heuristic interactive approach for solving discrete multiple criteria problems. *IEEE Transactions on Systems, Man, and Cybernetics* 18:2, 273–284

Malakooti, B. and Deviprasad, J. 1989. An interactive multiple criteria approach for parameter selection in metal cutting. *Operations Research* 37:5, 805–818.

Ramesh, R., Karwan, M.H., and Zionts, S. 1988. Theory of convex cones in multicriteria decision making, *Annals of Operations Research* 16, 131–148.

Steuer, R.E. 1977. An interactive multiple objective linear programming procedure. *TIMS Studies in the Management Sciences* 6, 225–239.

Taner, O.V. and Köksalan, M.M. 1991. Experiments and an improved method for solving the discrete alternative multiple-criteria problem. *Journal of the Operational Research Society* 42:5, 383–391.

Wymore, M.L. and Duckstein, L. 1989. Prioritizing factory automation investments with multicriterion Q analysis. in *Proceedings of the International Conference on Multiple Criteria Decision Making: Applications in Industry and Service*, M.T. Tabucanon and V. Chankong, eds., Asian Inst. of Tech., 317–331.

Zionts, S. and Wallenius, J. 1976. An interactive programming method for solving the multiple criteria problem. *Management Science* 22:6, 652–663

8
Outranking Methods

This chapter reviews outranking methods, focusing on two developed techniques: *ELECTRE* and *PROMETHEE*. These techniques seek to eliminate alternatives dominated according to a set of weights which is assumed to be given.

ELECTRE

A quite different approach to the alternative selection problem has been developed in France by B. Roy (initial work came from Benayoun, Roy, and Sussman [1966]). *ELECTRE* is an acronym for elimination and (et) choice translating algorithm. Given a set of alternatives on K objectives, this algorithm seeks to reduce the size of the nondominated set. It is assumed that the decision maker will also provide a set of weights reflecting the relative importance of the K objectives. The fundamen-tal idea of the *ELECTRE* techniques is that alternatives can be eliminated which are dominated by other alternatives to a specified degree. The method uses a concordance index to measure relative advantage of each alternative over all other alternatives, and a discordance index to measure relative disadvantages. These indices are used to determine a set of dominances. The **kernel** of the resulting graph is used to identify alternatives to present to the decision maker. Three versions of *ELECTRE* have been presented by Roy. *ELECTRE I* seeks to shrink the number of alternatives presented for decision maker consideration. *ELECTRE II* ranks nondominated alternatives. *ELECTRE III* is applicable to cases where a family of pseudo-criteria are to be aggregated. English publications of *ELECTRE III* are scarce.

Concordance Index: A concordance index for alternative A relative to alternative B is defined as the proportion of weights for which A is preferred to B. Let W^+ be the sum of weights for criteria where A is preferable to B, $W^=$ be the sum of weights of criteria where $A = B$, and W^- be the sum of weights where B is preferable to A. There are varying formulas for different versions of *ELECTRE*. In *ELECTRE I*, Roy used $C(A,B) = \Sigma(W^+ + .5\ W^=)/\Sigma\ (W^+ + W^= + W^-)$. In *ELECTRE II*, $C(A,B) = \Sigma(W^+ + W^=)/\Sigma\ (W^+ + W^= + W^-)$.

Discordance Index: A discordance index provides a measure of relative disadvantage of alternative A to alternative B. The discordance index is defined as the maximum ratio for each criterion: (criterion difference where B preferred to A)/(range of possible criterion difference)

$D(A,B)$ $= \mathrm{Max}\ \{[Z_{Bk} - Z_{Ak}]/[Z^*_k - Z^-_k]\}$ for all k where $B > A$

Z^*_k = optimal attainment for criterion k

Z^-_k = worst attainment for criterion k.

Note that Roy used scalar points for qualitative criterion. In this chapter, we will use $Z^*_k = 1$ and $Z^-_k = 0$, automatically giving a range of 1 for the divisor.

In *ELECTRE II*, Roy provided the option of a discordance index that could be set by the decision maker or analyst for each criterion independently. Here we will revert to the discordance index of *ELECTRE I*.

Slicing Planes: Key to the procedure are the limits required for concordance and discordance dominance. Parameters **p** and **q** are provided by the decision maker to set bounds on required concordance and discordance to identify dominance relationships. In *ELECTRE I*, alternative A dominates alternative B iff: $C(A,B) \geq$ **p** and $D(A,B) \leq$ **q**. The results of the analysis can be quite sensitive to the settings for **p** and **q**. Multiple *ELECTRE* runs varying **p** and **q** can be viewed as slicing planes.

Kernels: The next step is to determine the kernel of the dominance graph. The kernel consists of those alternatives which are not dominated by other members of the kernel. (1) Each element in the kernel is not outranked by any other element in the kernel. (2) Each element *not* in the kernel is outranked by at least one element in the kernel. Note that cycles can occur, where $A > B$ and $B > A$. Independent kernels can be determined in such cases (reduce the graph by taking out one of the elements in the cycle), with the union of these kernels presented to the decision maker.

This approach depends upon two sets of parameters assumed given by the decision maker. First, both concordance and discordance indices depend upon the relative criterion weights. Second, dominance relationships depend upon the limits **p** and **q**.

Rules

A workable set of rules for *ELECTRE I* and *ELECTRE II* are as follows:

ELECTRE I: Concordance index $= \Sigma(W^+ + .5\ W^-)/\Sigma(W^+ + W^- + W^-)$

Discordance index $= \mathrm{Max}\ \{[Z_{Bk} - Z_{Ak}]/[Z^*_k - Z^-_k]\}$ for all k where $B > A$

Outranking relationship – Concordance index $\geq$ **p**

Discordance index $\leq$ **q**

Selected set – kernel

ELECTRE II: For $0 <$ **p**$^- <$ **p**$^0 <$ **p**$^* < 1$ and $0 <$ **q**$^0 <$ **q**$^* < 1$

Concordance index $= \Sigma(W^+ + W^-)/\Sigma\ (W^+ + W^- + W^-)$.

Discordance index $= \mathrm{Max}\ \{[Z_{Bk} - Z_{Ak}]/[Z^*_k - Z^-_k]\}$ for all k where $B > A$

Strong outranking $\mathbf{RANK}_s$ – Concordance index $\geq \mathbf{p}^*$
Discordance index $\leq \mathbf{q}^*$
$\Sigma\ W^+ \geq \Sigma\ W^-$

OR   Concordance index $\geq \mathbf{p}^0$
Discordance index $\leq \mathbf{q}^0$
$\Sigma\ W^+ \geq \Sigma\ W^-$

Weak outranking $\mathbf{RANK}_w$ Concordance index $\geq \mathbf{p}^-$
Discordance index $\leq \mathbf{q}^*$
$\Sigma\ W^+ \geq \Sigma\ W^-$

For strong rankings, $\mathbf{RANK}_s$ is the iteration where an alternative passes the tests of not being outranked on the strong precedence relationships, as well as not being outranked by another member of this set on the weak precedence relationships. Members of this set are given $\mathbf{RANK}_s$ values of 1. This set is then deleted from the analysis, and the process continues until all alternatives are deleted. $\mathbf{RANK}_s$ is thus the iteration where an alternative was identified as passing the above test. $\mathbf{RANK}_w$ is obtained by reversing the original strong and weak precedence relationships, and the same procedure applied. Since rankings will be reversed, $\mathbf{RANK}_w$ is set equal to $1 + \text{Max}\{\text{all weak rankings}\}$ – the weak ranking for the alternative in question. For instance, assume $\mathbf{RANK}_s$ for three alternatives to be $A = 1$, $B = 2$, $C = 3$. The weak ranking, if perfect order were preserved, would be $C = 1$, $B = 2$, and $A = 3$, which is reversed. $\mathbf{RANK}_w$ for A would be $1 + 3$ (the maximum of all weak rankings) – 3 (the weak ranking for alternative A) yielding $\mathbf{RANK}_w$ of $A = 1$. A median ranking, $\mathbf{RANK}_m$, has been presented as $(\mathbf{RANK}_s + \mathbf{RANK}_w)/2$. The order of alternative attraction can then be estimated by ordering alternatives by $\mathbf{RANK}_m$. *ELECTRE II* thus provides a ranking of available alternatives.

Cellular Manufacturing Example

The first example presented in the preference cone chapter will be solved by *ELECTRE I*. The problem involved a cellular manufacturing system with 4 cells, 24 machines, and 50 parts to be assigned. For the example, 10 non-dominated solutions had to be compared.

Alternative	Z_1	Z_2	Z_3	Z_4
	Cost	Utilization Imbalance	% Shop Utilization	Exceptional Parts
#56	−738	−5.3	33.8	−15
#96	−702	−15.8	32.4	−15
#132	−815	−14.9	35.8	−15
#149	−612	−17.2	34.5	−13
#166	−752	−9.7	34.0	−14
#167	−698	−21.4	35.7	−16
#183	−686	−16.5	33.8	−14

#192	−914	−4.3	30.5	−20
#253	−878	−3.1	29.3	−16
#287	−633	−39.7	34.6	−14

Standardized scores for these solutions were developed:

Alternativ	S_1	S_2	S_3	S_4	
	Cost	Utilization Imbalance	% Shop Utilization	Exceptional Parts	Sum
#56	.5828	.9399	.6923	.7143	2.9293
#96	.7020	.6530	.4769	.7143	2.5462
#132	.3278	.6776	**1.0000**	.7143	2.7197
#149	**1.0000**	.6148	.8000	**1.0000**	**3.4148**
#166	.5364	.8197	.7231	.8571	2.9363
#167	.7152	.5000	.9846	.5714	2.7713
#183	.7550	.6339	.6923	.8571	2.9383
#192	.0000	.9672	.1846	.0000	1.1518
#253	.1192	**1.0000**	.0000	.5714	1.6906
#287	.9305	.0000	.8154	.8571	2.6030

With *ELECTRE* we need decision maker weights for the objectives. We will use .25 for each criterion.

ELECTRE I

Concordance Index: The concordance index by formula for *ELECTRE I* is:

	#56	#96	#132	#149	#166	#167	#183	#192	#253	#287
#56	—	.625	.625	.250	.500	.500	.375	.750	.750	.250
#96	.375	—	.375	.250	.250	.500	.250	.750	.750	.250
#132	.375	.625	—	.500	.250	.750	.500	.750	.750	.500
#149	.750	.750	.500	—	.750	.750	.750	.750	.750	.750
#166	.500	.750	.750	.250	—	.500	.625	.750	.750	.375
#167	.500	.500	.250	.250	.500	—	.250	.750	.625	.500
#183	.625	.750	.500	.250	.375	.750	—	.750	.750	.375
#192	.250	.250	.250	.250	.250	.250	.250	—	.250	.250
#253	.250	.250	.250	.250	.250	.375	.250	.750	—	.250
#287	.750	.750	.500	.250	.625	.500	.625	.750	.750	—

The concordance index element for **#56** versus **#96** would be developed as follows:

$$C(1,2) = .25(0) + .25(1) + .25(1) + .25(.5) = .625$$

where **#56** is preferable on K_2 (utilization imbalance) and K_3 (shop utilization) but **#96** is preferable on K_1 (*Cost*). The two alternatives are tied on K_4 (*Exceptional parts*).
The discordance index for this comparison is:

$$D(1,2) = Max\{(.7020 − .5828)/(1 − 0)\} = .1192$$

K_1 is the only element where **#56** < **#96**.

Discordance Index: Following the formula for *ELECTRE I*:

	#56	#96	#132	#149	#166	#167	#183	#192	#253	#287
#56	—	.119	.308	.417	.143	.292	.172	.027	.060	.348
#96	.287	—	.523	.323	.246	.508	.215	.314	.347	.338
#132	.262	.374	—	.672	.209	.387	.427	.290	.322	.603
#149	.325	.038	.200	—	.205	.185	.019	.352	.385	.015
#166	.120	.166	.277	.464	—	.261	.219	.148	.180	.394
#167	.440	.153	.178	.429	.320	—	.286	.467	.500	.286
#183	.306	.019	.308	.245	.186	.292	—	.333	.366	.175
#192	.714	.714	.815	1	.857	.800	.857	—	.571	.930
#253	.692	.583	1	.881	.723	.985	.692	.185	—	.815
#287	.940	.653	.678	.615	.820	.500	.634	.967	1	—

Kernel: The next step is to determine the kernel of the graph of outranking relationships. The kernel is sensitive to the selection of **p** (minimum concordance index required for outranking) and **q** (maximum discordance index needed for outranking. If there were no cycles ([A > B] and [B > A] simultaneously), the algorithm is quite simple. Search for alternatives that are not dominated by any other alternative (place these in set {kernel}). Eliminate alternatives dominated by this set (place these in set {not-kernel}). Iterate until all alternatives are in one of the two sets.

For example, if **p** = .6 and **q** = .5, outranking relationships for the cellular manufacturing model are:

#56 > {96 132 192 253}   all alternatives but **#149** are outranked

#96 > {192 253}
#132 > {167 192 253}   set kernel = {149}
#149 > {56 96 166 167 183 192 253 287}
#166 > {96 132 192 253}   eliminate those outranked by **#149**

#167 > {192}
#183 > {96 167 192 253}   set not-kernel = {56 96 166 167 183 192 253 287}

#253 > {192}

          #132 left   set kernel = {132 149}

If **p** = .6 and **q** = .75, there may be more outranking relationships. Here it makes no difference, as **#149** is still not outranked, and **#149** still does not outrank **#132**.

#56 > {96 132 192 253}   all alternatives but **#149** are outranked

#96 > {192 253}
#132 > { 96 167 192 253}   set kernel = {149}

#149 > {56 96 166 167 183 192 253 287}
#166 > {96 132 183 192 253}   eliminate those outranked
                                               by #149

#167 > {192}
#183 > {96 167 192 253}   set not-kernel = {56 96
                                               166 167 183 192 253 287}

#253 > {192}
#287 > {96 183}   #132 left   set kernel =
                                               {132 149}

If **p** = .6 and **q** = .25, there will be fewer outranking relationships.

  #56 > {96 192 253}   alternatives #56, #132 &
                                               #149 are not outranked
#149 > {96 166 167 183 287}   set kernel = {56 132 149}
#166 > {96 183 192 253}   eliminate those outranked
                                               by #56, #132 or #149
#183 > {96}   set not-kernel = {96 166
                                               167 183 192 253 287}
#253 > {192}   kernel = {56 132 149}

If **p** = .2 and **q** = .5, limits are slack enough that many cycles exist. Rather than enumerate all cycles, it would seem prudent to tighten the limits.

  #56 > {96 132 149 166 167 183 192 253 287}
  #96 > {56 149 166 183 192 253 287}
#132 > {56 96 166 167 183 192 253}
#149 > {56 96 132 166 167 183 192 253 287}
#166 > {56 96 132 149 167 183 192 253 287}
#167 > {56 96 132 149 166 183 192 253 287}
#183 > {56 96 132 149 166 167 192 253 287}
#253 > {192}
#287 > {167}

On the other hand, **p** = .8 and **q** = .5 yields no outranking relationships. Obviously, the limits need relaxing.

Automation Example

ELECTRE I can be applied to the automation example presented above. Proportional weights conforming to those presented above are:

	IRR	RISK	EDGE	QUAL	FLEX	CROS	LC	MGMT
Weight	.2	.1333	.1333	.1333	.0667	.1333	.0667	.1333

Concordance Index:

	#1	#2	#3	#5	#6	#7	#8	#9	#11
#1	—	.267	.300	.367	.367	.233	.467	.467	.567
#2	.733	—	.433	.467	.433	.300	.600	.533	.600
#3	.700	.567	—	.533	.633	.433	.700	.500	.600
#5	.633	.533	.467	—	.367	.300	.500	.433	.533
#6	.633	.567	.367	.633	—	.400	.533	.700	.667
#7	.767	.700	.567	.700	.600	—	.667	.633	.667
#8	.533	.400	.300	.500	.467	.333	—	.533	.533
#9	.533	.467	.500	.567	.300	.367	.467	—	.500
#11	.433	.400	.400	.467	.333	.333	.467	.500	—

Discordance Index:

	#1	#2	#3	#5	#6	#7	#8	#9	#11
#1	—	1	.667	.578	1	1	.640	1	1
#2	.500	—	1	.560	.500	.716	.880	.667	.500
#3	.500	1	—	.667	1	1	.667	1	1
#5	.500	1	1	—	1	1	.640	1	1
#6	.073	.092	.500	.651	—	.807	.640	.667	.500
#7	.333	.667	.500	.667	1	—	.667	.667	.333
#8	.500	1	.500	.615	1	1	—	1	1
#9	.500	.500	1	.844	.500	1	.640	—	.500
#11	.500	.667	1	.816	1	.973	1	.667	—

Kernel:

For $p = .6$ and $q = .5$, outranking relationships are:

2 > {1}	set kernel = {2 3 5 6 7 8 9}
3 > {1}	
5 > {1}	
6 > {1 11}	
7 > {1 11}	

For $p = .6$ and $q = .75$, outranking relationships are:

2 > {1}	7 eliminates {1 2 5 8 9 11}
3 > {1 8}	
5 > {1}	set kernel = {3 6 7}
6 > {1 5 9 11}	
7 > {1 2 5 8 9 11}	

In the first case, the decision maker would be presented with 7 alternatives to compare. The second set of limits would cut this to 3.

ELECTRE II: We will use $p^- = .3$, $p^0 = .5$, $p^* = .7$, $q^0 = .4$ and $q^* = .7$.

Concordance Index: This will be different than the concordance index for *ELECTRE I*.

	#1	#2	#3	#5	#6	#7	#8	#9	#11
#1	—	.333	.400	.533	.533	.333	.667	.600	.600

	#1	#2	#3	#5	#6	#7	#8	#9	#11
#2	.800	—	.533	.600	.667	.467	.800	.800	.733
#3	.800	.667	—	.667	.667	.600	.800	.533	.800
#5	.800	.667	.600	—	.533	.467	.800	.533	.533
#6	.800	.800	.400	.800	—	.667	.733	.867	.733
#7	.867	.867	.733	.867	.867	—	.800	.733	.867
#8	.733	.600	.400	.800	.667	.467	—	.667	.533
#9	.667	.733	.533	.667	.467	.467	.600	—	.667
#11	.467	.533	.600	.467	.400	.533	.467	.667	—

We will use the same discordance index as above. There is need for an additional matrix indicating the proportion of weights where $W_i > W_j$.

Weight Outrankings:

	#1	#2	#3	#5	#6	#7	#8	#9	#11
#1	—	.200	.200	.200	.200	.133	.267	.333	.533
#2	.667	—	.333	.333	.200	.133	.400	.267	.467
#3	.600	.467	—	.400	.600	.267	.600	.467	.400
#5	.467	.400	.333	—	.200	.133	.200	.333	.533
#6	.467	.333	.333	.467	—	.133	.333	.533	.600
#7	.667	.533	.400	.533	.333	—	.533	.533	.467
#8	.333	.200	.200	.200	.267	.200	—	.400	.533
#9	.400	.200	.467	.467	.133	.267	.333	—	.333
#11	.400	.267	.200	.467	.267	.133	.467	.333	—

Bold entries indicate alternative i (row) outranks alternative j (column) on weights.

Iteration 1

Strong Outranking

The initial iteration yields the following outrankings:

> #2 > {1 9 11}
> #3 > {1 8}
> #5 > {1 8}
> #6 > {1 2 5 8 9 11}
> #7 > {1 2 3 5 8 9 11}
> #8 > {1 5}

Weak Outranking

> #2 > {1 9 11}
> #3 > {1 5 8}
> #5 > {1 8}
> #6 > {1 2 5 8 9 11}
> #7 > {1 2 3 5 8 9 11}
> #8 > {1 5}
> #9 > {1 11}
> #11 > {9}

Alternatives with **no** precedents in the strong outranking are {6 7}. These two elements are not related in the weak outranking. Neither has a precedent in the weak outranking. **RANK**$_s$ **(6)** and **RANK**$_s$ **(7)** = 1.

Iteration 2

Alternatives **#6** and **#7** are deleted. Alternatives with **no** precedents in the strong outranking are now {2 3}. These two alternatives are not related in the weak outranking. Neither has a precedent in the weak outranking. **RANK**$_s$ **(2)** = 2 and **RANK**$_s$ **(3)** = 2.

Iteration 3

Alternatives **#3** and **#4** are deleted. Cycles cause complications at this iteration. When cycles are eliminated, alternatives with **no** precedents in the strong outranking are now {5 8 9 11}. Alternatives {5 8 9} are related in the weak outrankings. Alternatives in this set without a precedent in the weak outranking (after cycles are eliminated) are {5 8 9}. Therefore, **RANK**$_s$ **(5)** = 3, **RANK**$_s$ **(8)** = 3, **RANK**$_s$ **(9)** = 3 and **RANK**$_s$ **(11)** = 3.

Iteration 4

Only alternative **#1** is left. **RANK**$_s$ **(1)** = 4.
A second ranking **RANK**$_w$ is obtained by reversing the relationships for both strong and weak outranking. **RANK**$_w$ = 1 + maximum iteration − iteration of elimination.

Reversed Strong Outranking

> #1 > {2 3 5 6 7 8}
> #2 > {6 7}
> #3 > {7}
> #5 > {6 7 8}
> #8 > {3 5 6 7}
> #9 > {2 6 7}
> #11 > {2 6 7}

Reversed Weak Outranking

> #1 > {2 3 5 6 7 8 9}
> #2 > {6 7}
> #3 > {7}
> #5 > {3 6 7 8}
> #8 > {3 5 6 7}

#9 > {2 6 7 9}
#11 > {2 6 7 9}

Iteration 1

The set of alternatives with no strong precedents is {1 9 11}. After cycles are eliminated, only #1 and #9 are related in the weak outranking. Of these, #9 is outranked. Therefore, $R_w(1) = 1$ and $R_w(11) = 1$.

Iteration 2

Alternatives #1 and #11 are deleted. Only #9 has no strong precedent. $R_w(9) = 2$.

Iteration 3

Alternative #9 is deleted. Only #2 has no strong precedent. $R_w(2) = 3$.

Iteration 4

Alternative #2 is deleted. After elimination of cycles, #5 and #8 have no strong precedents. #5 outranks #8 in the weak relationship. $R_w(5) = 4$.

Iteration 5

Alternative #5 is deleted. Only #8 has no strong precedents. $R_w(8) = 5$.

Iteration 6

Alternative #8 is deleted. Alternatives #3 and #6 have no strong precedents. They are unrelated in the weak outrankings. $R_w(3) = 6$ and $R_w(6) = 6$.

Iteration 7

Only #7 is left. $R_w(7) = 7$.

Final Ranking

The weak ranking $RANK_w$ is calculated, and $RANK_w$ and $RANK_s$ are averaged. The final ranking $RANK_f$ is the order of the average ranking.

Alternative	R$_w$	RANK$_w$	RANK$_s$	Average	RANK$_f$
#1	1	7	4	5.5	9
#2	3	5	2	3.5	5 (tie)
#3	6	2	2	2	3
#5	4	4	3	3.5	5 (tie)
#6	6	2	1	1.5	2
#7	7	1	1	1	1
#8	5	3	3	3	4
#9	2	6	3	4.5	7
#11	1	7	3	5	8

Note that this ranking conforms fairly well with the kernels obtained above with *ELECTRE I*. It also selected the same recommended alternative (**#7**) as the preference cone method, although that is a matter of some chance, as the preference cone had an underlying utility not used by *ELECTRE*, and *ELECTRE* had a set of weights not used by the preference cone method.

Nuclear Dump Site Selection — *ELECTRE II*

The nuclear dump site selection problem with twelve alternative sites involved the following problem parameters:

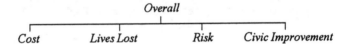

Note that here risk relates to the risk of a major catastrophe. While this obviously correlates with lives lost to some degree, in this analysis expected lives lost are under conditions where major catastrophes do not occur. Therefore, these criteria are independent. The alternatives are:

	Cost (bill)	Expected Lives Lost	Risk	Civic Improvement
1 Nome, AK	40	60	very high	low
2 Newark, NJ	100	140	very low	very high
3 Rock Springs, WY	60	40	low	high
4 Duquesne, PA	60	40	medium	medium
5 Gary, IN	70	80	low	very high
6 Yakima Flats, WA	70	80	high	medium
7 Turkey, TX	60	50	high	high
8 Wells, NE	50	30	medium	medium
9 Anaheim, CA	90	130	very high	very low
10 Epcot Center, FL	80	120	very low	very low
11 Duckwater, NV	80	70	medium	low
12 Santa Cruz, CA	90	100	very high	very low

ELECTRE II standardized scores as well as concordance and discordance indices, followed by relative weight advantages, are as follows:

Standardized Scores of Input

S   0.900 0.250 0.000 0.250
S   0.000 0.000 1.000 1.000
S   0.700 0.400 0.750 0.750
S   0.700 0.400 0.500 0.500
S   0.600 0.150 0.750 1.000
S   0.600 0.150 0.250 0.500
S   0.700 0.300 0.250 0.750
S   0.800 0.600 0.500 0.500
S   0.400 0.050 0.000 0.000
S   0.550 0.100 1.000 0.000
S   0.550 0.200 0.500 0.250
S   0.400 0.200 0.000 0.000

Concordance Indices

C   0.000 0.750 0.100 0.100 0.750 0.750 0.100 0.100 1.000 0.800 0.800 1.000
C   0.250 0.000 0.250 0.250 0.250 0.250 0.250 0.250 0.250 0.250 0.250 0.250
C   0.900 0.750 0.000 1.000 0.950 1.000 1.000 0.250 1.000 0.800 1.000 1.000
C   0.900 0.750 0.750 0.000 0.750 1.000 0.950 0.250 1.000 0.800 1.000 1.000
C   0.250 0.800 0.250 0.250 0.000 1.000 0.250 0.250 1.000 0.800 0.350 0.350
C   0.250 0.750 0.000 0.050 0.750 0.000 0.200 0.050 1.000 0.800 0.150 0.350
C   0.900 0.750 0.150 0.150 0.750 1.000 0.000 0.050 1.000 0.800 0.800 1.000
C   0.900 0.750 0.750 1.000 0.750 1.000 0.950 0.000 1.000 0.800 1.000 1.000
C   0.200 0.750 0.000 0.000 0.000 0.000 0.000 0.000 0.000 0.050 0.000 0.350
C   0.200 0.950 0.200 0.200 0.200 0.200 0.200 0.200 1.000 0.000 0.300 0.350
C   0.250 0.750 0.000 0.200 0.650 0.850 0.200 0.200 1.000 0.800 0.000 1.000
C   0.200 0.750 0.000 0.000 0.650 0.650 0.000 0.000 1.000 0.700 0.650 0.000

Discordance Indices

D   0.000 1.000 0.750 0.500 0.750 0.250 0.500 0.500 0.000 1.000 0.500 0.000
D   0.900 0.000 0.700 0.700 0.600 0.600 0.700 0.800 0.400 0.550 0.550 0.400
D   0.200 0.250 0.000 0.000 0.250 0.000 0.000 0.200 0.000 0.250 0.000 0.000
D   0.200 0.500 0.250 0.000 0.500 0.000 0.250 0.200 0.000 0.500 0.000 0.000
D   0.300 0.250 0.250 0.250 0.000 0.000 0.150 0.450 0.000 0.250 0.050 0.050
D   0.300 0.750 0.500 0.250 0.500 0.000 0.250 0.450 0.000 0.750 0.250 0.050
D   0.200 0.750 0.500 0.250 0.500 0.000 0.000 0.300 0.000 0.750 0.250 0.000
D   0.100 0.500 0.250 0.000 0.500 0.000 0.250 0.000 0.000 0.500 0.000 0.000
D   0.500 1.000 0.750 0.500 1.000 0.500 0.750 0.550 0.000 1.000 0.500 0.150
D   0.350 1.000 0.750 0.500 1.000 0.500 0.750 0.500 0.000 0.000 0.250 0.100
D   0.350 0.750 0.500 0.250 0.750 0.250 0.500 0.400 0.000 0.500 0.000 0.000
D   0.500 1.000 0.750 0.500 1.000 0.500 0.750 0.500 0.000 1.000 0.500 0.000

Weight Advantages

```
W   0.000 0.750 0.100 0.100 0.750 0.750 0.100 0.100 0.800 0.800 0.750 0.800
W   0.250 0.000 0.250 0.250 0.200 0.250 0.250 0.250 0.250 0.050 0.250 0.250
W   0.900 0.750 0.000 0.250 0.750 1.000 0.850 0.250 1.000 0.800 1.000 1.000
W   0.900 0.750 0.000 0.000 0.750 0.950 0.850 0.000 1.000 0.800 0.800 1.000
W   0.250 0.750 0.050 0.250 0.000 0.250 0.250 0.250 1.000 0.800 0.350 0.350
W   0.250 0.750 0.000 0.000 0.000 0.000 0.000 0.000 1.000 0.800 0.150 0.350
W   0.900 0.750 0.000 0.050 0.750 0.800 0.000 0.050 1.000 0.800 0.800 1.000
W   0.900 0.750 0.750 0.750 0.750 0.950 0.950 0.000 1.000 0.800 0.800 1.000
W   0.000 0.750 0.000 0.000 0.000 0.000 0.000 0.000 0.000 0.000 0.000 0.000
W   0.200 0.750 0.200 0.200 0.200 0.200 0.200 0.200 0.950 0.000 0.200 0.300
W   0.200 0.750 0.000 0.000 0.650 0.850 0.200 0.000 1.000 0.700 0.000 0.350
W   0.000 0.750 0.000 0.000 0.650 0.650 0.000 0.000 0.650 0.650 0.000 0.000
```

Using $p^- = .3$, $p^0 = .5$, $p^* = .7$, $q^0 = .2$ and $q^* = .8$, strong and weak outrankings obtained from *ELECTRE II* are:

ELECTRE II Strong Outrankings

```
 1 Dominates  5 6 9 11 12
 3 Dominates  1 2 4 5 6 7 9 10 11 12
 4 Dominates  1 2 5 6 7 9 10 11 12
 5 Dominates  2 6 9 10
 6 Dominates  2 9 10
 7 Dominates  1 2 5 6 9 10 11 12
 8 Dominates  1 2 3 4 5 6 7 9 10 11 12
10 Dominates  9
11 Dominates  2 6 9 10 12
12 Dominates  9
```

ELECTRE II Weak Outrankings

```
 1 Dominates  5 6 9 11 12
 3 Dominates  1 2 4 5 6 7 9 10 11 12
 4 Dominates  1 2 5 6 7 9 10 11 12
 5 Dominates  2 6 9 10
 6 Dominates  2 9 10
 7 Dominates  1 2 5 6 9 10 11 12
 8 Dominates  1 2 3 4 5 6 7 9 10 11 12
10 Dominates  9
11 Dominates  2 5 6 9 10 12
12 Dominates  6 9
```

This yields a ranking of: **8** Wells
                              3 Rock Springs
                              4 Duquesne
                              7 Turkey
                              1 Nome

11 Duckwater
5 Gary & **12** Santa Cruz
6 Yakima Flats
2 Newark & **10** Epcot Center
9 Anaheim

PROMETHEE

PROMETHEE (Brans & Vincke, 1985) is an offshoot of *ELECTRE*. Brans and Vincke noted that *ELECTRE* methods are rather intricate, requiring a lot of parameters which may have no meaning to the decision maker. *PROMETHEE* is a modification to *ELECTRE*, intended to be very simple and easy to understand. There are two versions of *PROMETHEE*: *PROMETHEE I* provides a partial outranking relation, recognizing that some alternatives are not comparable with others. *PROMETHEE II* provides a cardinal score for each alternative, which can be used to develop a complete ranking of alternatives.

The method begins with development of criteria scales to identify the intensity of preference of one alternative over another, converting the attainment levels for alternatives into a 0–1 scale (with 0 the worst and 1 the best). Six generalized criteria are given within *PROMETHEE*:

Criterion	(where **d** is difference in performance)	*Parameters*
I Usual criterion	0 if indifferent or worse,	
	1 if better	none
II Quasi-criterion	0 if **d** ≤ bound **q**,	
	1 if more	**q**
III Criterion w/linear		
preference	0 if indifferent or worse,	**p**
	d/p if advantage < bound **p** 1 if ≥ **p**	
IV Level criterion	0 if $|\mathbf{d}| \le \mathbf{q}$, ½ if $\mathbf{q} < |\mathbf{d}| \le \mathbf{p}$, 1 if $|\mathbf{d}| > \mathbf{p}$	**p,q**
V Criterion w/linear preference and indifference area		
	0 if $|\mathbf{d}| \le \mathbf{q}$, $(|\mathbf{d}|-\mathbf{q})/(\mathbf{p}-\mathbf{q})$ if $\mathbf{q} < |\mathbf{d}| \le \mathbf{p}$, 1 if $|\mathbf{d}| > \mathbf{p}$	**p,q**
VI Gaussian	0 if $\mathbf{d} < 0$, $1 - e^{-dxd/(2 \sigma x \sigma)}$ if $\mathbf{d} > 0$	σ (std dev)

These preference intensities can be expressed in a set of **n** x **n** tables, comparing all **n** alternatives with respect to each objective. A set of weights ($\mathbf{w}_j$ for all $j \in \mathbf{K}$ objectives) of relative importance of the objectives must be identified. As in *ELECTRE*, this is assumed to be a reasonable task for the decision maker. A multicriteria preference index is defined for all pairs of alternatives:

$$\Pi(a,b) = [\Sigma_{j \in K}\, \mathbf{w}_j\, P_j(a,b)]/[\Sigma_{j \in K}\, \mathbf{w}_j] \qquad\qquad \text{usually } \Sigma_{j \in K}\, \mathbf{w}_j = 1$$

From these calculations, an **n** x **n** table of $\Pi(a,b)$ for all alternatives can be developed. For each alternative *a*, the mean of preference intensities over all other alternatives is defined as $\Phi^+(a)$. $\Phi^+(a)$ is referred to as *outgoing flow*. In turn, the mean of preference intensities of all other alternatives over alternative a is defined as $\Phi^-(a)$. $\Phi^-(a)$ is referred to as *incoming flow*. *Net flow* $\Phi(a)$ is defined as $\Phi^+(a) - \Phi^-(a)$.

PROMETHEE I

Outranking relationships are defined as follows:

$a\,P^+\,b$ iff $\Phi^+(a) > \Phi^+(b)$ $a\,I^+\,b$ iff $\Phi^+(a) = \Phi^+(b)$
$a\,P^-\,b$ iff $\Phi^-(a) < \Phi^-(b)$ $a\,I^-\,b$ iff $\Phi^-(a) = \Phi^-(b)$

Alternative a outranks alternative b if $a\,P^+\,b$ and $a\,P^-\,b$ or $a\,P^+\,b$ and $a\,I^-\,b$ or $a\,I^+\,b$ and $a\,P^-\,b$.

Alternative a is indifferent to alternative b if $a\,I^+\,b$ and $a\,I^-\,b$. Alternatives a and b are incomparable in all other conditions.

PROMETHEE II

Outranking relationships are defined as:

Alternative a outranks alternative b iff $\Phi(a) > \Phi(b)$.
Alternative a is indifferent to alternative b iff $\Phi(a) = \Phi(b)$.

These techniques can be demonstrated on the cellular manufacturing example discussed with preference cones and *ELECTRE*. Criteria used and weights are:

Objective	Criteria	Parameters	Weights
Cost	III	p = 50	.5
Utilization imbalance	IV	p = 10, q = 5	.1
% Shop utilization	I	—	.2
Exceptional parts	II	q = 1	.2

For the *Cost* objective, criterion III is used. If an alternative has greater cost than another alternative, the score is 0. If an alternative has a cost 50 or more dollars less than the other alternative, the score is 1. Between these limits, the score equals the difference divided by 50. Alternative #56 will be used as the base alternative. It has a worse cost than alternatives #96, #149, #167, #183, and #287. Therefore, the scores for alternative #56 compared with each of the others on Cost is 0. Alternative #56 has a cost advantage of $77 over alternative #132 ($815 – $738). This difference is greater than **p** (set at 50), so the score for alternative #56 relative to alternative #132 is 1 with respect to Cost. This is also the case for alternatives #192 and #253. Alternative #166 has a cost of $752, compared with alternative #56's cost of $738. The difference is $14, and dividing by **p** of 50 yields a score of .28. The Cost preference intensities are:

Cost

$w_c = 6$	#56	#96	#132	#149	#166	#167	#183	#192	#253	#287
#56	—	0	1	0	0.28	0	0	1	1	0
#96	0.72	—	1	0	1	0	0	1	1	0
#132	0	0	—	0	0	0	0	1	1	0
#149	1	1	1	—	1	1	1	1	1	0.42
#166	0	0	1	0	—	0	0	1	1	0
#167	0.8	0.08	1	0	1	—	0	1	1	0
#183	1	0.32	1	0	1	0.24	—	1	1	0
#192	0	0	0	0	0	0	0	—	0	0
#253	0	0	0	0	0	0	0	0.72	—	0
#287	1	1	1	0	1	1	1	1	1	—

Criterion IV is to be used for the objective of minimizing utilization imbalance, with parameters of $p = 10$ and $q = 5$. For an advantage greater than 10, the score is 1. For an advantage between 5 and 10, the score is .5. Otherwise, the score is 0.

Utilization Imbalance

$w_u = .1$	#56	#96	#132	#149	#166	#167	#183	#192	#253	#287
#56	—	1	.5	1	0	1	1	0	0	1
#96	0	—	0	0	0	.5	0	0	0	1
#132	0	0	—	0	0	.5	0	0	0	1
#149	0	0	0	—	0	0	0	0	0	1
#166	0	.5	.5	.5	—	1	.5	0	0	1
#167	0	0	0	0	0	—	0	0	0	1
#183	0	0	0	0	0	0	—	0	0	1
#192	0	1	1	1	.5	1	1	—	0	1
#253	0	1	1	1	.5	1	1	0	—	1
#287	0	0	0	0	0	0	0	0	0	—

Criterion I will be used for the objective of maximizing the percentage of shop utilization. This criterion score is 1 if there is an advantage, and 0 otherwise.

% Shop Utilization

$w_s = .2$	#56	#96	#132	#149	#166	#167	#183	#192	#253	#287
#56	—	1	0	0	0	0	0	1	1	0
#96	0	—	0	0	0	0	0	1	1	0
#132	1	1	—	1	1	1	1	1	1	1
#149	1	1	0	—	1	0	1	1	1	0
#166	1	1	0	0	—	0	1	1	1	0
#167	1	1	0	1	1	—	1	1	1	1
#183	0	1	0	0	0	0	—	1	1	0
#192	0	0	0	0	0	0	0	—	1	0
#253	0	0	0	0	0	0	0	0	—	0
#287	1	1	0	1	1	0	1	1	1	—

For the exceptional parts objective, criteria II will be used. If there is a relative advantage greater than q (here set at 1), the score is 1. Otherwise, the score is 0.

Exceptional Parts

w_e=.1	#56	#96	#132	#149	#166	#167	#183	#192	#253	#287
#56	—	0	0	0	0	0	0	1	0	0
#96	0	—	0	0	0	0	0	1	0	0
#132	0	0	—	0	0	0	0	1	0	0
#149	1	1	1	—	0	1	0	1	1	0
#166	0	0	0	0	—	1	0	1	1	0
#167	0	0	0	0	0	—	0	1	0	0
#183	0	0	0	0	0	1	—	1	1	0
#192	0	0	0	0	0	0	0	—	0	0
#253	0	0	0	0	0	0	0	1	—	0
#287	0	0	0	0	0	1	0	1	1	—

The next step is to calculate the multicriteria preference indexes. Here, since the sum of the weights is set to equal 1, this is simply the sum of preference intensities multiplied by the respective weights. For instance, comparing **#56** with **#132**, the weighted sum is $.5 \times 0 + .1 \times 1 + .2 \times 1 + .2 \times 0 = .3$. Φ^+ is the mean of multicriteria preference indexes for an alternative (the row mean). Φ^- is the mean of multicriteria preference indexes of all other alternatives to the base alternative (column mean). Φ is Φ^+ for an alternative minus Φ^- for that alternative.

	#56	#96	#132	#149	#166	#167	#183	#192	#253	#287	ϕ^+
#56	—	.3	.55	.1	.14	.1	.1	.9	.7	.1	.332
#96	.36	—	.5	0	.5	.05	0	.9	.7	.1	.346
#132	.2	.2	—	.2	.2	.25	.2	.9	.7	.3	.350
#149	.9	.9	.7	—	.7	.7	.7	.9	.9	.31	.746
#166	.2	.25	.55	.05	—	.3	.25	.9	.9	.1	.389
#167	.6	.24	.5	.2	.7	—	.2	.9	.7	.3	.482
#183	.5	.36	.5	0	.5	.32	—	.9	.9	.1	.453
#192	0	.1	.1	.1	.05	.1	.1	—	.2	.1	.094
#253	0	.1	.1	.1	.05	.1	.1	.56	—	.1	.134
#287	.7	.7	.5	.2	.7	.7	.7	.9	.9	—	.667
ϕ^-	.384	.350	.444	.106	.393	.291	.261	.862	.733	.168	
ϕ	−.052	−.004	−.094	.640	.004	.191	.192	−.768	−.599	.499	

PROMETHEE I Calculations

A table of strong and weak relationships can be developed, following the rules presented above. A strong relationship of alternative a over alternative b requires $\Phi^+(a) > \Phi^+(b)$. A weak relationship of alternative a over alternative b requires $\Phi^-(a) < \Phi^-(b)$. (In both cases, if equality exists, strong or weak indifference exists). The following table identifies strong relationships (+) and weak relationships (−). There are no indifference cases in this example.

	#56	#96	#132	#149	#166	#167	#183	#192	#253	#287
#56			−		−			+−	+−	
#96	+−		−		−			+−	+−	
#132	+							+−	−	

	#56	#96	#132	#149	#166	#167	#183	#192	#253	#287
#149	+–	+–	+–		+–	+–	+–	+–	+–	+–
#166	+	+	+–					+–	+–	
#167	+–	+–	+–		+–		+	+–	+–	
#183	+–	+–	+–		+–	–		+–	+–	
#192										
#253								+–		
#287	+–	+–	+–		+–	+–	+–	+–	+–	

These relationships form the basis for the table of outrankings. In order for alternative a to outrank alternative b, (1) either both strong and weak relationship exists, or (2) a strong relationship and a weak indifference relationship exists, or (3) a weak relationship and a strong indifference relationship exists. Alternative a is indifferent to alternative b only if both a strong and weak indifference relationship exists. Otherwise, alternative a is incomparable with alternative b. In the following table, outranking relationships are indicated by >. (There are no indifference relationships.)

	#56	#96	#132	#149	#166	#167	#183	#192	#253	#287
#56								>	>	
#96	>							>	>	
#132								>	>	
#149	>	>	>		>	>	>	>	>	>
#166			>					>	>	
#167	>	>	>		>			>	>	
#183	>	>	>		>			>	>	
#192										
#253								>		
#287	>	>	>		>	>	>	>	>	

#56	#96	#132	#149	#166	#167	#183	#192	#253	#287
149→	287	167	183	96	166	56	132	253	192
	287→	167	183	96	166	56	132	253	192
		167→		96	166	56	132	253	192
			183→	96	166	56	132	253	192
				96→		56		253	192
					166→		132	253	192
						56→		253	192
							132→	253	192
								253→	192

Here **#149** outranks all other alternatives. Alternative **#192** is outranked by all other alternatives. There are some cases where alternatives are not comparable, such as **#167** and **#183**, as well as **#96** and **#166** and others.

PROMETHEE II Calculations

The calculations for *PROMETHEE II* are much easier, and also provide a complete ordering of alternatives. Brans and Vincke claim that this loses some of the information provided by *PROMETHEE I* (the incomparability). The ranking is simply in order of $\Phi\ (a)$.

Alternative	Φ^+	Φ^-	Φ
#149	6.71	.95	+5.76
#287	6.00	1.81	+4.19
#183	4.08	2.35	+1.73
#167	4.34	2.62	+1.72
#96	3.11	3.15	- .04
#166	3.50	3.54	- .04
#56	2.99	3.46	- .47
#132	3.15	4.00	- .85
#253	1.21	6.60	-5.39
#192	.85	7.76	-6.91

GAIA Output

GAIA is a graphical extension of *PROMETHEE* that allows the user to interactively manipulate relative weights to visually see the impact on the relative performance of the alternatives. The eigenvalues of the data matrix are calculated, and the first two eigenvectors used as a means to graph the data as in principal components analysis. This information will not be a perfect mapping of all original information, but will enable graphing in two dimensions. The criteria are graphed, as well as a Π variable, representing the weighted overall impact of the criteria. The degree to which the criteria correlate is readily apparent from this display. The alternatives are also plotted on this graph. The relative performance of each alternative on each criterion is identifiable from the relative position of the eigenvalues for each alternative relative to the criterion scales.

In this problem, the first two eigenvalues contained 90.32% of the data information. Criterion and alternative scores are:

	First eigenvector	Second eigenvector
Criteria		
Cost	0.57877	−0.52706
Utilization imbalance	−0.52250	−0.00943
% Shop utilization	0.51919	0.78965
Exceptional parts	0.34995	−0.31395
Alternatives		
#56	−0.51442	−0.10862
#96	−0.02314	−0.57247
#132	0.28474	1.08404
#149	1.09297	−0.43656
#166	−0.14645	0.11347
#167	0.68916	0.56841
#183	0.37535	−0.48599
#192	−1.69188	0.20363
#253	−1.48136	−0.26548
#287	1.41504	−0.10043
Resultant of weights	0.41096	−0.31395

In this problem, graphing these eigenvectors indicates that criteria *Cost* and *Exceptional Parts* are very positively correlated. On the other hand, the other two criteria, *% Shop Utilization* and *Utilization Imbalance*, are well dispersed from the other two criteria. Using the resultant of the weights the graph shows **#149** and **#287** as performing well on the relative scales. For each individual criterion, relative performance is indicated. On the scale of *Utilization Imbalance*, **#192** and **#253** are shown to perform very well, while **#287** has very poor performance on this criterion. Alternatives **#132** and **#167** perform very well on the criterion of *Shop Utilization*, while alternative **#253** does very poorly.

Nuclear Dump Site Selection — *PROMETHEE*

The nuclear dump site selection problem support from *PROMETHEE* follows. Input parameters for the four criteria were:

	Weight	*Type*	*Parameter* *p*	*Values* *q*
Cost	.20	V	50	10
Lives	.65	III	90	
Risk	.10	IV	4	1
Improvement	.05	IV	4	1

The resulting preference indices, followed by preference flows and rankings from *PROMETHEE I* and *PROMETHEE II* were:

Nuclear dump preference indices

Site	Nome	Newa	Rock	Duqu	Gary	Yaki	Turk	Well	Anah	Epco	Duck	Sant
Nome	—	0.62	0.00	0.00	0.14	0.14	0.00	0.00	0.51	0.43	0.07	0.29
Newark	0.08	—	0.00	0.08	0.00	0.08	0.05	0.08	0.08	0.03	0.08	0.08
Rock Spr	0.22	0.65	—	0.00	0.29	0.34	0.12	0.00	0.72	0.60	0.24	0.51
Duquesne	0.19	0.65	0.00	—	0.29	0.29	0.07	0.00	0.72	0.60	0.22	0.51
Gary	0.08	0.43	0.00	0.03	—	0.08	0.05	0.03	0.44	0.31	0.03	0.22
Yakima Fl	0.00	0.43	0.00	0.00	0.00	—	0.00	0.00	0.39	0.31	0.00	0.17
Turkey	0.10	0.65	0.00	0.00	0.22	0.22	—	0.00	0.60	0.53	0.17	0.39
Wells	0.27	0.65	0.07	0.07	0.36	0.36	0.14	—	0.72	0.67	0.29	0.58
Anaheim	0.00	0.07	0.00	0.00	0.00	0.00	0.00	0.00	—	0.00	0.00	0.00
Epcot Cen	0.05	0.14	0.00	0.05	0.00	0.05	0.05	0.05	0.12	—	0.05	0.05
Duckwate	0.05	0.51	0.00	0.00	0.07	0.07	0.00	0.00	0.48	0.36	—	0.27
Santa Cru	0.00	0.29	0.00	0.00	0.00	0.00	0.00	0.00	0.22	0.14	0.00	—

Here the partial ranking is: Wells   Rock Springs

Duquesne
Turkey
Nome
Duckwater
Gary
Yakima Flats
Santa Cruz
Epcot Center

Anaheim   Newark

PROMETHEE II Complete Ranking

Rank	Action	Phi	Phi+	Phi–
1.	A..8 Wells	0.3679	0.3816	0.0136
2.	A..3 Rock Sprin	0.3295	0.3361	0.0066
3.	A..4 Duquesne	0.3023	0.3225	0.0202
4.	A..7 Turkey	0.2164	0.2609	0.0444
5.	A..1 Nome	0.1072	0.2006	0.0934
6.	A..5 Gary	0.0277	0.1525	0.1248
7.	A.11 Duckwater	0.0612	0.1647	0.1035
8.	A..6 Yakima Fla	–0.0291	0.1184	0.1475
9.	A.12 Santa Cruz	–0.2184	0.0591	0.2775
10.	A.10 Epcot Cen	–0.3078	0.0561	0.3639
11.	A..2 Newark	–0.4087	0.0545	0.4632
12.	A..9 Anaheim	–0.4482	0.0066	0.4548

GAIA can provide some useful insight to decision makers. GAIA software calculates eigenvalues for criteria and alternatives, making visual display of relative performance possible. The eigenvalues for this problem contain 90.1% of the information. Therefore, the plots on these two dimensions are not perfect representations of relative alternative performance, but this approach provides a powerful visualization tool. Relative scores in order of the *PROMETHEE II* ranking are:

	First eigenvalue	Second eigenvalue
Criteria:		
Cost	0.00675	–0.01638
Lives	0.97427	–0.11893
Risk	–0.04061	0.74211
Civic impr	0.22159	0.65944
Alternatives:		
Wells	0.54949	–0.00237
Rock Spr	0.48398	0.26447
Duquesne	0.45108	0.00965
Turkey	0.39234	–0.02590
Nome	0.18926	–0.38275
Duckwater	0.05628	–0.09818
Gary	0.05166	0.41086
Yakima Fl	–0.00223	–0.10255
Santa Cruz	–0.31345	–0.41471
Epcot Cent	–0.57733	0.12010
Newark	–0.62319	0.59405
Anaheim	–0.65789	–0.37267

The plots of these eigenvalues give an indication of the relative correlation among criteria. Here *Risk* and *Civic Improvement* are correlated. These two criteria are almost perpendicular to the plot for *Lives Lost*, indicating almost no correlation.

The plots of the alternatives along with the criterion plots indicate which alternatives do well on which criteria. Wells does well on *Lives Lost*, explaining why it was ranked first (this criterion had the heaviest weight). Rock Springs did almost as well on *Lives Lost*, while doing better on *Risk* and *Civic*

Improvement. Newark and Anaheim cost a relatively large amount, and involved the risk of many more lives than other alternatives, and thus were ranked at the bottom. GAIA includes the ability to interactively change weights on criteria, visually demonstrating the impact while giving scores of each alternative. This provides a form of sensitivity analysis.

Applications of Outranking Methods

Unlike *ELECTRE*, there are quite a number of applications of *PROMETHEE* published in English. It seems to be a viable method, which has been used for expert systems (DuBois, et al., 1991; Mareschal and Brans, 1991; Pasche, 1991) as well as other applications. These other applications include location analysis (Mladineo and Margeta, 1987), investment analysis (Ribarovic and Mladineo, 1987), hospital service analysis (d'Avignon & Mareschal, 1989) and nuclear waste management (Briggs, et al., 1990). The method has been extended to incorporate visual technology in *PROMETHEE-GAIA* (Mareschal and Brans, 1988). This software package is available from Professor Brans, and is a very easily used system which includes features providing visual interactive ability to change relative criterion weights.

Conclusions

The outranking methods were originated by the works of Roy [1971, 1975, 1978] and coworkers [Roy and Vincke, 1981; Skalka, et al., 1983]. Both the method of preference cones and *ELECTRE* provide viable means of supporting selection from a finite set of alternatives. *ELECTRE* has been modified a number of times, with versions I through IV existing. There also have been modifications of the general *ELECTRE* approach developed by Professor Duckstein of Arizona University (see Szidarovszky, et al. 1986; Wymore and Duckstein, 1989), as well as others. *PROMETHEE* is another extension, based upon the fundamental ideas of *ELECTRE*, but appearing to be much easier to implement. Brans, Mareschal and others [1985, 1986, 1992] developed *PROMETHEE*.

ELECTRE is a bit limited with respect to the number of compared alternatives, as large numbers of indices would need calculation. However, the decision maker would be asked to do very little (only set the relative weights on the K objective functions, and await results). Since the process could be automated, the upper bound on the number of considered alternatives could also be quite large in theory. *PROMETHEE* provides much of the good features of *ELECTRE*, with much less mystery.

Note that an alternative means of selecting from a set of given nondominated alternatives would be to take the weights from the techniques presented in Chapter 7, and simply score each alternative. That, of course, would require use of a linearized utility function.

References

Benayoun, R., Roy, B. and Sussman, B. 1986. ELECTRE: Une Methode Pour Guider le Choixe en Presence de Points de Vue Multiples. *SEMA* Note 49, (June).

Brans, J.P. and Mareschal, B. 1992. PROMETHEE V: MCDM Problems with Segmentation Constraints. *INFOR* **30**:2, 85–96.

Brans, J.P. and Vincke, Ph. 1985. A preference ranking organization method: The PROMETHEE method. *Management Science* **31**, 647–656.

Brans, J.P. Vincke, P. and Mareschal, B. 1986. How to select and how to rank projects: The PROMETHEE method. *European Journal of Operational Research* **24**, 228–238.

Briggs, T., Kunsch, P.L. and Mareschal, B. 1990. Nuclear waste management: An application of the multicriteria PROMETHEE method. *European Journal of Operational Research* **44**, 1–10.

d'Avignon, G.R. and Mareschal, B. 1989. Specialisation of hospital services in Québec: An application of the PROMETHEE and GAIA methods. *Mathematical and Computer Modelling* **12**, 1393–1400.

DuBois, P., Brans, J.P., Cantraine, F. and Mareschal, B. 1991. MEDICIS: An expert system for computer-aided diagnosis using the PROMETHEE multicriteria method. *European Journal of Operational Research* **52**, 224–234.

Mareschal, B. and Brans, J.P. 1988. Geometrical Representations for MCDA. *European Journal of Operational Research* **34**, 69–77.

Mareschal, B. and Brans, J.P. 1991. BANKADVISER: An industrial evaluation system. *European Journal of Operational Research* **54**, 318–324.

Mladineo, N. and Margeta, J. 1987. Multicriteria ranking of alternative locations for small scale hydro plants. *European Journal of Operational Research* **31**, 215–222.

Pasche, C. 1991. EXTRA: An expert system for multicriteria decision making. *European Journal of Operational Research* **52**, 224–234.

Ribarovic, Z. and Mladineo, N. 1987. Application of multicriteria analysis to the ranking and evaluation of the investment programmes in the ready mixed concrete industry. *Engineering Costs and Production Economics* **12**, 367–374.

Roy, B. 1971. Problems and methods with multiple objective functions. *Mathematical Programming* **1**:2, 239–266.

Roy, B. 1975. Why multicriteria decision aid may not fit in with the assessment of a unique criteria. In *Multiple Criteria Decision Making: Kyoto 1975*, M. Zeleny, ed. New York: Springer-Verlag. 280–283.

Roy, B. 1978. ELECTRE III: Un algorithme de classement fonde sur une representation floue des preferences en presence de criteres multiple. *Cahiers du Centre Etudes Recherche Operationelle* **20**, 3–24.

Roy, B. and Vincke, P. 1981. Multicriteria analysis: Survey and new directions. *European Journal of Operational Research* **8**, 207–218.

Skalka, J.M., Bouyoussou, D. and Bernabeu, Y.A. 1983. ELECTRE III et IV: Aspect methodologique et guide d'utilisation. *Cahier du LAMSADE 25*. Universite Paris-Dauphine.

Szidarovszky, F., Gershon, M.E. and Duckstein, L. 1986. *Techniques for multiobjective decision-making in systems management*. New York: Elsevier Science Publishing Co.

Wymore, M.L. and Duckstein, L. 1989. Prioritizing factory automation investments with Multicriterion-Q Analysis. *Proceedings of the International Conference on Multiple Criteria Decision Making: Applications in Industry and Service*. Bangkok: Asian Institute of Technology.

9
ZAPROS

ZAPROS is a multicriteria selection aid based on qualitative judgments. Using the principles given by Larichev [1982], Larichev and Moshkovich [1988, 1991], Larichev et al. [1974], and Moshkovich [1988], *ZAPROS* provides a means to construct a quasi-order on large sets of alternatives described over multiple attributes. Larichev [1992] has argued that human ability to consistently express preference is limited. The safest way to acquire preference information is to present the decision maker with two alternatives, differing on only two criteria. Rational decision makers are assumed to have preferential independence across criteria values other than the two criteria that are varied in a tradeoff. Decision problems are assumed to be adequately described by categorical measures. A finite number of decision categories describe the decision problem, and minor differences in attainment levels are considered to be immaterial. *ZAPROS* is an implementation of this philosophy.

ZAPROS is based on development of a joint ordinal scale (JOS), a list of boundaries between groups of alternatives. Because each attainment level is describable in categories (no more than seven and usually fewer, as that is proposed as the limit of human differentiation between objects [Payne 1976; Slovic et al. 1977]), the selection problem can be simplified to comparison of a finite set of alternatives. The JOS is in preference order. *ZAPROS* only guarantees a partial ordering of alternatives, because only those tradeoffs adjacent to the ideal solution are tested. The full development of all possible tradeoffs would be too time consuming. The partial ordering *ZAPROS* provides makes it possible for decision makers to focus on a much smaller set of potentially useful alternatives rather than an original large set.

The *ZAPROS* procedure seeks to develop at least part of the matrix of relationships between alternatives. Knowledge acquisition is the process of determining relative preference among those alternatives adjacent to the ideal solution. The partial order of real alternatives is conducted applying four principles:

1. Sequential selection of non-dominated alternatives (All non-dominated alternatives are assigned rank 1 and eliminated from consideration; of all remaining alternatives, those that are non-dominated with respect to the remaining set are assigned rank 2 and eliminated from consideration; and so forth.)

2. Sequential selection of non-dominating alternatives (All alternatives that do not dominate any other alternative in the set are given rank 1 and eliminated from consideration; of those remaining alternatives, those that do not dominate any other member of the remaining set are assigned rank 2 and eliminated from consideration; and so forth—then the rank orders for this analysis are inverted.)

3. Sequential selection of alternatives dominating the maximum number of other alternatives (Using the matrix of pairwise comparisons for each alternative, the number of alternatives dominating each member is identified—rank 1 is assigned to alternatives that dominate the maximum number of other alternatives.)

4. Sequential selection of alternatives dominated by the least number of other alternatives (the reverse process from the prior operation).

The average ranking from these four principles can be used for rank ordering of real alternatives.

Pairwise preference questions ask the decision maker to select between two alternatives differing on only two criteria. A tradeoff is present; where relative to the first alternative, the second alternative has a better performance on one criteria and a worse performance on the second. The order in determining which alternatives are compared is based on adjacency of alternatives to the ideal (111 in our example). In addition, the system can ask for preferences among pairs of alternatives adjacent to the *Nadir* (333) reference point as a basis for testing preferential independence.

The *ZAPROS* system assures consistency by checking for intransitivity each time new preference information is added. For instance, if $(21X)$ is stated to be preferred to $(12X)$, and prior information had implied that $(12X)$ was preferable to $(21X)$, the decision maker is alerted to the discrepancy, and asked to reconsider. If the last bit of preference information is considered erroneous by the decision maker, it is changed with no need to change the prior stored information. On the other hand, if the current assessment is considered valid, this implies an error in the previously stored information. That preference information contradicting the current information is changed. Furems and Gnedenko [1992] discuss an error detection method.

Once sufficient information is gathered to make a partial ranking of alternatives, the system ceases asking the decision maker pairwise preference questions. Alternatives are then ranked.

Demonstration Model

A fund has received a large number of proposed projects for consideration of funding. The fund's manager is responsible for the effective management of the fund in furthering a research program outlined by the board of directors. The manager developed a form for the use of referees in their review and evaluation of proposals. In an attempt to quickly screen projects after their review, and to guarantee that the fund's objectives are attained, four criteria were identified as critically important. These criteria and the attainments of the first twelve proposals on these criteria are given in Table 9.1.

TABLE 9.1 Criteria and attainments

Proposals	Attributes			
	Originality	Prospects	Quality	Level
01	1	2	4	3
02	3	3	1	1
03	2	1	2	2
04	2	1	3	2
05	3	3	2	1
06	3	3	4	3
07	4	1	2	2
08	2	1	1	3
09	3	4	4	3
10	3	4	2	3
11	3	2	3	3
12	3	4	4	3

Attributes are scored on a scale where 1 is best.

Project originality
   1 - absolutely new idea and/or approach
   2 - there are new elements in the proposal
   3 - further development of previous ideas
   4 - accumulation of additional data for previous
       research
Prospects for success
   1 - high probability of success
   2 - success is moderately probable
   3 - there is some possibility of success
   4 - success is improbable
Proposer qualifications
   1 - proposer qualification is high
   2 - proposer qualification is normal
   3 - proposer qualification is unknown
   4 - proposer qualification is low
Level of proposed work
   1 - the proposed work is high level
   2 - the proposed work is middle level
   3 - the proposed work is low level

The decision maker wants to develop a decision rule that considers these attributes. Experts will provide evaluations of each proposal on these attributes. The decision rule can then be used to classify proposals objectively and efficiently.

The main idea of the method *ZAPROS* (Larichev and Moshkovich, 1991) is the concept of a joint ordinal scale built according to the preferences of the decision maker. The joint ordinal scale (JOS) gives a basis for rank-ordering all possible combinations of attributes reflecting the preferences of the decision maker. This ordinal scale can effectively be used for pairwise comparison of alternatives. Usually it is assumed that values on each attribute scale are rank-ordered for the decision maker on his or her preferences. For each attribute scale, values are rank-ordered from the most to the least preferable. This means that the score of 1 is the most preferable, 2 the second most preferable, and so on.

To construct the joint ordinal scale it is necessary to make ordinal tradeoffs for each pair of attributes and for each pair of possible values. For ordinal tradeoffs, the decision maker is asked questions of the form "What do you prefer: to have the best level upon attribute Q and the second upon attribute $Q+1$, or the best level upon attribute $Q+1$ and the second level upon attribute Q?" For our example we ask "What do you prefer in a proposal: to have an original idea with only probable success, or only some new elements with a high probability of success?"

It is clear that the analogous question when levels are changed from the best to the worst attribute level correspond to the routine questions in the classical procedure for determination of attribute weights (von Winterfeldt and Edwards, 1986). However, with *ZAPROS* it is not necessary to obtain quantitative estimation.

The questions used to determine the joint ordinal scale are fairly easy, but formulations are a bit too complicated. The same information can be obtained much easier in the form of comparison of two hypothetical alternatives that differ in levels on only two attributes. This type of judgment is considered valid by Larichev (1992). In our example, the decision maker is asked to compare the following alternatives with three options:

> You are to compare the following alternatives:
>
> 1. Absolutely new idea and/or approach
> 2. High probability of success
>
> ALTERNATIVE 1
>
> 3. Proposer qualification is normal
> 4. The proposed work is high level
>
> ALTERNATIVE 2
>
> 3. Proposer qualification is high
> 4. The proposed work is middle level
>
> Possible answers:
> 1. Alternative 1 is more preferable than alt. 2.
> 2. Alternative 1 and 2 are equally preferable.
> 3. Alternative 2 is more preferable than alt. 1.

As this figure demonstrates, values on all attributes except the two under consideration are held at the best level.

We can construct a set of hypothetical alternatives **L** including vectors from **Y** for such comparisons. Set **L** has the feature that all attributes have the best characteristic on each attribute except one at most. In our example, the set **L** consists of the following 12 vectors: (1111), (2111), (3111), (4111), (1211), (1311), (1411), (1121), (1131), (1141), (1112), and (1113). Vector (1211) represents the hypothetical proposal that is rated as an absolutely original idea, with moderately probable success probability, a highly qualified proposer, and high level work. The *ZAPROS* system operates by filling in the matrix of size $\mathbf{M} \times \mathbf{M}$ with the results of pairwise comparisons of alternatives from set **L**.

In any interview with a decision maker, there is a possibility of errors in responses. Therefore, a special procedure for detection and elimination of contradictions is needed. Possible contradictions in decision maker responses are determined as violations of transitivity of relations **P** and **I** (in general as violations of transitivity of **R**). After each comparison of vectors from **L**, this information can be extended on the basis of transitivity (transitive closure of the binary relation defined on the set **L** being built).

After closure is obtained, the decision maker is presented with the next pair of vectors from **L** for which a binary relation has not been defined. When the decision maker's response is obtained, transitivity is checked. This procedure assures a transitive system of relationships.

To test decision maker responses, the decision maker could be presented with additional pairs of vectors for comparison on the basis of the following principle: the relation between each pair of vectors from **L** is to be defined directly by a decision maker's response, or indirectly from transitive closure, no less than two times. This requirement means that if a decision maker response is verified, then this relationship is considered to be proven. If the relationship between two vectors from **L** has only defined one, and that only on the basis of transitive closure, then this pair is to be presented to the decision maker for comparison. If the decision maker's response does not conflict with the previous information, then the judgment is considered to be correct. If there is some difference, the triple of vectors for which a pairwise comparison contradicts the transitivity of **L** is identified. It is always possible to detect such a triple, because after each of the decision maker's responses we have assured transitive closure. When the triple is detected, the decision maker is asked to reconsider the situation, and to change one (or more) of the previous responses in order to eliminate the intransitivity. After the corrected responses are obtained, they are incorporated into the information on the decision maker's preferences.

The assumed transitivity of preferences and rank orderings of attribute levels make it possible to construct an effective procedure of pairwise comparisons, which essentially reduces the number of required comparisons from $M \times (M-1)/2$. For our example, the following 13 responses from a decision maker were enough to complete the matrix of pairwise comparisons from **L**:

1. (2111) is preferred over (1211)
2. (2111) is preferred over (1121)
3. (1112) is preferred over (2111)
4. (1113) is preferred over (1211)
5. (3111) is preferred over (1211)
6. (1121) is preferred over (3111)
7. (3111) is preferred over (1131)
8. (1211) is preferred over (4111)
9. (4111) is preferred over (1311)
10. (1131) is preferred over (4111)
11. (4111) is preferred over (1141)
12. (1131) is preferred over (1211)
13. (1141) is preferred over (1311)

Three additional pairwise comparisons were made to check this information.

1. (1211) is preferred over (1141)
2. (1141) is preferred over (1411)
3. (1121) is preferred over (1113)

This third answer contradicts the previous information.

(1311) was preferred over (2111)
(2111) was preferred over (1121)

Therefore,

(1113) was preferred over (1121).

Now, the decision maker has selected

(1121) is preferred over (1113).

In this case, the decision maker may have responded to this prompt by changing the relationship between (1113) and (2111).

(2111) is preferred over (1113)

The system recalculates the matrix of pairwise comparisons and no further questions are required.

In experiments conducted by Larichev, et al. [1993] for a task with five attributes, four with three levels and one with four levels (giving an $\mathbf{M} = 11$ and $\mathbf{M} \times (\mathbf{M}-1)/2 = 55$), the number of questions varied from around 18 to 20 with a maximum of 25.

We now discuss how the judgments obtained by this procedure can lead to identification of a linear quasi-order on the set $\mathbf{L}$. This rank-order is called the joint ordinal scale (JOS).

Rank	Joint Ordinal Scale (Ordered Values)	Vector
1	absolutely new idea and/or approach, high probability of success, proposer qualifications are high, the proposed work is high level	1111
2	the proposed work is middle level	1112
3	there are new elements in the proposal	2111
4	the proposed work is low level	1113
5	the proposer's qualifications are normal	1121
6	further development of previous ideas	3111
7	proposer's qualifications are unknown	1131
8	moderate probability of success	1211
9	accumulation of additional data for previous research	4111
10	proposer's qualifications are low	1141
11	there is some possibility of success	1311
12	success is improbable	1411

We can formulate the following rule for comparison of a pair of vectors from $\mathbf{Y}$:

Definition 1

Alternative A is not less preferable for the decision maker than alternative B, if for each attribute Q there exists attribute $T(Q)$ such that $(1,1,..,1,AQ,1,..,1)$ is not less preferable than $(1,1,..,1,BT(Q),1,..,1)$.

The correctness of such a rule in case of preferential independence of all pairs of attributes has been proven in Larichev and Moshkovich [1991].

Vectors from the set **L** differ from the best possible alternative in only one component. Therefore, we can consider the place, obtained by the vector in this ranking, to be the place of this unique component in the JOS. That is why the rule for comparison of vectors from Y may be reformulated as follows:

Definition 2

Alternative A is not less preferable than alternative B, if for each component of vector X there exists a component of vector Y with a less preferable value on the JOS (binary relation **R**).

The procedure of comparison of two vectors from Y may be accomplished as follows. Let us mark $\mathbf{R}(AQ)$ as the rank which vector $B = (1,1,..,1,AQ,1,..,1)$ obtained in the joint ordinal scale. Then alternative A can be represented by vector of ranks $R(A) = (R1(A),R2(A),...,RQ(A))$. We can rearrange ranks in a vector in a non-descending manner: the first $R1 = \text{Min }(R(AQ))$, where $Q=1,2,...,Q$; the second rank–the smallest from the rest, and so on. As a result we have $R(A) = (R1(A),R2(A),..., RQ(A))$ for A, and $R(B) = (R1(B),R2(B),...,RQ(B))$ for B, and A is not less preferable than B, if $RQ(A) \leq RQ(B)$, $Q=1,2,...,Q$. This procedure guarantees the requirement of definition 1.

Let us assume the twelve proposals given in Table 9.1. We change each component of a vector by the corresponding rank in the JOS. The result is presented in the next-to-last column of Table 9.2. We then rewrite these vectors with values in non-descending order (the last column of Table 9.1). Now we are able to compare these alternatives, as shown in Table 9.2.

We can see a rather large number of incomparable alternatives. This leads us to the question of how to rank-order alternatives on the basis of this matrix. There are several approaches possible. *ZAPROS* repeats the rules presented earlier.

1. Sequential selection of non-dominated alternatives
2. Sequential selection of non-dominating alternatives

TABLE 9.2 Criteria and attainments

Proposals	Vectors	Ranks in JOS				Rearranged ranks			
01	1243	1	8	10	4	1	4	8	10
02	3311	6	11	1	1	1	1	6	11
03	2122	3	1	5	2	1	2	3	5
04	2132	3	1	7	2	1	2	3	7
05	3321	6	11	5	1	1	5	6	11
06	3343	6	11	10	4	4	6	10	11
07	4122	1	8	10	4	1	4	8	10
08	2113	3	1	1	4	1	1	3	4
09	3443	6	12	10	4	4	6	10	12
10	3423	6	12	5	4	4	5	6	12
11	3233	6	8	7	4	4	6	7	8
12	3443	6	12	10	4	4	6	10	12

3. Sequential selection of alternatives that dominate the maximum of other alternatives

4. Sequential selection of alternatives that dominate the minimum of other alternatives

To see the results of applying these principles to our example,

Rank	Alternatives	
1	0008	
2	0002	0003
3	0004	
4	0007	0011
5	0001	0005
6	0006	0010
7	0009	0012

We see that we are unable to form a complete ranking of alternatives. However, we obtain a fairly stable partial ordering that can effectively be used in decision making. In the example, alternative 8 is consistently a leading choice. A second group includes alternatives 2, 3, and 4. The next group consists of alternatives 1, 5, 7, and 11. Although we have some additional information about the comparison of alternatives within these groups, this is not crucial for decision making in this task, because the aim is to support proposals of good quality, not just identify the best choice.

It would be easy to obtain explanations for comparison of any two alternatives from the JOS. If the alternatives are incomparable on the basis of this rule, then the resulting relationship between them is explained with the help of additional alternatives. Let alternative X have some smaller rank than alternative Y in the final ranking. At the same time, on the basis of the JOS, alternatives X and Y are incomparable. Then, if the ranking was conducted according to the principle of sequential selection of non-dominated or non-dominating alternatives, alternative X is searched for, which is incomparable with alternative Y but is more preferable than alternative Z.

If the ordering is according to the number of dominated (dominating) alternatives, then alternative Z is searched for, which is dominated by X but is not dominated by Y.

Examples of possible messages for explanation of results of comparison of real alternatives are as follows:

Alternative 7 (4122)
   is more preferable than
Alternative 6 (3343)
   because as a result of the interview it was stated that:

Value 4 on attribute 1 (alt 7) is more preferable than
Value 3 on attribute 2 (alt 6);

Value 1 on attribute 2 (alt 7) is more preferable than
Value 3 on attribute 2 (alt 6);
Value 2 on attribute 3 (alt 7) is more preferable than
Value 4 on attribute 3 (alt 6);

Value 2 on attribute 4 (alt 7) is more preferable than
Value 3 on attribute 4 (alt 7);

Alternative 2 (3311)
    more preferable than
Alternative 1 (1243)
    they are incomparable on the basis of JOS

but

the least preferable alternative 8 dominating alternative 2,
has smaller rank than
the least preferable alternative 7 dominating alternative 1.

Nuclear Dump Site Selection

We have solved a problem involving selection of a nuclear dump site using other techniques. Here we will demonstrate how *ZAPROS* could be used to support this decision.

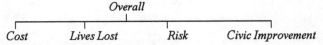

Note that here risk relates to the risk of a major catastrophe. While this obviously correlates with lives lost to some degree, in this analysis expected lives lost are under conditions where major catastrophes do not occur. Therefore, these criteria are independent. The alternatives are:

	Cost (bill)	Expected Lives Lost	Risk	Civic Improvement	Vector
Nome, AK	40	60	very high	low	1243
Newark, NJ	100	140	very low	very high	4411
Rock Springs, WY	60	40	low	high	2122
Duquesne, PA	60	40	medium	medium	2133
Gary, IN	70	80	low	very high	3321
Yakima Flats, WA	70	80	high	medium	3343
Turkey, TX	60	50	high	high	2142
Wells, NE	50	30	medium	medium	2133
Anaheim, CA	90	130	very high	very low	3443
Epcot Center, FL	80	120	very low	very low	3413
Duckwater, NV	80	70	medium	low	3233
Santa Cruz, CA	90	100	very high	very low	3443

The problem measures need to be converted to categorical scales. An example is:

Variable	Category 1 (best)	Category 2	Category 3	Category 4
Cost	≤ 40	41–65	66–99	≥ 100
Lives Lost	≤ 50	51–70	71–90	≥ 91
Risk	very low	low	medium	high or very high
Civic Improvement	very high	high	medium or low	

Input files are given in the appendix. The pairwise comparison questions and a set of responses are:

pairwise comparison 1	alt. 1 (2111) is preferred over alt. 2 (1211)
pairwise comparison 2	alt. 1 (2111) is preferred over alt. 2 (1121)
pairwise comparison 3	alt. 2 (1112) is preferred over alt. 1 (2111)
pairwise comparison 4	alt. 1 (1113) is preferred over alt. 2 (2111)
pairwise comparison 5	alt. 2 (3111) is preferred over alt. 1 (1311)
pairwise comparison 6	alt. 2 (1121) is preferred over alt. 1 (3111)
pairwise comparison 7	alt. 1 (3111) is preferred over alt. 2 (1131)
pairwise comparison 8	alt. 1 (4111) is preferred over alt. 2 (1211)
pairwise comparison 9	alt. 1 (1131) is preferred over alt. 2 (4111)
pairwise comparison 10	alt. 2 (4111) is preferred over alt. 1 (1141)
pairwise comparison 11	alt. 1 (1141) is preferred over alt. 2 (1211)
pairwise comparison 12	alt. 2 (1141) is preferred over alt. 1 (1311)
pairwise comparison 13	alt. 2 (1113) is preferred over alt. 1 (1121)

This yields the following partial rank ordering:

Layer 1:	0002 Newark	(4411)
	0003 Rock Springs	(2122)
Layer 2:	0004 Duquesne	(2133)
	0007 Turkey	(2142)
	0008 Wells	(2133)
Layer 3:	0001 Nome	(1243)
	0005 Gary	(3321)
	0010 Epcot Center	(3413)
	0011 Duckwater	(3233)
Layer 4:	0006 Yakima Flats	(3343)
Layer 5:	0009 Anaheim	(3443)
	0012 Santa Cruz	(3443)

Note that Newark is selected despite terrible costs and expected *Lives Lost* because it is rated so high on *Risk* and *Civic Improvement*, and is therefore not dominated by any other alternative. *ZAPROS* is intended to focus the decision maker's attention to a smaller set of alternatives rather than identify a particular best solution. *ZAPROS* explanation facilities rank Newark above layer 2 and 3 elements because Newark is not directly comparable with any of those alternatives, and Rock Springs outranks all level 2 and level 3 alternatives, while nothing outranks Newark.

House Selection

The last example we will present involves the purchase of a house. Criteria considered include monetary considerations (*Fiscal*—consisting of *Payment* as well as *Investment*), *Appearance*, and *Convenience* (consisting of distance to *School* and distance to *Work*). The first tradeoff is for the *Fiscal* goal. The decision maker would like monthly *Payment* to be as low as possible. On the other hand, purchase of the house as an *Investment*, anticipating increase in the value of the house over time, has an opposing effect. As the value of the house goes up, *Investment* becomes more attractive. The hierarchy of goals and measures is:

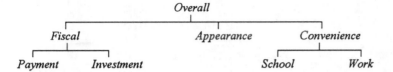

There are five alternatives under consideration. Alternatives and measures are:

Alternative (units)	Payment (dollars)	Investment (thousand dollars)	Appearance (categorical)	School (blocks)	Work (miles)
Ramshackle	400	50	0	1	10
Baltic Avenue	500	55	.2	8	3
Tennessee Avenue	650	70	.5	7	15
Illinois Avenue	800	90	.6	15	25
Park Place	1000	120	.9	12	45

Categorical scales could be:

	Category 1 (best)	Category 2	Category 3	Category 4
Payment	≤ 500	501–650	651–800	> 800
Investment	> 85	61–85	≤ 60	
Appearance	good	average	poor	
Distance to school	< 5	5–10	≥ 11	
Distance to work	≥ 30	11–29	≤ 10	

The input files for this problem are appended. The pairwise comparison questions and a set of responses are:

pairwise comparison 1	alt. 1 (21111) is preferred over alt. 2 (12111)
pairwsie comparison 2	alt. 1 (21111) is preferred over alt. 2 (11211)
pairwise comparison 3	alt. 1 (21111) is preferred over alt. 2 (11121)
pairwise comparison 4	alt. 2 (11112) is preferred over alt. 1 (21111)
pairwise comparison 5	alt. 2 (11113) is preferred over alt. 1 (21111)
pairwise comparison 6	alt. 2 (11113) is preferred over alt. 1 (31111)
pairwise comparison 7	alt. 1 (31111) is preferred over alt. 2 (13111)
pairwise comparison 8	alt. 2 (11211) is preferred over alt. 1 (31111)
pairwise comparison 9	alt. 1 (31111) is preferred over alt. 2 (11311)
pairwise comparison 10	alt. 2 (11121) is preferred over alt. 1 (31111)
pairwise comparison 11	alt. 1 (31111) is preferred over alt. 2 (11131)
pairwise comparison 12	alt. 2 (13111) is preferred over alt. 1 (41111)
pairwise comparison 13	alt. 1 (41111) is preferred over alt. 2 (11311)
pairwise comparison 14	alt. 2 (11131) is preferred over alt. 1 (41111)
pairwise comparison 15	alt. 1 (12111) is preferred over alt. 2 (11211)
pairwise comparison 16	alt. 1 (12111) and alt. 2 (11121) are equally preferable
pairwise comparison 17	alt. 1 (13111) and alt. 2 (11131) are equally preferable
pairwise comparison 18	alt. 2 (11121) is preferred over alt. 1 (11211)

The resulting partial rank ordering is:

Layer 1:	Tennessee Avenue	(22222)
	Illinois Avenue	(31232)
	Park Place	(41131)
Layer 2:	Ramshackle	(13313)
Layer 3:	Baltic Avenue	(13323)

Conclusions

ZAPROS is a selection method seeking to use the most accurate human inputs to discriminate among choices presented to them. *ZAPROS* provides a very sound theoretical means to aid selection problems involving multiple criteria. It provides a partial rank-ordering, not guaranteeing that a complete rank-ordering will be obtained. However, those alternatives assigned to the same level appear to be equivalent in value. *ZAPROS* can be applied to problems involving large numbers of alternatives, as value relationships are analyzed and can be applied over any number of alternatives. *ZAPROS* is limited relative to the number of attributes that can be considered and the number of categories used to describe each attribute. This is due to the combinatoric problem when large numbers of possible descriptions are allowed. However, human behavioral research indicates that humans accurately discriminate among a relatively small subset of categories anyway. *ZAPROS* provides a very usable, sound method to aid selection decision making for problems involving a large number of real alternatives. *ZAPROS* does not seek to identify any one best alternative, but rather to identify a short list of nondominated real alternatives that the decision maker can apply more focused analysis to.

References

Furems, E.M. and Gnedenko, L.S. 1992. Interactive procedure for non-transitivity revealing and correcting under pairwise comparisons. *Information Systems and Operations Research* 4:1, 118–126.

Gnedenko, L.S., O.I. Larichev, H.M. Moshkovich and E.M. Furems. 1986. Procedure for construction of a quasi-order on the set of multiattribute alternatives on the base of reliable information about the decision maker's preferences. *Automatica i Telemechanica* 9, 104–113 (in Russian).

Larichev, O.I. 1982. A method for evaluating R&D proposals in large research organizations. Collaborative paper CP-82-75, IIASA.

Larichev, O.I. 1984. Psychological validation of decision methods. *Journal of Applied Systems Analysis* 11, 37–46.

Larichev, O.I. 1992. Cognitive validity in design of decision-aiding techniques. *Journal of Multi-Criteria Decision Analysis* 1:3, 127–138.

Larichev, O.I. and H.M. Moshkovich. 1988. Limits to decision-making ability in direct multi-attribute alternative evaluation. *Organizational Behavior and Human Decision Processes* 42, 217–233.

Larichev, O.I. and H.M. Moshkovich. 1991. ZAPROS: A method and system for ordering multiattribute alternatives on the base of a decision-maker's preferences. preprint, All-Union Research Institute for Systems Studies, Moscow .

Larichev, O.I., H.M. Moshkovich, A.I. Mechitov and D.L. Olson. 1993. Experiments comparing qualitative approaches to rank ordering of multiattribute alternatives. *Journal of Multi-Criteria Decision Analysis* **2**, 5–26.

Larichev, O.I., O.A. Polyakov and A.D. Nikiforov. 1987. Multicriterion linear programming problems (Analytical Survey). *Journal of Economical Psychology* **8**, 389–407.

Larichev, O.I., Y.A. Zuev and L.S. Gnedenko. 1974. Method for classification of applied R&D Projects. In Perspectives in Applied R&D planning, S.V. Emelyanov, ed., Nauka Press, pp. 28–57 (in Russian).

Moshkovich, H.M. 1988. *Interactive System ZAPROS (for ordering of multiattribute alternatives on the base of decision maker's preferences.* VNIISI press **11**, 13–21 (in Russian).

Payne, J.W. 1976. Task complexity and contingent processing in decision making: An information search and protocol analysis. *Organizational Behavior and Human Processes* **16**, 366–387.

Slovic, P., B. Fishhoff and S. Lichtenstein. 1977. Behavioral decision theory. *Annual Psychological Review* **28**, 1–39.

vonWinterfeldt, D. and W. Edwards. 1986. *Decision Analysis and Behavioral Research.* Cambridge University Press, New York.

Appendix: Input Files

Nuclear Waste Site Selection Problem Input Files

The INPUT1 file:

```
 4  4  4  4  3 12
0001 0002 0003 0004 0005 0006 0007 0008 0009 0010 0011 0012
1Cost is low
1Cost is medium
1Cost is high
1Cost is very high
1Expected lives lost is low
1Expected lives lost is medium
1Expected lives lost is high
1Expected lives lost is very high
1Risk is very low
1Risk is low
1Risk is medium
1Risk is high
1Civic improvement is very high
1Civic improvement is high
1Civic improvement is medium at best
```

The INPUT2 file:

Criterion 1: Cost
1. Cost is low.
2. Cost is medium.

3. Cost is high.
4. Cost is very high.

Criterion 2: Expected lives lost
1. Expected lives lost is low.
2. Expected lives lost is medium.
3. Expected lives lost is high.
4. Expected lives lost is very high.

Criterion 3: Risk
1. Risk is very low.
2. Risk is low.
3. Risk is medium.
4. Risk is high.

Criterion 4: Civic Improvement
1. Civic improvement is very high.
2. Civic improvement is high.
3. Civic improvement is medium at best.

The INPUT3 file:

4
1. This site is very attractive.
2. This site is acceptable.
3. This site is unattractive.
4. The situation is contradictory.

The xxxxI1 file:

	12				
0001 0002 0003 0004 0005 0006 0007 0008 0009 0010 0011 0012					
1243	4411	2122	2133	3321	3343
2142	2133	3443	3413	3233	3443

House Selection Example Input Files

INPUT1

```
5  4  3  3  3  5
0001 0002 0003 0004 0005
1Payment is low
1Payment is medium
1Payment is high
1Payment is very high
1Investment is good
1Investment is average
```

1 Investment is poor
1 Appearance is good
1 Appearance is average
1 Appearance is poor
1 School is close
1 School is average distance
1 School is far away
1 Work is a nice distance away
1 Work is an average distance away
1 Work is too close

INPUT2

Criterion 1. Payment

1. Payment is low
2. Payment is medium
3. Payment is high
4. Payment is very high

Criterion 2. Investment

1. Investment is good
2. Investment is average
3. Investment is poor

Criterion 3. Appearance

1. Appearance is good
2. Appearance is average
3. Appearance is poor

Criterion 4. Distance to school

1. Distance to school is very good
2. Distance to school is average
3. Distance to school is too far

Criterion 5. Distance to work

1. Distance to work is very good
2. Distance to work is average
3. Distance to work is too close

HOUSI1

5
0001 0002 0003 0004 0005
    13313   13323   22222   31232   41131

10
Aspiration-Level Interactive Model

The aspiration-level interactive model (AIM-Lotfi, Stewart and Zionts, 1992) method is based on the idea of providing decision makers a means to explore efficient solutions, in order to gain better understanding of the tradeoffs involved in the decision. In order to do this, AIM utilizes a number of the ideas we have seen in other methods. AIM is intended to aid selection of one alternative from a large set. We may think of the problem as forming a matrix, with the rows representing alternatives and the columns criteria. The idea is to adjust aspiration levels of the objectives and obtain feedback regarding the feasibility of the aspiration levels, separately and jointly. As the aspiration levels are adjusted, the nearest non-dominated solution based on the levels changes.

Weights are generated by the aspiration levels, and various additional options may also be used. These include identifying (and perhaps eliminating) dominated solutions, ranking of alternatives, identifying "neighbor" solutions (alternatives similar in performance) to the nearest solution, and a convergence procedure that may be used to narrow the selection of alternatives to a single choice. The latter approach, down played by the developers, uses preference or dominance cones to elimiate alternatives.

Methodology

AIM operates by establishing problem features (defining objectives, their direction and measures, defining alternatives and their attainments on each objective). This is followed by identification of decision maker aspiration levels. The system identifies the solution closest to the aspiration levels following either the Tchebycheff or Euclidean metrics. The decision maker is provided with (1) a report of the proportion of alternatives satisfying the ideal levels, (2) the aspiration levels, (3) the set of attainment levels one level better than the aspiration levels, and (4) the set of attainment levels one level worse than the aspiration levels. Levels considered are those found in the set of available alternatives. The intent of this step is that the decision maker can change aspiration levels and thus learn the potential attainment levels available. The decision maker can then solve the problem with the intent of identifying the best alternative from the perspective of the decision maker's preference function. All alternatives in the data set may be rank ordered by the weights generated by the aspiration levels. The system can eliminate dominated alternatives, and can apply the preference (cone dominance) method to identify a preferred solution via pairwise comparison of alternatives.

A closer description of the steps involved in AIM follows.

Problem Definition:

Objectives of four types are allowed: maximization, minimization, minimization of deviations from targets, and qualitative objectives. For each objective, three attainment levels are established.

1. The "must" level is a constraint level that must be satisfied. This allows the decision maker to set mandatory requirements.
2. The "want" level expresses the aspiration level of the decision maker with respect to each objective.
3. Finally, an "ignore" level better than the "want" level establishes a threshold attainment level beyond which the decision maker gains no further value.

Target objectives are those for which a target is sought. For example, a home buyer may want to be close to schools but not too close. The perfect distance may be between one and two miles. Closer than a mile and further than two miles would be less desirable. Ideal objective levels are established by identifying either the threshold level or best attainment level on this objective in the data set. (The minimum of the threshold level or greatest attainment level for maximization; the maximum of the threshold level or the least attainment level for minimization; the best level for qualitative objectives). Nadir objective levels are established by identifying the minimum attainment level in the data set for maximizations, the maximum attainment level in the data set for minimizations, and the worst attainment level for qualitative objectives. The difference between the ideal and nadir points establish the working distance over which objective attainments are evaluated. A measure as good or better than the ideal receives a measure of 1.0 on this objective. A measure as poor or worse than the nadir receives a measure of 0.0 on this objective. Any measure between these levels receives a proportional score.

Solution Procedure:

For each objective k, the attainment of alternative X_j ($j = 1$ to the number of available alternatives) is measured, yielding Z_{jk}. These attainments are ordered from least to most preferred for each objective. The system then identifies median and quartile values for each objective. The decision maker is provided:

a) The current aspiration level A_k for each objective, initially set to the median, along with the proportion of alternatives X_j simultaneously satisfying this set of attainment levels, both individually and jointly.
b) The aspiration level one level better on each objective than A_k, with the proportion of available alternatives simultaneously satisfying this set of

attainment levels; and the aspiration level one level worse on each objective than A_k, with the proportion of available alternatives simultaneously satisfying this set of attainment levels.

c) The ideal I_k and nadir N_k values for each objective.

d) The nearest nondominated solution is presented, as well as the implied set of weights for each objective. The nearest nondominated solution is defined following the scalarizing function proposed by Wierzbicki [1979]. The set of weights is identified by dividing the distance from the aspiration level to the nadir level by the distance between the ideal level and the nadir level: $(A_k - N_k)/(I_k - N_k)$. This set of $\mathbf{k}$ values is normalized by dividing each ratio by the sum of the ratios.

Nuclear Dump Site Selection

The nuclear dump site selection problem with twelve alternative sites involved the following problem parameters:

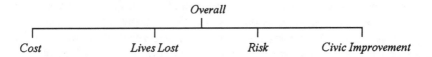

In AIM, categorical ratings can be expressed with the adjectives *Awful, Poor, Fair, Good, Great,* and *Superb.* We had two qualitative objectives, risk of catastrophe and civic improvement. The previous ratings of very high risk will be rated as *Awful,* high risk to *Poor,* medium risk to *Fair,* low risk to *Good* and very low risk to *Great.* A similar change in ratings for civic improvement is applied, although in the reverse direction. Very high civic improvement translates to *Great,* high civic improvement to *Good,* medium to *Fair,* low to *Poor,* and very low to *Awful.* We will not use *Superb* for this problem. The data required for expressing the objectives is:

Objective Name	Objective Type	Minimum Desired	Maximum Desired	Absolute Minimum	Absolute Maximum
Cost	**Decrease**	40	99999	0	99999
Lives	**Decrease**	0	99999	0	99999
Risk	Qual	*Awful*	*Great*	*Awful*	*Great*
Improve	Qual	*Awful*	*Great*	*Awful*	*Great*

After naming the objectives and entering the objective type, the minimum desired level (for minimization) or maximum desired level (for maximizations) is entered. This entry should be the ideal level (the best level found in the data set) or the threshold level (the point at which maximum value is attained). Here we use the ideal level for **Cost** and the threshold level for **Lives**. This indicates that the maximum value with respect to cost ends at 40 billion, which may be viewed as the cheapest reasonable price that could be attained. On the other hand, reducing lives lost is viewed as valuable all the way to zero, even though that level is lower than any attainment levels found in the available data set. The absolute limits are available as hard constraints. These can be left at their default levels unless the decision maker wants to eliminate alternatives that have attainment levels beyond the absolute levels expressed. The alternatives with their measures over the four objectives are:

	Cost (bill)	Expected Lives Lost	Risk	Civic Improvement
1 Nome, AK	40	60	Awful	Poor
2 Newark, NJ	100	140	Great	Great
3 Rock Springs,	60	40	Good	Good
4 Duquesne, PA	60	40	Fair	Fair
5 Gary, IN	70	80	Good	Great
6 Yakima Flats,	70	80	Poor	Fair
7 Turkey, TX	60	50	Poor	Good
8 Wells, NE	50	30	Fair	Fair
9 Anaheim, CA	90	130	Awful	Awful
10 Epcot Center,	80	120	Great	Awful
11 Duckwater, NV	80	70	Fair	Poor
12 Santa Cruz, CA	90	100	Awful	Awful

Set Aspiration Levels:

We assume aspiration levels of $60 billion, 60 lives, and attainments of *Good* for both risk and civic improvement. We adjust these levels to explore our desires. The AIM system now displays the ideal, nadir, current aspiration level, and one step better and worse than the current aspiration level. The proportion of alternatives passing the current aspiration level as well as the two adjacent levels is provided. The proportion of alternatives with attainments at least as good as each of the current objective aspiration levels is also provided. In this case, no alternatives equal the set of attainment levels one step better than the current aspirations. Only 8% (1 alternative) meets the current aspiration levels. One quarter of the alternatives are at least as good as the next worse set of levels. Of the costs in the alternative set, 42% are at least as good as the current aspiration level of $60 billion, and 42% of the lives lost measures are at least as good as the current aspiration level of 60. One third of the alternatives have attainments at least as good as the current aspiration levels for risk and civic improvement.

Current aspiration levels are the basis for weights W_t. These weights are used to generate a temporary ranking of available alternatives. (Note that the weights merely serve as a basis for the order in which alternatives are presented to the learning decision maker, and do not serve any other major purpose.) First the proportional distance of aspirations relative to the range of possibilities is calculated.

1. For *Cost*, I_{cost} = 40 billion, and N_{cost} = 100 billion, giving a range of possibilities of 60 billion.
2. The aspiration level is 60 billion, and the calculation for *Cost* is $(60 - 100)/(40 - 100) = 0.667$.
3. I_{lives} = 30, N_{lives} = 140, and A_{lives} = 60, yielding $(60 - 140)/(30 - 140) = 0.727$.
4. I_{risk} = 5 (*Great*), N_{risk} = 1 (*Awful*), and A_{risk} = 4 (*Good*), yielding $(4 - 1)/(5 - 1) = 0.75$.
5. I_{impr} = 5 (*Great*), N_{impr} = 1 (*Awful*), and A_{impr} = 4 (*Good*), yielding $(4 - 1)/(5 - 1) = 0.75$.
6. The sum of these relative scores = $0.667 + 0.727 + 0.75 + 0.75 = 2.894$.
7. Dividing each by this total yield W_{cost} = 0.667/2.894 = 0.230, W_{lives} = 0.727/2.894 = 0.251, W_{risk} = 0.75/2.894 = 0.259, and W_{impr} = 0.75/2.894 = 0.259.

The last information provided by *AIM* at this stage is the alternative nearest to the aspiration levels. That is Rock Springs, the only alternative meeting all of the four aspiration levels.

Explore:

AIM allows the user to explore alternatives. This is the central purpose of the method, giving the decision maker a means to better see the tradeoffs involved in the decision. The decision maker has the choice of measuring distance of each alternative from the current aspiration levels by either the Tchebycheff norm (minimize maximum distance) or the Euclidean norm (minimize squared distance). The **Explore** option rank orders the alternatives by this distance. Distance is defined as proportional attainment over the range *Aspiration – Nadir*, or $S_{jk} = (X_{jk} - N_{jk})/(A_{jk} - N_{jk})$, with a maximum score of 1.0 (no extra credit is given for exceeding the current aspiration level A_{jk}). The scores for Nome are:

$$S_{Nome,cost} = (40 - 100)/(60 - 100) = 1.5, \text{ so } S_{nome,cost} = 1.0, \text{ the maximum}$$
$$S_{Nome,lives} = (60 - 140)/(60 - 140) = 1.0$$
$$S_{Nome,risk} = (Awful - Awful)/(Awful - Good) = (1 - 1)/(4 - 1) = 0$$
$$S_{Nome,impr} = (Poor - Awful)/(Awful - Good) = (2 - 1)/(4 - 1) = 0.33$$

The Tchebycheff norm would select the worst of these four scores, or 0, as the overall score for alternative Nome. These calculations are internal to the system, but are presented here in order to demonstrate how the method works. The full set of scores for the twelve alternatives are:

Alternative	Cost	Lives	Risk	Improve	Overall (min)
Nome	1	1	0	0.33	0
Newark	0	0	1	1	0
Rock Springs	1	1	1	1	1
Duquesne	1	1	0.67	0.67	0.67
Gary	0.75	0.75	1	1	0.75
Yakima	0.75	0.75	0.33	0.67	0.33
Turkey	1	1	0.33	1	0.33

Wells	1	1	0.67	0.67	0.67
Anaheim	0.25	0.12	0	0	0
Epcot	0.5	0.25	1	0	0
Duquesne	0.5	0.87	0.67	0.33	0.33
Santa Cruz	0.25	0.5	0	0	0

The rankings provided by AIM at this stage are in this order:

Alternative	Cost	Lives	Risk	Improve
CG levels	60	60	good	good
Rock Springs	60	40	good	good
Gary	70	80	good	great
Duquesne	60	40	fair	fair
Wells	50	30	fair	fair
Turkey	60	50	poor	good
Yakima	70	80	poor	fair
Duckwater	80	70	fair	poor
Newark	100	140	great	great
Nome	40	60	awful	poor
Epcot	80	120	great	awful
Santa Cruz	90	100	awful	awful
Anaheim	90	130	awful	awful

Further Exploration:

The purpose of the system is to give the decision maker a chance to see the impact of changing aspiration levels and to see potential attainment within the alternative set. The impact of changing aspiration levels are displayed for the decision maker. In this example, if the aspiration levels were changed to the following, new weights would be implied, resulting in a new ranking.

Set Aspiration Levels:

After seeing the relative performance of available alternatives, the decision maker can adjust aspiration levels. Such adjustment reflects the process of learning. In our example, let us assume the decision maker resets aspirations to more ambitious levels:

Cost = 40   **Lives** = 30   **Risk** = $Good$ **Improve** = $Fair$

This set of aspirations reflects very strong relative emphasis on **Cost** and **Lives**, both set at or near their ideal levels; slightly less importance is igned to **Risk** (at its second best level), while **Improve** is left at its medium level. The set of implied weights is:

Cost = 0.308   **Lives** = 0.308   **Risk** = 0.231   **Improve** = 0.154

The resulting rankings of alternatives is:

Alternative	Cost	Lives	Risk	Improve
CG levels	40	30	good	fair
Wells	50	30	fair	fair
Rock Spgs	60	40	good	good
Duquesne	60	40	fair	fair
Turkey	60	50	poor	good
Gary	70	80	good	great
Yakima	70	80	poor	fair
Nome	40	60	awful	poor
Duckwater	80	70	fair	poor
Epcot	80	120	great	awful
Santa Cruz	90	100	awful	awful
Anaheim	90	130	awful	awful
Newark	100	140	great	great

By using the **Explore** option, the adjacent solutions to the nearest solution, Wells, are identified. These adjacent solutions are Rock Springs, Duquesne, and Gary. Note that Turkey has a higher ranking than Gary, but that Turkey has greater difference from Wells in attainment levels on **Risk** and **Improve** than does Gary.

Invoke Convergence:

The user can now select the INVOKE CONVERGENCE option from the menu, which will access the preference, OR CONE DOMINANCE, algorithm. This step is optional. The method does not have to use the preference cone method as a basis for identifying a recommended solution. The user is asked if the convergence option is desired. This option will weed out dominated solutions. In this case, there are six dominated solutions: Duquesne, Yakima, Turkey, Anaheim, Duckwater, and Santa Cruz. All of these six are dominated by Rock Springs, while some are dominated by other solutions as well.

The remaining six alternatives can be analyzed using the preference cone algorithm. This step is not necessary for the system, which is intended to show the decision maker the tradeoffs involved. If desired, the decision maker can use the preference cone approach to reach closure. In this case, the first pair of alternatives presented to the decision maker is:

	Rock Springs	Gary
Cost	60	70
Lives	40	80
Risk	good	good
Improvement	good	great

The decision maker is asked to select the preferred alternative, with the option of expressing indifference between them. Here we picked Rock Springs as the preferred alternative. The preference cone is applied to the remaining four alternatives to see if any of them are eliminated. In this case, all four remain in the analysis.

The second pair of alternatives presented to the decision maker is:

	Rock Springs	Nome
Cost	60	40
Lives	40	60
Risk	*good*	*awful*
Improvement	*good*	*poor*

Here we picked Rock Springs as the preferred alternative. The preference cone is applied to the remaining three alternatives to see if any of them are eliminated. In this case, all three remain in the analysis.

The third pair of alternatives presented to the decision maker is:

	Rock Springs	Newark
Cost	60	100
Lives	40	140
Risk	*good*	*great*
Improvement	*good*	*great*

Here we picked Rock Springs as the preferred alternative. The preference cone is applied to the remaining two alternatives to see if any of them are eliminated. In this case, one was eliminated (Duquesne), leaving only Wells as an alternative to Rock Springs.

The fourth pair of alternatives presented to the decision maker is:

	Rock Springs	Wells
Cost	60	50
Lives	40	30
Risk	*good*	*fair*
Improvement	*good*	*fair*

In this case, the decision maker selected Wells.

Cellular Manufacturing Example

The first example presented in the preference cone chapter (Chapter 7) will be solved by AIM. The problem involved a cellular manufacturing system with 4 cells, 24 machines, and 50 parts to be assigned. For the example, 10 nondominated solutions had to be compared.

Alternative	Z_1	Z_2	Z_3	Z_4
	Cost	Utilization Imbalance	% Shop Utilization	Exceptional Parts
#56	738	5.3	33.8	15

#96	702	15.8	32.4	15
#132	815	14.9	35.8	15
#149	612	17.2	34.5	13
#166	752	9.7	34	14
#167	698	21.4	35.7	16
#183	686	16.5	33.8	14
#192	914	4.3	30.5	20
#253	878	3.1	29.3	16
#287	633	39.7	34.6	14

The data required for expressing the objectives is:

Objective name	Objective type	Minimum desired	Maximum desired	Absolute Minimum	Absolute Maximum
Cost	Decrease	700	99999	0	99999
Imbalance	Decrease	15	99999	0	99999
Utilize	Increase	-99999	35	99999	0
Exception	Decrease	15	99999	0	99999

Each objective is named. The default assumption is maximization. To make an objective a minimization, replace "Increase" with "Decrease." For minimizations, the aspiration levels are entered in the Minimum Desired column. For maximizations, aspirations are entered in the "Maximum Desired" column. Absolute minimums and maximums can be entered, but are taken from the data set.

Once the data is entered, the user can select "SOLVE" from the menu. The basic display is presented:

Objective	Cost	Imbalance	Utilize	Exception	Proportion
Ideal Point	700	15	35	15	
Next Better	700		34.5		0
Current Goal	702	15	34	15	0
Proportion	0.5	0.5	0.5	0.7	
Next Worse	738	15.8	33.8	16	0.1
Nearest Solution	686	16.5	33.8	14	#183
Nadir Point	914	39.7	29.3	20	

This table presents the decision maker with basic information. There are no alternatives satisfying the current goal. Ten percent of the alternatives satisfy the next worse set of attainment levels. The nearest solution is calculated either by the Euclidean distance or the Tchebycheff distance. Here we selected the Euclidean distance. The calculation of weights, as formulated above, is

Objective	A_k	N_k	I_k	$(A_k-N_k)/(I_k-N_k)$	Normalized
Cost	702	914	700	0.991	0.26
Imbalance	15	39.7	15	1	0.262
Utilize	34	29.3	35	0.825	0.216
Exception	15	20	15	1	0.262
				3.816	

The set of aspirations was well within attainable levels, but no alternative satisfied all of them simultaneously. Distance d_{jk} for each alternative X_j is calculated $(X_{jk}-N_k)/(I_k-N_k)$.

Alternative	Cost	Imbalance	Utilize	Exception	$\Sigma w_k d_{jk}$
Weight	0.26	0.262	0.216	0.262	
#56	0.83	1	0.96	1	0.947
#96	1	0.97	0.66	1	0.919
#132	0.46	1	1	1	0.862
#149	1	0.91	1	1	0.976
#166	0.76	1	1	1	0.938
#167	1	0.74	1	0.8	0.879
#183	1	0.94	0.96	1	0.976
#192	0	1	0.26	0	0.318
#253	0.17	1	0	0.8	0.516
#287	1	0	1	1	0.738

The alternative with the greatest score is **#183,** making it the nearest solution to the set of aspiration levels. The user can ask for a number of options, including identifying neighboring solutions to #183. Here there are five identified, **#56, #96, #149, #166** and **#167**. With respect to the current aspiration targets, there are two dominated alternatives, **#192** and **#253**. (Note that neither is dominated in an absolute sense.)

Selection of the best alternative is supported by the "Invoke Convergence" option from the menu. This places the user in a preference cone operation. The first pair of alternatives presented is:

#183 vs. #56	**#183** selected because of cost.	
	This cone eliminates one other alternative.	
#183 vs. #132	**#183** selected because of cost.	
#183 vs. #149	*#183* selected because of higher minimums.	
	This cone eliminates two other alternatives	
#183 vs. #166	**#166** selected, slightly better cost.	

For this decision maker, the method led to selection of alternative **#166.**

Summary

The AIM method provides a technique useful to help decision makers learn about the tradeoffs among criteria considered in the selection of alternatives from large sets of available choices. The technique uses a number of multiple criteria decision making principles and techniques. Aspiration levels are used as working targets for decision makers. The system provides decision makers a view of the possibilities of attaining these aspiration levels. The system presents the decision maker a basic display, including the ideal attainment level and nadir attainment level for each criterion. This display also includes the next better set of attainment levels along with the proportion of available alternatives that satisfy these levels, the current set of attainment levels nearest to the expressed set of aspiration levels along with the proportion of alternatives satisfying these levels, and finally the next worse set of attainment levels and the proportion of alternatives satisfying them. The nearest solution is determined by calculating a score for each alternative over which the alternatives can be ranked. Both the Tchebycheff norm and Euclidean norms are available for this measurement. The nearest solution is that solution with the highest score. Concordance and discordance measures are used to identify neighbor solutions. Dr. Zionts likes to present outranking as one alternative being at least as good as another in most (or at least sufficiently many) respects (concordance), but not too much worse in any one respect (discordance). Dominated solutions are identified, but are retained for the learning process. Dr. Zionts considers that there may be other considerations not expressed in the current set of criteria, which could eliminate a solution that was very close to an alternative that dominated it, and which might be preferable for other reasons. Finally, while not a necessary component of the system, the preference cone method is available to aid the decision maker in obtaining a nondominated selection from the set of available alternatives.

References

Lotfi, V., T.J. Stewart, and S. Zionts. 1992. An aspiration-level interactive model for multiple criteria decision making. *Computers and Operations Research* 19:7 671–681.

Wierzbicki, A.P. 1979. The use of reference objectives in multiobjective optimization. Working Paper 79-66, Laxenburg, Austria: International Institute for Applied Systems Analysis.

11
Visual Interactive Method

The Visual Interactive Method for Decision Analysis (*VIMDA*) was developed with the aim of providing an easy to use and easy to understand method for decision makers to examine efficient alternatives with no restrictive assumptions about the underlying utility function of the decision maker (Korhonen, 1988). *VIMDA* was designed for dealing with problems where many alternatives were available (purchasing a house, purchasing an appliance, selecting the best candidate for an award). The method allows preliminary screening of alternatives using aspiration levels as bounds, retaining the possibility of considering these alternatives later in the analysis. A computer graphics system presenting the attainments of a small subset of alternatives to the decision maker is the heart of *VIMDA*. The decision maker can select the preferred alternative from this small set, with the implied preference information providing a basis for elimination of many of the remaining alternatives. User friendliness is emphasized in the system. Decision makers are allowed to change their minds about the quality of solutions, hence, allowing a free search of alternatives.

VIMDA Overview

VIMDA requires that alternatives be expressed numerically. Up to ten criteria are allowed. The method will systematically search for the most preferred alternative using the reference direction approach (Wierzbicki, 1980). The user implements this principle by specifying aspiration levels for each of the criteria. The system identifies a subset of nondominated alternatives for decision maker consideration, presenting them graphically by attainment, with the corresponding numeric values given at the top of the screen. The user can move the cursor back and forth to consider several alternatives, and finally to make a selection. This selected alternative becomes the basic solution of the next iteration, and the process continues until the most preferred solution is identified.

VIMDA Procedure

The *VIMDA* procedure rests on the fundamental principle of the **reference direction**. A reference direction is the space (measuring criteria attainment) moving from a basic alternative describing a preferable change for the decision maker. An **achievement function** is the set of criteria attainments for a given alternative or set of aspirations. In *VIMDA*, the reference direction is determined by identifying the direction from the current alternative to the set of decision maker aspiration levels. The reference direction is projected onto the set of efficient points by using an achievement function (Wierzbicki, 1980). Once the decision maker has specified aspiration levels, an efficient solution minimizing the value of the achievement function is identified. When the achievement function is applied to the reference direction, a set of efficient solutions is obtained.

Once the set of efficient solutions is obtained, a subset (up to 8) is visually presented to the decision maker for consideration. The current basic alternative is shown on the left of the screen. A color coded and continuous line is used for each criterion, with the best attainment at the top of the display and the worst at the bottom. The decision maker can move the cursor to display the numeric attainments for the highlighted alternative. This visual display provides the decision maker with a holistic comparison of alternatives.

Step 0: The decision maker specifies criteria to be used in the analysis, as well as a set of aspiration levels, one for each criterion. Relative criterion weights (W) are obtained by dividing by the range of criterion attainments between the worst attainment level and the aspiration level for each criterion k in order to get rid of differences of scale. (This assumes that all criteria are maximizations, which can be accomplished by multiplying minimization attainments by -1.) If this range is 0, W_k is defined as 1. An efficient solution is obtained by optimizing one of the criteria.

Step 1: Find a reference direction. The reference direction is obtained by subtracting the current solution attainment levels from the set of aspiration levels for each objective provided by the decision maker.

Step 2: Order alternatives. An algorithm is used to parametrically determine the set of alternatives that could minimize the distance to the ideal solution as defined by the set of aspiration levels. This algorithm assures that nondominated solutions are obtained. These candidate alternatives are ordered. If more than eight are identified, the first eight are presented to the decision maker. If less than eight of these alternatives are generated, the full set is presented to the decision maker.

Step 3: Decision maker exploration and selection. The system graphically presents the set of alternatives identified in Step 2 by attainment level. Each alternative displayed is assigned a column, with the left column reserved for the current solution. Each criterion has a uniquely colored and patterned line that depicts attainment on this criterion. The best attainment levels are displayed on the top (minimum values for minimization criteria, maximum values for maximization criteria). The decision maker can thus see the tradeoffs among this set of alternatives. The system displays the numeric attainment levels for the current column. The decision maker can move to other columns by using the keyboard arrows. The numeric attainment levels change to the column identified by the arrows. After weighing tradeoffs, the decision maker moves the arrows to the preferred combination of attainment levels, and indicates completion of this iteration by pressing the F10 key.

This returns the user to a menu, allowing the user to change aspiration levels, or quit with the last selected alternative as the solution. Should the decision maker reset aspiration levels, a new set of alternatives will be presented for consideration. Note that alternatives are not eliminated by the selection process, but are retained for further decision maker consideration in light of new aspiration level settings. Only dominated alternatives are eliminated from consideration.

Nuclear Dump Site Selection

While *VIMDA* was meant for problems with a large set of alternatives, it can be used to analyze problems comparing a small set of alternatives as well. We can demonstrate *VIMDA* using the nuclear dump site selection problem with twelve alternative sites involved the following problem parameters:

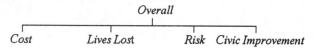

In AIM (Chapter 10), categorical ratings can be expressed with the adjectives *awful*, *poor*, *fair*, *good*, *great*, and *superb*. We will convert our previous ratings of very high risk and very low improvement to *awful*, high risk and low improvement to *poor*, medium on both scales to *fair*, low risk and high improvement to *good*, and very low risk and very high civic improvement to *great*. We will not use *superb* for this problem. The alternatives with their measures over the four objectives are:

	Cost (bill)	Expected Lives Lost	Risk	Civic Improvement
1 Nome, AK	40	60	awful	poor
2 Newark, NJ	100	140	great	great
3 Rock Springs, WY	60	40	good	good
4 Duquesne, PA	60	40	fair	fair
5 Gary, IN	70	80	good	great
6 Yakima Flats, WA	70	80	poor	fair
7 Turkey, TX	60	50	poor	good
8 Wells, NE	50	30	fair	fair
9 Anaheim, CA	90	130	awful	awful
10 Epcot Center, FL	80	120	great	awful
11 Duckwater, NV	80	70	fair	poor
12 Santa Cruz, CA	90	100	awful	awful

Step 1: The initial step in this application is to set aspiration levels. We assume initial aspiration levels of spending no more than $70 billion dollars, with no more than 40 lives lost, and ratings of at least fair (3 on a 5 point scale) for risk and civic improvement.

Step 2: VIMDA screens the set of alternatives, weeding out the six dominated solutions. By parametrically varying a distance multiplier, three solutions are identified for presentation to the decision maker. These solutions and their attainment vectors are Newark [100 140 5 5], Rock Springs [60 40 4 4] and Wells [50 30 3 3]. The other three nondominated solutions were never found to be closest to the set of aspiration levels.

Step 3: The decision maker looks at the graphically displayed information and selects the preferred alternative. In this case, we selected Wells, as it had lower cost and lives lost measures.

The decision maker can then return to the aspiration level setting option. We changed aspiration levels to a more ambitious $40 billion cost, 30 lives, and attainment levels of good for both risk and civic improvement. The same three alternatives were presented by the system. In fact, for all of the aspiration levels we entered, we always were presented with these three alternatives.

Cellular Manufacturing Example

The first example presented in the preference cone chapter (Chapter 7) presented a set of nondominated solutions among proposals for a cellular manufacturing project. The problem involved a cellular manufacturing system with 4 cells, 24 machines, and 50 parts to be assigned. The criteria considered were cost (to be minimized), utilization imbalance (to be minimized), shop utilization (to be maximized), and exceptional parts (to be minimized).

Alternative	Z_1 Cost	Z_2 Utilization Imbalance	Z_3 % Shop Utilization	Z_4 Exceptional Parts
#56	−738	−5.3	33.8	−15
#96	−702	−15.8	32.4	−15
#132	−815	−14.9	35.8	−15
#149	−612	−17.2	34.5	−13
#166	−752	−9.7	34.0	−14
#167	−698	−21.4	35.7	−16
#183	−686	−16.5	33.8	−14
#192	−914	−4.3	30.5	−20
#253	−878	−3.1	29.3	−16
#287	−633	−39.7	34.6	−14

Note that while only ten alternatives are presented here, there were 100 alternatives in the original problem, filtered down to these ten nondominated solutions. Therefore, the data set anticipates one of the steps of *VIMDA*.

The *VIMDA* system asks for the range of possible attainment levels. Here we used costs between $500 thousand and $1000 thousand, imbalance percentages between 0 and 100, utilization percentages between 20 and 40, and exceptional parts between 10 and 25.

Step 1: Aspiration levels are set. We start out with aspiration levels of no more than $800 thousand, no more than 10% imbalance, at least 30% shop utilization, and no more than 10 exceptional parts.

Step 2: VIMDA uses these aspiration levels and the range of attainment levels to determine the solutions minimizing a distance function to the set of aspiration levels. Four solutions are graphically presented (**#92**, **#56**, **#149**, and **#166**). After reviewing the relative attainments, (both **#56** and **#166** satisfied all of the aspiration levels), **#56** was selected on the basis of cost and imbalance.

In the next iteration, new aspiration levels were set. These were costs of no more than $700 thousand, imbalance of no more than 5%, utilization of at least 35%, and no more than 15 exceptional parts.

The system responded with five solutions (**#56**, **#166**, **#149**, **#167**, and **#132**). Costs below aspiration levels were provided by **#149** and **#167**, utilization below aspiration levels were attained by **#132** and **#167**, and exceptional parts below aspiration levels were attained by **#56**, **#149**, and **#166**. Upon consideration, **#149** was selected. This selection indicates a change of mind on the part of the decision maker, who had this alternative available in the first iteration, but selected **#56** instead at that time. In this instance, **#149** has less cost than **#56**, but a higher imbalance. The new set of aspiration levels tightened the cost aspirations while relaxing the aspiration level for imbalance. Part of the purpose of *VIMDA* is to aid decision maker learning.

New aspiration levels were again set, at no more than $650 thousand cost, no more than 15% utilization imbalance, at least 34% utilization, and no more than 14 exceptional parts.

The system responded with solutions **#56**, **#92**, **#149**, **#183**, and **#253**. Note that only **#149** satisfies the cost aspiration level, while **#56**, **#92**, and **#253** all satisfy the imbalance aspiration level. Only **#149** satisfies the utilization aspiration, and only **#183** satisfies the new exceptional parts aspiration level. After examining the choices presented, the decision maker selected **#149**, and decided to quit.

Summary

The idea behind *VIMDA* is to use aspiration levels [Wierzbicki, 1980, 1986] as an anchor upon which to visually display alternative performance on criteria. Korhonen [1988] working with Laakso [1986a, 1986b] and Wallenius [1989] has developed the system used in this chapter. *VIMDA* is very strong in ease of use, relying on graphical presentation to improve communication with the decision maker. It is very easy to set aspiration levels and to balance tradeoffs among the alternatives presented by the system. *VIMDA* relies on dominance to cut down the number of alternatives considered, and then minimizes a distance function to select the alternatives presented to the decision maker.

More than any of the other systems examined, *VIMDA* relies on the learning process. This has an impact in the way the system operates. No dominated solutions are eliminated from consideration, even though some alternatives are selected instead of other alternatives. As demonstrated in the last example, this can support cases where the decision maker is learning about possibilities and changes his or her mind.

VIMDA is intended for problems involving many alternatives. It provides a means to focus on a subset of nondominated alternatives. The decision maker does not have to compare more than eight alternatives at a time.

References

Korhonen, P. 1988. A visual reference direction approach to solving discrete multiple criteria problems. *European Journal of Operational Research* **34**:2, 152–159.

Korhonen, P. and J. Laakso. 1986a. A visual interactive method for solving the multiple criteria problem. *European Journal of Operational Research* **24**:2, 277–287.

Korhonen, P. and J. Laakso.1986b. Solving generalized goal programming problems using a visual interactive approach. *European Journal of Operational Research* **26**:3, 355–363.

Korhonen, P. and J. Wallenius. 1989. *A visual multiple criteria decision support system.* NumPlan: Helsinki.

Wierzbicki, A. 1980. The use of reference objectives in multiobjective optimization. in G. Fandel and T. Gal, eds. *Multiple Criteria Decision Making: Theory and Application.* New York: Springer-Verlag.

Wierzbicki, A. 1986. On the completeness and constructiveness of parametric characterizations to vector optimization problems. *OR Spektrum* **8**, 73–87.

12
Models with Uncertain Estimates

In many cases, decision makers may be able to express a range for the relative importance of one alternative or criterion over another without being that confident of a precise numerical value. For instance, in buying a house, someone might feel that interior arrangement might be 2 to 4 times as important as the exterior appearance. The methods we have looked at so far have either expected the decision maker to state a specific value (interior is 3 times as important as exterior) or provided means to obtain such a specific value. This chapter discusses two methods (*ARIADNE* and *HIPRE 3+*) that allow decision makers to input ranges for relative advantage or performance.

ARIADNE

ARIADNE is a system that was developed by Sage and White [1984] and implemented by Burden [1987]. It has been tested extensively by Goicoechea [1990] and Goicoechea, et al. [1992]. The *ARIADNE* system is explained and demonstrated in Goicoechea and Li [1994].

The idea behind *ARIADNE* is that for each alternative, a small linear programming model is run to determine the maximum value function for that alternative, as well as the minimum value function for that alternative, given the range of relative weights for each criterion.

Maximize $\Sigma_{k=1,K} w_k v_{ik}$ w = weight, v = value, K = number of criteria
st. $\Sigma_{k=1,K} w_k = 1$
lower bound $\leq w_k \leq$ upper bound   for each **i**
$w_k \geq 0$

and in turn:

Minimize $\Sigma_{k=1,K} w_k v_{ik}$
st. $\Sigma_{k=1,K} w_k = 1$
lower bound $\leq w_k \leq$ upper bound   for each **i**
$w_k \geq 0$

where **i** is the subscript for each alternative, and **k** is the subscript for each criterion.

Note that this formulation is solved for each alternative, and here assumes one level in the criterion hierarchy. If more than one hierarchical level exists, the solution procedure would be to work up from the bottom of the hierarchy, inserting the bounds obtained into the mathematical programming models for the higher levels in sequence.

The value functions v_{ik} for each alternative on each criterion can be directly entered, can be identified by a linear function as in *SMART*, or can be entered as a range. If the uncertain range option is selected, the solution models become nonlinear (quadratic programming).

Parking Example

Simple examples used in prior chapters will be used to demonstrate *ARIADNE*. The first we will use involves an educational institution that has a lot of students where parking is a major problem. Currently, parking is assigned to a series of small asphalt lots spread throughout campus (*Lot*). This is relatively inexpensive, but land is becoming scarce. The other options are to build a parking garage (*Garage*) or to utilize a system of perimeter lots and shuttle buses (*Shuttle*).

- *Lot*: Expansion of the current system of asphalt lots to wherever lots will fit
- *Garage*: Construction of a parking garage near facilities
- *Shuttle*: A shuttle bus system which would utilize asphalt lots at some distance from facilities

Objectives in the decision have been identified as:

- *Service*: The ideal system would provide close parking facilities for at least 2000 customers.
- *Convenience*: Building the system should minimize disruption of activities.
- *Cost*: Cost for customers should be minimized.
- *Control*: There should be some way of alleviating behavioral problems by adequately enforcing order.
- *Investment*: Cost for the system should be minimized.

The three alternatives have the following measured or rated characteristics:

	Service	Convenience	Cost	Control	Investment
Lot	800	medium	$100/yr	very poor	$2,000,000
Garage	2000	high	$150/yr	excellent	$6,000,000
Shuttle	1200	low	$50/yr	poor	$500,000

Following the *SMART* approach, we will assign direct values (where 1 is ideal performance and 0 is no value) yielding the following:

	Service	Convenience	Cost	Control	Investment
Lot	.1	.2	.3	.1	.2
Garage	.7	.75	.2	.7	.1
Shuttle	.2	.1	.5	.2	.7

A hierarchy of these objectives is developed, grouping those objectives relating to customer service, convenience, and cost. The hierarchy for this problem is:

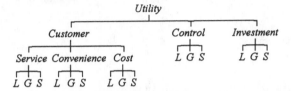

The first model solved is for the alternative *Lot*:

Max/Min .1 *Service* + .2 *Convenience* + .3 *Cost* + .1 *Control* + .2 *Investment*
s.t.   *Service* + *Convenience* + *Cost* + *Control* + *Investment* = 1

Service	≥ .2	*Service*	≤ .5
Convenience	≥ .05	*Convenience*	≤ .2
Cost	≥ .1	*Cost*	≤ .3
Control	≥ .2	*Control*	≤ .3
Investment	≥ .05	*Investment*	≤ .15

The maximized objective function to this model is 0.19. The same model is solved minimizing the objective function, yielding an objective function value of 0.13. Here the objective function is the contribution to value. The results indicate that the value of the *Lot* alternative is somewhere between 0.13 and 0.19 in terms of the decision maker's preference function. Solutions to linear programming models for *Garage* are 0.63 for the maximization model, and 0.4625 for the minimization model, while *Shuttle* had a value of 0.36 for the maximization model and 0.235 for the minimization model. Taken together, these results indicate that the worst preference value for *Garage* is better than the best possible value function for *Lot* or for *Shuttle*. This indicates that *Garage* is the choice preferred by the decision maker, given the ranges on weights provided.

Nuclear Waste Disposal Siting Problem

In prior chapters, a nuclear waste disposal problem was used for demonstration. The same problem can be solved with *ARIADNE*. The hierarchy for the problem was:

```
                        Overall
         ┌─────────────────┼───────────┬─────────────────┐
        Cost         Lives Lost        Risk      Civic Improvement
```

Data for the problem was as follows:

	Cost (bill)	Expected Lives Lost (transport local)	Risk	Civic Improvement
Nome, AK	40	60	very high	low
Newark, NJ	100	140	very low	very high
Rock Springs, WY	60	40	low	high
Duquesne, PA	60	40	medium	medium
Gary, IN	70	80	low	very high

Assume decision maker value function attainments (between 0 and 1, with 1 the most preferred) as follows:

	Cost	Lives	Risk	Improvement
Nome	.9	.2	0	.2
Newark	0	0	.1	.1
Rock Springs	.7	.4	.75	.75
Duquesne	.7	.4	.5	.5
Gary	.6	.15	.75	1.0

Solution to the linear programming models yield:

	Maximization	Minimization
Nome	0.355	0.2075
Newark	0.350	0.1
Rock Springs	0.5675	0.465
Duquesne	0.49	0.43
Gary	0.44	0.255

Note that here the final solution is not clear. There is some overlap between Rock Springs and Duquesne. However, given the bounds on the weight ranges provided, Rock Springs clearly is preferred to Nome, Newark, and Gary.

A feature of the uncertainty model is that it reflects the approximation of the parameters input into value models. However, there is another feature that this approach does not pick up. In this case, Duquesne was inferior or the same to Rock Springs on every one of the four criteria. Yet the range of uncertainty was large enough that an apparent overlap between Rock Springs and Duquesne exists. Because of the dominance relationship, we know that when Rock Springs has a low score, Duquesne has a lower score.

Uncertain Value Contributions

In the examples we have presented, we have assumed ranges for the relative weights w_k, but have had precise estimates for v_{ik}. Note that while we have dealt with specific given values for each of the v_{ik}, they could have been obtained from linear value functions (as in *SMART* or *Logical Decision*) with the same result. Here we would like to demonstrate the model when the decision maker provides a range for the v_{ik}, just as for the w_k. The operative result is that we now have a nonlinear programming model.

We return to the parking model presented first in this chapter. The only difference is that instead of point estimates for the value of each alternative on each criterion, we now have ranges. We assume the same ranges as before on the w_k.

	Variable	Service C_1	Convenience C_2	Cost C_3	Control C_4	Investment C_5
Lot	L	.05–.15	.1–.25	.2–.35	.05–.15	.1–.25
Garage	G	.5–.9	.6–.9	.1–.3	.6–.8	.05–.1
Shuttle	S	.1–.3	.05–.1	.4–.7	.1–.3	.6–.8

For alternative LOT the model is:

$$
\begin{aligned}
\text{Max/Min} \quad & L_1 \times C_1 + L_2 \times C_2 + L_3 \times C_3 + L_4 \times C_4 + L_5 \times C_5 \\
\text{st.} \quad & C_1 + C_2 + C_3 + C_4 + C_5 = 1
\end{aligned}
$$

$C_1 \geq .2$	$C_1 \leq .5$
$C_2 \geq .05$	$C_2 \leq .2$
$C_3 \geq .1$	$C_3 \leq .3$
$C_4 \geq .2$	$C_4 \leq .3$
$C_5 \geq .05$	$C_5 \leq .15$
$L_1 \geq .05$	$L_1 \leq .15$
$L_2 \geq .1$	$L_2 \leq .25$
$L_3 \geq .2$	$L_3 \leq .35$
$L_4 \geq .05$	$L_4 \leq .15$
$L_5 \geq .1$	$L_5 \leq .25$

The solution to this nonlinear (quadratic programming) maximization model is a value of 0.24. The solution to all of the models are:

	Maximization	Minimization
Lot	0.240	0.070
Garage	0.780	0.337
Shuttle	0.485	0.145

Note that here there is a little overlap between *Garage* and *Shuttle*. This reflects the greater degree of uncertainty in the data entered.

House Buying Example

The last example we will use to demonstrate *ARIADNE* has the feature of multiple hierarchical levels. The hierarchy is:

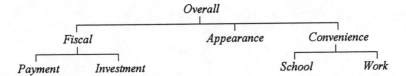

Available alternatives are:

Alternative (units)	Payment (dollars)	Investment (thousand dollars)	Appearance (categorical)	School (blocks)	Work (miles)
Ramshackle	400	50	very poor	1	10
Baltic Avenue	500	55	poor	8	3
Tennessee Avenue	650	70	average	7	15
Illinois Avenue	800	90	good	15	25
Park Place	1000	120	very good	12	45

Assume that the decision maker assigns values for each alternative **i** on attribute **k** as follows:

Criterion	Ramshackle	Baltic	Tennessee	Illinois	Park Place
Payment	1.0	0.4	0.1	0.8	0.3
Investment	0.8	0.5	0.3	0.4	0.1
Appearance	0.6	0.6	0.7	0.5	0.5
School	0.4	0.7	0.8	0.0	0.9
Work	0.0	0.8	0.9	0.1	1.0

In *ARIADNE*, multiple hierarchical levels are dealt with by working up from the bottom. For instance, in this case there are two second hierarchical level clusters. The first splits *Fiscal* factors into *Payment* and *Investment*. The second cluster splits *Convenience* into *School* and *Work* factors. *ARIADNE* operates by identifying the range of values for *Fiscal* and *Convenience*, which are then used as in the prior examples we have demonstrated on the first hierarchical level.

The *Fiscal* cluster analysis would require the decision maker to specify ranges on relative weights. Assume *Payment*'s weight is specified to be between 0.2 and 0.4, while *Investment*'s weight is specified to be between 0.6 and 0.8. For the alternative on Ramshackle Avenue, this would yield the LP model:

$$\text{Max/Min } 1\,P + .4\,I$$
$$\text{st} \qquad P + I = 1$$
$$P \geq .2 \qquad P \leq .4$$
$$I \geq .6 \qquad I \leq .8$$

The solution to this model is a maximum value of 0.64, while minimizing the objective function yields a value of 0.52. These values become the bounds on estimated weights for *Fiscal*. The minimum and maximum values for each of the alternatives on both the *Fiscal* and *Convenience* clusters are as follows:

	Fiscal max	min	Convenience max	min
Ramshackle	0.640	0.520	0.550	0.450
Baltic Avenue	0.620	0.560	0.250	0.190
Tennessee Avenue	0.600	0.600	0.500	0.500
Illinois Avenue	0.640	0.580	0.630	0.450
Park Place	0.640	0.480	0.730	0.550

This results in the overall model (for Ramshackle) of:

$$\text{Max/Min} \quad v_{fis}\, w_{fis} + v_{app}\, w_{app} + v_{con}\, w_{con}$$
$$\text{st} \qquad w_{fis} + w_{app} + w_{con} = 1$$
$$w_{fis} \geq .6 \qquad w_{fis} \leq .9 \qquad v_{fis} \geq .52 \qquad v_{fis} \leq .64$$
$$w_{app} \geq 0 \qquad w_{app} \leq .1 \qquad v_{app} \geq .45 \qquad v_{app} \leq .55$$
$$w_{con} \geq .05 \qquad w_{con} \leq .2$$

The solutions to these geometric programming models are a maximum of 0.631 and a minimum of 0.464. The results for all five alternatives provide *ARIADNE* its output for this problem:

	Minimum	Maximum
Ramshackle	0.464	0.631
Baltic Avenue	0.440	0.583
Tennessee Avenue	0.530	0.590
Illinois Avenue	0.506	0.639
Park Place	0.445	0.658

The analysis indicates quite a bit of overlap, with none of the alternatives eliminated. Park Place has an especially diverse result, while Tennessee Avenue has much less variance.

HIPRE 3+

Like *ARIADNE, HIPRE 3+* allows decision makers to specify weight ranges as well as point values. And like *ARIADNE, HIPRE 3+* operates by solving a pair of linear programming models, a maximization and a minimization, for each alternative over the feasible set of weights. The primary difference is that *HIPRE 3+* is interactive, eliciting information from the decision maker until the minimum value score for the highest scored alternative is greater than the maximum score for all other alternatives.

As in *ARIADNE*, as many hierarchical levels as desired can be used. As in Saaty's [1977] version of AHP, alternative performance on each attribute is estimated by the method. The analysis works from the bottom up, solving a series of mathematical programming models to obtain minimum and maximum value scores for each alternative.

The linear programming formulation to be solved derives from the decomposition of AHP models. The value function in AHP consists of relative contributions from alternatives weighted by relative importance of criteria. The value for alternative $i = \Sigma_{k=1,K} v_{ik} w_k$. In *ARIADNE*, variables v_{ik} and w_k were treated as separate variables. In *HIPRE 3+*, these variables are joined, so that $v_{ik}w_k$ is a specific variable. The sum of these variables over all alternatives adds to 1.0. Constraints are placed on the relative contributions reflecting ranges of ratio importances or preferences.

$$\text{Max/Min} \quad \Sigma_{k=1,K} v_{ik} w_k \quad \text{for each alternative } i;$$
$$\text{st} \quad \Sigma_{i=1,N} \Sigma_{k=1,k} v_{ik} w_k = 1$$
$$\text{bounds on specific variable sets}$$

The *HIPRE 3+* procedure is iterative. Initial bounds on relative importances and preferences are obtained, and a set of linear programming models with these constraints is solved (maximizing and minimizing each alternative's value function in turn). The maximum and minimum value functions for each alternative are obtained. Let the alternative with the highest maximum be labeled **X**. If alternative **X**'s minimum is greater than all other alternatives' maxima, then stop, identifying alternative **X** as the preferred choice. If not, obtain additional information from the decision maker and reiterate.

Note that a complication that can be encountered is model infeasibility. In this case, the least important (presumably the last) information entered is removed until the infeasibility is resolved. If a preferred alternative has not been identified, an uncertain ranking must be used as the final result.

Parking Example

We apply *HIPRE 3+* to the parking example presented with *ARIADNE*. There are three alternatives (*Lot*—**L**, *Garage*—**G**, and *Shuttle*—**S**) and five criteria (*Service*—**S**, *Convenience*—**V**, *Cost*—**C**, *Control*—**N**, and *Investment*—**I**). We will therefore have 15 variables for the *HIPRE 3+* model:

Max/Min   LS + LV + LC + LN + LI   for the *Lot* alternative
st.   LS + LV + LC + LN + LI + GS + GV + GC + GN + GI + SS + SV + SC + SN + SI = 1
bounds on relative preferences of alternatives with respect to specific criteria
all variables ≥ 0

In this case, we will impose bounds as follows, reflecting direct values assigned following the SMART approach.

with respect to *Service*:
Garage between 6 and 8 times as useful as *Lot*	6LS – GS ≤ 0	8LS – GS ≥ 0
Shuttle between 1 and 3 times as useful as *Lot*	LS – SS ≤ 0	3LS – SS ≥ 0
Garage between 3 and 4 times as useful as *Shuttle*	3SS – GS ≤ 0	4SS – GS ≥ 0

with respect to *Convenience*:
Garage between 3 and 4 times as useful as *Lot*	3LV – GV ≤ 0	4LV – GV ≥ 0
Lot between 1 and 3 times as useful as *Shuttle*	SV – LV ≤ 0	3SV – LV ≥ 0
Garage between 7 and 8 times as useful as *Shuttle*	7SV – GV ≤ 0	8SV – GV ≥ 0

with respect to *Cost*:
Lot between 1 and 2 times as attractive as *Garage*	GC – LC ≤ 0	2GC – LC ≥ 0
Shuttle between 1 and 2 times as good as *Lot*	LC – SC ≤ 0	2LC – SC ≥ 0
Shuttle between 2 and 3 times as good as *Garage*	2GC – SC ≤ 0	3GC – SC ≥ 0

with respect to *Control*:
Garage between 6 and 8 times as good as *Lot*	6LN – GN ≤ 0	8LN – GN ≥ 0
Shuttle between 1 and 3 times as good as *Lot*	LN – SN ≤ 0	3LN – SN ≥ 0
Garage between 3 and 4 times as good as *Shuttle*	3SN – GN ≤ 0	4SN – GN ≥ 0

with respect to *Investment*:
Lot between 1 and 3 times as attractive as *Garage*	GI – LI ≤ 0	3GI – LI ≥ 0
Lot between 3 and 4 times as good as *Shuttle*	3SI – LI ≤ 0	4SI – SI ≥ 0
Shuttle between 6 and 8 times as good as *Garage*	6GI – SI ≤ 0	8GI – SI ≥ 0

The solutions to this series of LPs are as follows:

	Minimum	*Maximum*
Lot	0.400	0.086
Garage	0.800	0.086
Shuttle	0.727	0.086

There is a great deal of overlap. Therefore, additional preference information is elicited from the decision maker. Here we rank order the five criteria (arbitrarily, but generally following earlier chapter results):

Service > *Control* > *Cost* > *Convenience* > *Investment*

This yields additional constraints:

Service	*> Control*	LS + GS + SS ≥ LN + GN + SN
Control	*> Cost*	LN + GN + SN ≥ LC + GC + SC
Cost	*> Convenience*	LC + GC + SC ≥ LV + GV + SV
Convenience	*> Investment*	LV + GV + SV ≥ LI + GI + SI

This yielded the following set of solutions:

	Maximum	*Minimum*
Lot	0.246	0.086
Garage	0.727	0.411
Shuttle	0.397	0.176

Note that the ranges of value functions are now much tighter, and there is no overlap between *Garage* (with a minimum of .411) and the other two alternatives (with a maximum of .397). The conclusion is that the decision maker would prefer the garage option. This result, of course, is directly dependent on the relative preferences input by the decision maker.

Nuclear Dump Site Example

The nuclear dump site example used with *ARIADNE* can be dealt with by *HIPRE 3+* as well. There are five alternatives and four criteria, yielding 20 variables. The first variable character indicates the location (N-Nome, W-Newark, R-Rock Springs, D-Duquesne, and G-Gary), while the second variable character indicates the criterion (*C-Cost, L-Lives lost, R-Risk*, and *I-Improvement*). The model is:

Max/Min   NC + NL + NR + NI   for alternative NOME

st   NC + NL + NR + NI + WC + WL + WR + WI + RC + RL + RR + RI + DC + DL + DR + DI + GC + GL + GR + GI = 1

The following bounds are assumed. The resulting limits are given to the right, reflecting direct values assigned following the *SMART* approach used in the *ARIADNE* example.

with respect to COST:

NOME at least 9 times as costly as NEWARK		NC - 9WC ≥ 0
NOME between 1 and 2 times as costly as ROCK	NC - 2RC ≤ 0	NC - RC ≥ 0
NOME between 1 and 2 times as costly as DUQUESNE	NC - 2DC ≤ 0	NC - DC ≥ 0
NOME between 1 and 2 times as costly as GARY	NC - 2GC ≤ 0	NC - GC ≥ 0
NEWARK at least 7 times as costly as ROCK	7WC - RC ≤ 0	
NEWARK at least 7 times as costly as DUQUESNE	7WC - DC ≤ 0	
NEWARK at least 6 times as costly as GARY	6WC - DC ≤ 0	
ROCK between .5 and 2 times as costly as DUQUESNE	RC - 2DC ≤ 0	2RC - DC ≥ 0
ROCK between .5 and 2 times as costly as GARY	RC - 2GC ≤ 0	2RC - GC ≥ 0
DUQUESNE between .5 and 2 times as costly as GARY	DC - 2GC ≤ 0	2DC - GC ≥ 0

with respect to LIVES:

NOME at least 2 times as good as NEWARK		NL -2WL ≥ 0
ROCK between 1 and 3 times as good as NOME	NL - RL ≤ 0	3NL - RL ≥ 0
DUQUESNE between 1 and 3 times as good as NOME	NL - DL ≤ 0	3NL - DL ≥ 0
GARY between 1 and 2 times as good as NOME	NL - GL ≤ 0	2NL - GL ≥ 0
ROCK at least 4 times as good as NEWARK		RL - 4WL ≥ 0
DUQUESNE at least 4 times as good as NEWARK		DL - 4WL ≥ 0
GARY at least 2 times as good as NEWARK		GL - 2WL ≥ 0
ROCK between .5 and 2 times as good as DUQUESNE	RL - 2DL ≤ 0	2RL - DL ≥ 0
ROCK between 2 and 3 times as good as GARY	RL - 3GL ≤ 0	RL -2GL ≥ 0
DUQUESNE between 2 and 3 times as good as GARY	DL - 3GL ≤ 0	DL -2GL ≥ 0

with respect to RISK:

NEWARK at least as good as NOME	NR − WR ≤ 0
ROCK at least 7 times as good as NOME	NR − 7RR ≤ 0
DUQUESNE at least 5 times as good as NOME	NR − 5DR ≤ 0
GARY at least 7 times as good as NOME	NR − 7GR ≤ 0
ROCK between 7 and 8 times as good as NEWARK	7WR − RR ≤ 0 8WR − RR ≥ 0
DUQUESNE between 4 and 6 times as good as NEWARK	4WR − DR ≤ 0 6WR − DR ≥ 0
GARY between 7 and 8 times as good as NEWARK	7WR − GR ≤ 0 8WR − GR ≥ 0
ROCK between 1 and 2 times as good as DUQUESNE	RR − 2DR ≤ 0 RR − DR ≥ 0
ROCK between .5 and 2 times as good as GARY	RR − 2GR ≤ 0 2RR − GR ≥ 0
GARY between 1 and 2 times as good as DUQUESNE	DR − GR ≤ 0 2DR − GR ≥ 0

with respect to IMPROVEMENT:

NOME is between 1 and 3 times better than NEWARK	NI − 3WI ≤ 0 NI − WI ≥ 0
ROCK is between 3 and 4 times better than NOME	3NI − RI ≤ 0 4NI − RI ≥ 0
DUQUESNE is between 2 and 3 times better than NOME	2NI − DI ≤ 0 3NI − DI ≥ 0
GARY is between 4 and 6 times better than NOME	4NI − GI ≤ 0 6NI − GI ≥ 0
ROCK is between 7 and 8 times better than NEWARK	7WI − RI ≤ 0 8WI − RI ≥ 0
DUQUESNE is 4 to 6 times better than NEWARK	4WI − DI ≤ 0 6WI − DI ≥ 0
GARY is between 9 and 11 times better than NEWARK	11WI − GI ≤ 0 9WI − GI ≥ 0
ROCK is between 1 and 2 times better than DUQUENSE	RI − 2DI ≤ 0 RI − DI ≥ 0
GARY is between 1 and 2 times better than ROCK	RI − GI ≤ 0 2RI − GI ≥ 0
GARY is between 1 and 3 times better than DUQUESNE	DI − GI ≤ 0 3DI − GI ≥ 0

Solutions to these models are as follows:

	Maximum	Minimum
Nome	0.400	0
Newark	0.077	0
Rock	0.429	0.140
Duquesne	0.429	0.140
Gary	0.443	0.105

This involves a great deal of overlap. Therefore, additional constraints are added to the model. Here we impose restrictions, forcing the weight on *Lives* (NL+WL+RL+DL+GL) to be at least as great as the weight on *Risk* (NR+WR+RL+DL+GL), the weight on *Risk* to be at least as great as the weight on COST (NC+WC+RC+DC+GC), and the weight on *Cost* to be at least as great as the weight on *Improvement* (NI+WI+RI+DI+GI). These additional constraints yielded the following results:

	Maximum	Minimum
Nome	0.286	0.059
Newark	0.077	0
Rock	0.429	0.227
Duquesne	0.429	0.178
Gary	0.336	0.105

There is still some overlap. The problem is that Rock and Duquesne are very similar alternatives, but Rock dominates Duquesne on *Risk* and *Improvement*. Additional constraints were unable to yield results where the minimum score on Rock exceeded the maximum score on Duquesne. However, the method would highlight the need for the decision maker to focus on these two alternatives.

Summary

The uncertainty models presented allow less precise data inputs. The *ARIADNE* model is based on *SMART* concepts, while *HIPRE 3+* is based on AHP. Both allow ranges for the relative advantages of alternatives or criteria, a very realistic approach. The cost, of course, is a corresponding degree of uncertainty in the results obtained. Both methods could ultimately yield a single recommendation, but could require a great deal of input.

Note that both *ARIADNE* and *HIPRE 3+* have very good user interfaces. Buede [1992] reviews *HIPRE 3+*. *ARIADNE*, with documentation, can be obtained from Dr. Ambrose Goicoechea, STATCOM, Inc., 7921 Jones Branch Drive, Suite 445, McLean, VA 22102. *HIPRE 3+* can be obtained from Scandinavian Softline Technology, Inc., Innopoli, SF-02150 Espoo, Finland.

References

Buede, D.M. 1992. Software review—Three packages for AHP: Criterium, Expert Choice and HIPRE 3+. *Journal of Multi-Criteria Decision Analysis* 1:1, 119-121.

Burden, E.M.,1987. Design and implementation of a diverse, user-friendly decision support software package in "C" utilizing ARIADNE. masters thesis. School of Information Technology and Engineering, George Mason University.

Goicoechea, A. 1990. Experimental evaluation of decision support systems and their use in situations involving multiple criteria and uncertainty. Report S-11 to the U.S. Army Corps of Engineers. STATCOM, Inc., McLean, VA.

Goicoechea, A. and F. Li. 1994. Evaluating alternative systems with ARIADNE: Uncertainty assessment, software architecture and user-system interface design. presented at the XIth International Conference on Multiple Criteria Decision Making (MCDM), Coimbra, Portugal. (August).

Goicoechea, A., E.Z. Stakhiv, and F. Li. 1992. Experimental evaluation of multiple criteria decision models for application of water resources planning. *Water Resources Bulletin* 28:1.

Saaty, T.L. 1977. A scaling method for priorities in hierarchical structures. *Journal of Mathematical Psychology* 15:3, 234-281.

Sage, A.P. and C.C. White. 1984. ARIADNE: A knowledge-based interactive system for planning and decision support. *IEEE Transactions* **SMC-14**:1.

Salo, A. and R.P. Hämäläinen. 1990. Processing interval judgments in the analytic hierarchy process. *Proceedings of the IXth International Conference on MCDM*. (August). Fairfax, VA.

13
Comparisons

The twelve systems we have looked at all support selection problems, but they vary in the specific type of selection decision they were meant to support. This chapter compares the kinds of problems where each technique would be expected to have an advantage, and the kind of decision maker effort required. Techniques will be compared on the dimensions of:

- Task Type
- Task Dimensionality
- Task Uniqueness
- Decision Maker Cognitive Effort required

Task Type

Decision aids can support a variety of task types. These possible task types include identifying the best alternative from a given set, selecting a short list from that set (sorting the alternatives into a partial order of ranking), and providing a means to rank order all of the alternatives (full order ranking). The biggest divergence in approach is found in the outranking systems and in *ZAPROS*, where the emphasis is on providing decision makers with a partial order. This approach is popular in France, with Professor Roy as its primary exponent. The philosophical underpinning seems to be that the decision aid should filter a large list of multiattribute alternatives down to a short list for the decision maker to concentrate on. The *ELECTRE I* and *PROMETHEE I* approaches emphasize selection of those alternatives that have salient advantages on one or more attributes, with corresponding disadvantages on one or more attributes. The *ZAPROS* system from Russia also adopts this partial order philosophy. *VIMDA* uses a similar approach, generating up to eight nondominated alternatives an iteration for decision makers to select from.

The *ARIADNE* method recognizes uncertainty about the relative importance of criteria, as well as the relative performance of alternatives on these criteria. This approach yields output rankings that can easily overlap. Therefore, *ARIADNE* does not guarantee a complete ranking at all. In this sense it is very close in philosophy to the *ELECTRE* approach.

The preference cone method is unique among the techniques we have reviewed in that it is only capable of identifying the best alternative from the given set. The preference cone method operates using a process of elimination, identifying a tighter and tighter preference cone that can be used to mathematically eliminate alternatives on the basis of past preferences. This cone, along with the rejection of alternatives directly from the pairwise comparisons, finally ends up with one winning alternative. There is no inference made about the relative ranking of the rejected alternatives. *HIPRE 3+* intends to accomplish the same thing (in the same uncertain environment as *ARIADNE*) through logical elimination of all alternatives except one.

The other techniques we have looked at generally provide some mechanism for obtaining a full order. This is done by using a value function, where a higher number indicates a better alternative. MAUT (and *SMART*), AHP, and *REMBRANDT* all provide such a numeric value that is used as the basis for full rank ordering. *ELECTRE II* and *PROMETHEE II* were developed to provide a similar full rank ordering capability for those systems.

Task Dimensionality

Multiattribute selection tasks have two basic dimensions: the number of attributes and the number of alternatives.

Number of Attributes

Hierarchical structures can be used to provide some means of organizing and therefore controlling the complexity of decisions involving many attributes. MAUT, AHP, *REMBRANDT*, the outranking methods *ELECTRE* and *PROMETHEE*, and *VIMDA* all are more complex when there are many attributes, simply because there are more coefficients to identify. Fischer [1979] concluded that the predictive validity of multiattribute models was adequate only when there were fewer than five attributes. However, the hierarchical structure provides a mechanism to allow the decision maker to focus on specific subsets of these attributes sequentially.

The number of attributes has a more significant impact on the other systems. In preference cones, when there are a large number of attributes it becomes nearly impossible to find a cone that will eliminate any but dominated alternatives. There are just too many dimensions so that the probability of an alternative performing in an inferior manner to another on at least one criterion becomes very high. *ZAPROS* and *HIPRE 3+* both suffer from the same limitation. The number of pairwise comparisons required to reach a conclusion grow exponentially with the number of alternatives. *ARIADNE* is also affected, because when there are a large number of attributes, the ranges of alternate performance are more likely to overlap.

Number of Alternatives

Multiattribute utility theory and analytic hierarchy process were intended for comparison of a small (seven or less) number of alternatives. Both approaches are explained in a context where the relative ratings are a function of the alternatives being considered. In each of these systems, however, a formula is developed which could be applied to a data set of measurements reflecting any number of alternatives. Application of these methods to large sets of alternatives is not recommended by their proponents, because part of the analysis is intended to be specific ratings of the features of specific alternatives. The *REMBRANDT* method was developed as a series of modifications to AHP. Therefore, it has the same capabilities and limitations of AHP with respect to the number of alternatives that could be considered. In both AHP and *REMBRANDT*, the number of pairwise comparisons necessary grow exponentially with the number of alternatives considered, and therefore there is a practical limit on the size of problem that can be considered. Yet if scores reflecting alternative performance on each attribute are developed as in *SMART*, the value formulas reflecting the relative importance of attributes can be used to consider large databases of alternatives. Therefore, these approaches could be used to consider problems with many alternatives, although we note that this approach contradicts the philosophic underpinnings of these methods.

Preference cones and *HIPRE 3+* operate by eliminating all other alternatives by establishing the ultimate best choice as logically superior to each of the others. You would not want to use preference cones unless there were a large set of alternatives, because it operates by asking the decision maker to select the preferred alternative of two presented. This simple process of elimination could quickly yield the preferred choice in **n**–1 comparisons without going through the complexity of the mathematical programs used in preference cones. If **n** is small, there would be no point in identifying the cone.

HIPRE 3+ is different in this aspect. Instead of asking the decision maker to select the preferred alternative, in *HIPRE 3+* the decision maker is asked to give ranges on the relative preference of attributes, or of alternative performance on attributes. Therefore, the impact of large numbers of alternatives is that the number of questions required of the decision maker can be expected to grow with larger **n**.

ARIADNE was developed using *SMART* approaches as the basis of value functions for each alternative on each attribute, and using interval preference statements for the relative importance of each attribute. This approach is less affected by large numbers of alternatives than are the other methods. *VIMDA*, *ELECTRE* and *PROMETHEE* have much the same performance as *ARIADNE* with respect to the number of alternatives considered. All of these methods could handle large numbers of alternatives, although the likelihood of overlapping value function ranges or partial order rankings would be expected to be greater when more alternatives were considered.

ZAPROS is highly suitable to problems with large numbers of alternatives. The amount of input required in *ZAPROS* is a function of the number of attributes. Once the decision maker's preference mapping is identified, *ZAPROS* results could be applied to any number of alternatives.

Task dimensionality is a very important factor in method appropriateness. MAUT, AHP, and *REMBRANDT* are better when there are few alternatives. Large numbers of attributes can be dealt with using any of these methods. On the other hand, preference cones, *AIM*, and *ZAPROS* are more suitable in the reverse case, where there are few attributes and many alternatives. *VIMDA*, *ARIADNE* and *HIPRE 3+* as well as the outranking methods *ELECTRE* and *PROMETHEE*, can be applied in either setting, although the partial order idea of the outranking methods implies problems with large numbers of alternatives.

Task Uniqueness

MAUT, AHP, and *REMBRANDT* focus on the unique task of comparing the defined set of alternatives over a value function reflecting attribute importance. As we have stated before, these techniques generate cardinal formulas which could be applied in a general fashion. But the intent of the method is to focus on the comparison of available alternatives. *HIPRE 3+* is more limited, in that the relative performances of alternatives are entered as ranges on relative advantage. Therefore, the analysis is specific to the set of alternatives considered.

Outranking methods (*ELECTRE* and *PROMETHEE*) focus on criteria independent of the number of alternatives available (much the same as *VIMDA* and *ZAPROS*). But the results are a function of the alternatives evaluated. The outranking relationships will change if additional alternatives are considered. Therefore, the analysis is specific rather than universal. *VIMDA* is also specific, in that the decision maker directly selects an alternative from the nondominated set presented by the system.

Preference cones and *ZAPROS* develop the decision maker's preference structure. Preference cones operate by making inferences based on selections from available alternatives, and *ZAPROS* by making inferences based on selections from selected members of all possible alternatives. They are both general with respect to task, in that additional alternatives could be added. In the case of *ZAPROS*, no additional preference information would be required. In the case of preference cones additional work may be required. These methods are universal as opposed to specific.

In *ARIADNE*, the *SMART* approach can be used to determine alternative value on each criterion. If only attribute weights are described by ranges, the same information could be applied to new sets of alternatives. In this sense, *ARIADNE* could be universally applied.

Decision Maker Cognitive Effort

This section will consist of two evaluations. The first is based on the theoretical work of Larichev [1992], followed by general comments based on experience with student subjects.

Larichev published a view of psychological validity of elementary operations required of decision makers by various multicriteria decision aids. Larichev felt that the scientific validity of multicriteria methods depends upon the kinds of input demanded of decision makers. Elementary operations were classified in four ways: complex, admissible, admissible for small dimensions, and uncertain (due to either admissibility or to complexity).

1. An operation was classified as complex if psychological research indicates that in performing such operations the decision maker displays many inconsistencies and makes use of simplified strategies.
2. An operation was classified as admissible if psychological research indicated that people were capable of performing these operations with minor inconsistencies, and if they could employ complex strategies.
3. Operations that are admissible but for small dimension are those that research indicates can be performed with minor inconsistencies given that the number of criteria, alternatives, or multiattribute estimates are small enough that they can be dealt with without major inconsistencies.
4. Those operations classified as uncertain were those where insufficient psychological research had been conducted in order to evaluate admissibility or complexity.

Each of the techniques we have discussed include some elementary operations classified by Larichev. Here I will review each technique in order, and give Larichev's classifications for operations that apply.

Multiattribute Utility Theory

MAUT includes the elementary operations of decomposing complex criteria into simple ones during hierarchical structuring. Larichev rates this activity as complex. MAUT also involves determination of quantitative equivalents of a lottery during the phase where criteria are compared with each other. Larichev rates this operation as complex. MAUT includes the step of identifying the quantitative tradeoff value for two criteria estimates, which Larichev rates as uncertain relative to complexity. Therefore, Larichev would rate MAUT as challenging the cognitive capabilities of human decision makers.

The *SMART* method places less burden on decision makers, who can directly assign both weights and scores of alternatives on attributes. Larichev argued that this was a complex task for decision makers, but swing weights provide a means to improve the accuracy of these assessments.

Analytic Hierarchy Process

AHP also includes hierarchical structuring of criteria, exactly as in MAUT. As we have seen, Larichev rated this as a complex task. AHP involves assignment of quantitative equivalents for qualitative concepts, reflecting subjective comparisons through ratio values. Larichev classified this activity as uncertain in complexity. AHP can also be viewed as the qualitative comparison of two estimates taken from two criteria scales, which Larichev rates as admissible. Saaty's nine-point scale provides a simple way of quantifying qualitative concepts. However, Larichev would respond that this is an heuristic activity. Therefore, while AHP is not relatively complex relative to decision maker tasks, it is viewed by Larichev (and others) as heuristic.

REMBRANDT

REMBRANDT essentially involves the same operations as AHP, although Lootsma would argue that it uses a more natural scale. The other differences are really transparent to the user. Therefore, the same complexity ratings would apply as in AHP.

Uncertain Methods

With respect to input information, *HIPRE 3+* follows AHP, allowing less precise specification of relative advantage. *ARIADNE* uses the same type of input for expression of relative importance of attributes. The specification of ranges of relative weights was rated as a complex operation by Larichev.

Outranking Methods

Both *ELECTRE* and *PROMETHEE* involve assignment of quantitative criteria weights, which Larichev rates as complex. Outranking methods involve assignment of quantitative equivalents for qualitative estimates during the definition phase, where the decision maker is given a number of alternative means of scaling values for criterion attainment levels. This is rated as uncertain relative to complexity by Larichev. This same step can involve assignment of satisfactory levels by criterion, which Larichev rates as uncertain relative to admissibility. The most complex task involved in outranking methods is the assignment of criteria weights by decision makers as initial inputs. This is the output for most of the other techniques.

Preference Cones

Preference cones require decision makers to compare two alternatives viewed as a set of estimates by criteria and select the preferred of the two. Larichev rates this as an admissible operation for small dimensions. In other words, if there are two criteria varying (as in *ZAPROS*), this is considered an admissible operation. However, if there are three or more criteria varying, this task becomes increasingly difficult.

VIMDA

VIMDA requires decision makers to make the same selection as is made with preference cones, only instead of selecting the preferred combination of attainments from two alternatives, in *VIMDA* the decision maker is presented with up to eight choices (on up to ten criteria). Larichev rated this as a more difficult task. *VIMDA* also requires users to set aspiration levels, or targets, a task Larichev considered humans to be unreliable at.

ZAPROS

ZAPROS is designed specifically to require only those tasks of the decision maker that can be performed without introducing inconsistencies or requiring complex strategies. All that is asked of the decision maker is to select from pairs of alternatives differing on only two criteria. Furthermore, each criterion's performance is measured on a categorical scale.

Based on Larichev's evaluation of psychological validity, *ZAPROS* is based on the most dependable human input. Preference cones are considered a little less reliable if more than two criteria are present (most likely the case), because decision makers are asked to compare two things that vary on more than two dimensions. The outranking methods involve tasks easily within human decision maker ability to be accurate except for the assignment of weights. MAUT involves even more challenging tasks in identification of lottery tradeoffs and value identification. *ARIADNE* and *HIPRE 3+* involve interval assessments of ratio advantage. This is considered complex by Larichev, only slightly better than the ratio assessments required in AHP (and *REMBRANDT*).

Human Subject Responses

Hobbs [1986] found that decision makers preferred simpler methods because they felt more in control and could better understand the process. Larichev's theoretical analysis of what humans are capable of doing accurately concluded that the actions required by each method would rank in the following order, with the methods based on the most reliable methods listed first:

- *ZAPROS*
- Preference cones (*AIM*)
- *VIMDA*
- *ELECTRE* and *PROMETHEE*
- *SMART*
- MAUT
- *ARIADNE* and *HIPRE 3+*
- AHP and *REMBRANDT*

This rank ordering does not match the findings reported relative to subject ratings of the ease of use and trust in these methods. In conjunction with other researchers, I have had student subjects use a number of these systems (*ZAPROS*, preference cones, *Logical Decision*, and AHP, with some exposure to *PROMETHEE*). These subjects tend to find AHP the easiest to understand, although they do not like large numbers of pairwise comparisons. I myself find that after the twentieth pairwise comparison, I have a tendency to use less effort in obtaining accuracy and more effort on obtaining speed. The subjects find *ZAPROS* hard to understand, because the decision maker is asked to focus on controlled, abstract alternatives. But they have evaluated *ZAPROS* as being easier to use than AHP (see Larichev, et al. [1993]). *Logical Decision* has been used in a number of experiments. I find that package to be very well done, and quite self-explanatory. Subjects have had a number of complaints, however. They are willing to use that package's means of assigning alternative scores on attributes. But they do not feel at all comfortable making lottery tradeoffs. Preference cones have been used on fewer occasions, when comparing 30 alternatives. This method was not rated highly by the subjects at all, because they felt that while the method went very quickly, they got no feedback about why the conclusion was reached by the method. They simply entered their responses, and suddenly the computer gave the winner. *PROMETHEE* has more recently been used with subjects. Primary comments were that these subjects did not feel comfortable with the output given to them by that system. *SMART* was not used in its pure form, although a method where subjects simply entered weights and scores was. Subjects found that method extremely easy to use and understand.

Based on these experiences, the methods considered would be ranked as follows relative to ease of use and understandability:

- *SMART*
- *VIMDA*
- AHP
- *ZAPROS*
- *Logical Decision* (MAUT)
- *PROMETHEE* (outranking)
- preference cones

AIM, *REMBRANDT*, *HIPRE 3+*, and *ELECTRE* were not included, as they were not used extensively by student subjects. Note that this ranking for the systems used is quite different from the theoretical ranking.

Aid to Decision Maker Learning

Vanderpooten [1990] called for consideration of the ability of multicriteria methods to aid decision maker learning. The contention is that decision makers may often start off with only an initial impression of what they want from alternatives. As the analysis proceeds, decision makers can more accurately form their preferences.

Each of the methods reviewed differs relative to supporting decision maker learning. Some, such as MAUT, preference cones, and *ZAPROS*, assume a clear underlying preference function to be elicited from the decision maker. *Logical Decision* gives the decision maker a means to express measures of how well each alternative performs on each criterion, as well as means to measure tradeoffs among criteria. Initially, preferences are assumed to be fixed, with the problem focus on accurate elicitation of this preference structure. In that sense, *Logical Decision* does not consider learning very highly. However, *Logical Decision* includes excellent sensitivity features which enable the decision maker to explore the relative importance of each input. Further, the system allows changes in inputs to be made very expeditiously.

Preference cones are a little dangerous with respect to changes in decision maker preferences. The cone defined by decision maker selections can quickly eliminate vast regions of feasible alternatives. *ZAPROS* uses a similar treatment of preference structure, but because it gathers information on all preference tradeoffs adjacent to the ideal point, no final conclusions are made until all of the evidence is gathered. If there are shifts in preference structure resulting in inconsistencies with past preference statements, *ZAPROS* identifies these inconsistencies and provides the decision maker a means to rectify the entire system.

AHP and *REMBRANDT* do not directly consider learning (any more than MAUT or preference cones do). *Expert Choice* and *Criterium* both include ample sensitivity routines, just as *Logical Decision* does. In a sense, *ELECTRE* requires sensitivity analysis of a type by changing analysis parameters until the distinction between alternatives became clear.

PROMETHEE provides a good deal of output to support decision makers learning about their preference structures. The *GAIA* subroutine of *PROMETHEE* provides a very attractive visual means of aiding this learning process. Initially, a principle components analysis plot showing the relative performance of each alternative on each criterion is given. The decision maker can then explore the impact of changing weights in a dynamic visual display.

AIM and *VIMDA* provide the most direct implementation of learning. These methods help the decision maker by selecting a list of alternatives. *AIM* uses aspiration level settings by the decision maker to infer relative criteria importance, and displays the attainments of the best solution according to these settings as well as levels of attainment one step above and one step below. *AIM* does not eliminate nondominated alternatives during the learning stage, reflecting the possibility that there may be other unexpressed criteria. *VIMDA* has the same idea as *AIM*, seeking to present tradeoffs. While *AIM* presents these tradeoffs in tabular form, *VIMDA* uses graphics. Unlike *AIM*, *VIMDA* screens alternatives to insure that only nondominated choices are considered. The decision maker can set aspiration levels and see the impact of these choices. No nondominated solutions are discarded, so that if the decision maker changes preference indications after looking at the results of prior selections, old solutions that were not considered attractive can still show up for decision maker consideration.

Synthesis

The decision aids we have looked at all seek to help decision makers select multiattribute choices that best match their preference function. But, we have seen that these methods vary in the types of problems they deal with, to include various dimensions of problem size and the specificity of the analysis. The methods also vary in the inputs required from decision makers. Table 13.1 compares these methods.

TABLE 13.1

	MAUT	SMART	AHP	Prefc	Outrank	ZAPROS	ARIADNE	Learn
Task Type	pick best	pick best	pick best	pick best	partial order	partial order	either	pick best
Task dimension								
Alternatives	few	few	few	many	many	many		many
Criteria				few		few	few	≤10
Task uniqueness	spec	spec	spec	univers	spec	univers	univers	spec
Cognitive effort								
Theoretical rank	6	5	8	2	4	1	7	3
Subject rank	6	1	3	8	7	5	4	2

* In this table, AHP represents Analytic hierarchy process, *REMBRANDT* and *HIPRE 3+*; outrank represents *ELECTRE* and *PROMETHEE*; and learn represents *AIM* and *VIMDA*.
"spec" stands for specific application, while "univers" stands for universal.

Fischer [1979] stated that MAUT lost its validity with five or more criteria. Actually, the same argument could be made for all of the methods, in that the accuracy of the technique would be suspect with more criteria. However, the mechanics of some of these methods are adversely affected by more criteria. AHP and its related methods have an exponential growth in the number of required comparisons with more criteria. ZAPROS is also affected, but on a different scale. The number of pairwise comparisons required grows exponentially with the number of criteria, as well as the number of categories upon which each criterion is graded. Preference cones also involve more decision maker pairwise comparisons with more criteria.

Task uniqueness refers to the ability to extend the analysis to alternatives not yet described. Specific applications apply only to those alternatives that were considered in the preference development. Universal applications would involve identification of a formula that can be applied to any alternative described by its attributes. Expert systems are an example of a universal application. Of the methods considered, only preference cones and *ZAPROS* was designed for universal application. The other techniques are argued to be specific, although those that generate value formulas could be applied universally (*ARIADNE*), given a means to objectively measure the performance of each alternative on each attribute (as in *SMART*).

Conclusion

Decision aids are very useful tools to aid decision makers. There are a number of diverse software products that have been developed to deliver these techniques. These techniques vary significantly in the type of problems they are suitable for, in the amount of information required, and in the type of conclusion reached.

All of the decision aids covered in this book are useful, sound methods. I personally have used all of them, and like any other user, I have some personal preferences. But I would not say that any one technique should be avoided. All eight techniques reviewed have useful potential for some decision makers.

The clearest distinction is on task type. MAUT, AHP (and related methods), and preference cones are meant to select a best choice. *ZAPROS* and outranking methods are meant to focus the decision maker's attention on a short list of alternatives from an initial large set. This distinction is clouded by the fact that MAUT and AHP can and have been used to deal with large sets of alternatives.

Use of any of the techniques is an enlightening exercise. Readers are encouraged to try them. The previous chapters demonstrated how each technique worked. This chapter has sought to identify some of the difficulties in using each of the techniques under various circumstances.

References

Fischer, G.W. 1979. Utility models for multiple objective decisions: Do they accurately represent human preferences? *Decision Sciences* **10**, 451–479.

Hobbs, B.F. 1986. What can we learn from experiments in multiobjective decision analysis? *IEEE Transactions on Systems, Man, and Cybernetics* **SMC-16**:3, 384–394.

Larichev, O.I. 1992. Cognitive validity in design of decision-aiding techniques. *Journal of Multi-Criteria Decision Analysis* **1**:3, 127–138.

Larichev, O.I., Moshkovich, H.M., Mechitov, A.I. and Olson, D.L. 1993. Experiments comparing qualitative approaches to rank ordering of multiattribute alternatives. *Journal of Multi-Criteria Decision Analysis* **2**:1, 5–26.

Vanderpooten, D. 1990. The interactive approach in MCDA: A technical framework and some basic conceptions. *Mathematical and Computer Modelling* **12**, 1213–1220.

Bibliography

AUTHOR NOTE: This Bibliography is grouped into specific disciplines and further sub-grouped by areas within those disciplines. The entries appear in the order in which they were published.

Multiattribute Utility Theory

Theory

Von Neumann, J. and O. Morgenstern. 1947. *Theory of Games and Economic Behavior*, 2nd ed. Princeton, NJ: Princeton University Press.

Herstein, I.N. and J. Milnor. 1953. An Axiomatic Approach to Measurable Utility. *Econometrica* **21** (April) 291–297.

Debreu, G. 1959. *Theory of value: An axiomatic analysis of economic equilibrium*. New Haven, CT: Yale University Press.

Arrow, K.J. 1965. *Aspects of the theory of risk bearing*. Helsinki: Yrjo Jahnssonis Saatio.

Fishburn, P.C. 1970. *Utility theory for decision making*. New York: John Wiley & Sons.

Keeney, R.L. and H. Raiffa. 1976. *Decisions with multiple objectives: Preferences and value tradeoffs*. New York: John Wiley & Sons.

Edwards, W. 1977. How to use multiattribute utility measurement for social decision making. *IEEE Transactions on Man and Cybernetics* **SMC–7**, 326–340.

Fishburn, P.C. and G.A. Kochenberger. 1979. Two-piece von Neumann-Morgenstern utility functions. *Decision Sciences* **10**:4, 503–518.

Krzysztofowicz, R. 1983. Risk attitude hypotheses of utility theory. In *Foundations of Utility and Risk Theory with Applications*, B.P. Stigum & F. Wenstop, eds., Dordrecht Holland: D. Reidel Publishing Company. 326–348.

Bunn, D.W. 1984. *Applied Decision Analysis*. New York: McGraw-Hill.

Fishburn, P.C. 1984. Multiattribute nonlinear utility theory. *Management Science* **30**:11, 1301–1310.

Larichev, O.I. 1984. Psychological validation of decision methods. *Journal of Applied Systems Analysis* **11**, 37–46.

Kahneman, D. and A. Tversky. 1984. Choices, values, and frames. *American Psychologist* **39**:4, 341–350.

Decision Making

Georgescu–Roegen, N. 1954. Choice, expectations and measurability. *Quarterly Journal of Economics* #**468**:4, 503–534.

Lindblom, C.E. 1959. The Science of 'Muddling Through'. *Public Administration Review* **19**:2, 79–88.

Morgenstern, O. 1972. Thirteen critical points in contemporary economic theory: An interpretation. *Journal of Economic Literature* **10** December 1163–1189.

Tversky, A. 1972. Elimination by aspects: A theory of choice. *Psychological Review* 281–299.

March, J.G. 1978. Bounded rationality, ambiguity, and the engineering of choice. *The Bell Journal of Economics* **9**:2, 587–608.

Simon, H.A. 1979. Rational decision making in business organizations. *The American Economic Review* **69**:4, 493–513.

March, J.G. and Z. Shapira. 1987. Managerial perspectives on risk and risk taking. *Management Science* **33**:11, 1404–1418.

Clemen, R.T. 1991. *Making hard decisions: An introduction to decision analysis.* Boston: PWS–Kent.

Keeney, R.L. 1992. *Value-focused thinking: A path to creative decisionmaking.* Cambridge, MA: Harvard University Press.

MAUT Empirical

Green, P.E. 1963. Risk attitudes and chemical investment decisions. *Chemical Engineering Progress* **59**:1, 35–40.

Swalm, R.D. 1966. Utility theory-insights into risk taking. *Harvard Business Review* **47**, November–December, 123–136.

Boussard, J.-M. and M. Petit. 1967. Representation of farmers' behaviour under uncertainty with a focus-loss constraint. *Journal of Farm Economics* **49**, 869–880.

Grayson, C.J. 1970. *Decisions under uncertainty: Drilling decisions by oil and gas operators.* Cambridge, MA: Harvard University Graduate School of Business.

Cummings, L.L., Harnett, D.L. and O.J. Stevens. 1971. Risk, fate, conciliation and trust: An international study of attitudinal differences among executives. *Academy of Management Journal* **14**, 285–304.

Halter, A.N. and G.W. Dean. 1971. *Decisions under uncertainty.* Cincinnati, OH: Southwestern Publishing Company.

Lorange, P. and V.D. Norman. 1973. Risk preference in Scandinavian shipping. *Applied Economics* **5**, 49–59.

Barnes, J.D. and J.E. Reinmuth. 1976. Comparing imputed and actual utility functions in a competitive bidding setting. *Decision Sciences* 7:4, 801–812.

Shoemaker, P.J.H. 1980. *Experiments on decisions under risk: The expected utility hypothesis*. Boston, MA: Nijhoff.

Brockhous, R.H., Sr. 1980. Risk taking propensity of entrepreneurs. *Academy of Management Journal* 23, 509–520.

Laughhunn, D.J., Payne, J.W. and R. Crum. 1980. Managerial risk preferences for below target returns. *Management Science* 26, 1238–1249.

Krinsky, I. 1985. Mean-variance utility functions, flexible functional forms, and the investment behaviour of canadian life insurers. *The Journal of Risk and Insurance* 52 (June) 241–268.

MacCrimmon, K.R. and D.A. Wehrung. *Taking risks: The management of uncertainty*. New York: Free Press.

Adelman, L., Sticha, P.J. and M.L. Donnell. 1986. An experimental investigation of the relative effectiveness of two techniques for structuring multiattributed hierarchies. *Organizational Behavior and Human Decision Processes* 37 (April) 188–196.

Farmer, T. 1987. Testing the robustness of multiattribute utility theory in an applied setting. *Decision Sciences* 18 (Spring) 178–193.

Larichev, O.I. and H.M. Moshkovich. 1988. Limits to decision-making ability in direct multiattribute alternative evaluation. *Organizational Behavior and Human Decision Processes* 42 (October) 217–233.

MacCrimmon, K.R. and D.A. Wehrung. 1990. Characteristics of risk taking executives. *Management Science* 36:4, 422 –435.

MAUT Technique

Keeney, R.L. 1972. An illustrated procedure for assessing multiattributed utility functions. *Sloan Management Review* 14, 37–50.

Cohon, J.L. and D.H. Marks. 1973. Multiobjective analysis in water resource planning. *Water Resources Research* 9:4, 333–340.

Keeney, R.L. 1977. The art of assessing multiattribute utility functions. *Organizational Behavior and Human Performance* 19, 267–310.

Bodily, S.E. 1977. A multiattribute decision analysis for the level of frozen blood utilization. *IEEE Transactions on Systems, Man and Cybernetics* SMC–7, 683–694.

Krzysztofowicz, R. and L. Duckstein. 1980. Assessment errors in multiattribute utility functions. *Organizational Behavior and Human Performance* 26:3, 326–348.

Hershey, J.C., Kunreuther, H.C. and P.J.H. Shoemaker. 1982. Sources of bias in assessment procedures for utility functions. *Management Science* 28:8, 936–954.

McCord, M.R. and R. de Neufville. 1983. Empirical demonstration that expected utility decision analysis is not operational. In *Foundations of Utility and Risk Theory with Applications*, B.P. Stigum & F. Wenstop, eds., Dordrecht Holland: D. Reidel Publishing Company. 181–199.

McCord, M.R. and R. de Neufville. 1983. Fundamental deficiency of expected utility decision analysis. *Multi-objective Decision Making*, S. French et al., eds., San Diego, CA: Academic Press. 279–306.

Farquhar, P.H. 1984. Utility assessment methods. *Management Science* **30**:11, 1283–1300.

McCord, M.R. and R. de Neufville. 1984. Utility dependence on probability: An empirical demonstration. *Journal of Large Scale Systems* **6**, 91–103.

Wehrung, D.A., MacCrimmon, K.R. and K.M. Brothers. 1984. Utility assessment: Domains, stability, and equivalence procedures. *Infor* **22**, 98–115.

Krinsky, I. 1985. Mean-variance utility functions, flexible functional forms, and the investment behaviour of Canadian life insurers. *The Journal of Risk and Insurance* **52** (June) 241–268.

McCord, M. and R. de Neufville. 1985. Assessment response surface: Investigating utility dependence on probability. *Theory and Decision* **18**, 263–285.

McCord, M. and R. de Neufville. 1987. 'Lottery Equivalents': Reduction of the certainty effect problem in utility assessment. *Management Science* **32**:1, 56–60.

Buede, D.M. 1986. Structuring value attributes. *Interfaces* **16**:2, 52–62.

Stillwell, W.G., von Winterfeldt, D. and R.S. John. 1987. Comparing hierarchical and nonhierarchical weighting methods for eliciting multiattribute value models. *Management Science* **33** (April) 442–450.

Brownlow, S.A. and S.R. Watson. 1987. Structuring multi-attribute value hierarchies. *Journal of the Operational Research Society* **38**:4, 309–317.

Louviere, J.J. and G.J. Gaeth. 1987. Decomposing the determinants of retail facility choice using the method of hierarchical information integration: A supermarket illustration. *Journal of Retailing* **63** (Spring) 25–48.

Laskey, K.B. and G.W. Fischer. 1987. Estimating utility functions in the presence of response error. *Management Science* **33** (August) 965–980.

de Neufville, R. and P. Delquie. 1988. A model of the influence of certainty and probability effects on the measurement of utility. In *Risk, Decision and Rationality*, B. Munier, ed., Dordrecht Holland: D. Reidel Publishing Company. 189–205.

Desvousges, W.H. and V.K. Smith. 1988. Focus groups and risk communication: The 'Science' of listening to data. *Risk Analysis* **8**:4, 479–484.

Holbrook, M.B. and W.J. Havlena. 1988. Assessing the real-to-artificial generalizability of multiattribute attitude models in tests of new product designs. *Journal of Marketing Research* **25** (February) 25–35.

McCord, M. and C. Leotsarakos. 1988. Investigating utility and value functions with an assessment cube. In *Risk, Decision and Rationality*, B. Munier, ed., Dordrecht Holland: D. Reidel Publishing Company. 59–75.

Oral, M. and O. Kettani. 1989. Modelling the process of multiattribute choice. *Journal of the Operational Research Society* **40** (March) 281–291.

Salminen, P., Korhonen, P. and J. Wallenius. 1989. Testing the form of a decision-maker's multiattribute value function based on pairwise preference information. *Journal of the Operational Research Society* **40** (March) 299–302.

Keeney, R.L., von Winterfelt, D. and T. Eppel. 1990. Eliciting public values for complex policy decisions. *Management Science* **36**:9, 1011–1030.

Fraser, J.M. and R.P. Fynn. 1990. A new method to teach multi-attribute utility assessment. *The Engineering Economist* **36**:1, 11–20.

MAUT Application

Folayen, J.I., Hoeg, K. and J.R. Benjamin. 1970. Design of fill for San Francisco Bay. *ASCE Journal of Soil Mechanics and Foundations Division* **96** (July) 1127–1141, also in *Systems planning and design: Case studies in modeling, optimization, and evaluation*, R. de Neufville and D.H. Marks, eds., 1974. Englewood Cliffs, NJ: Prentice Hall. 338–348.

de Neufville, R. and R.L Keeney. 1974. Use of decision analysis in airport development for Mexico City. In *Systems Planning and Design: Case Studies in Modeling, Optimization, and Evaluation*. R. de Neufville and D.H. Marks, eds., Englewood Cliffs, NJ: Prentice Hall. 349–369.

Major, D.C. 1974. Multiobjective redesign of the big walnut project. In *Systems Planning and Design: Case Studies in Modeling, Optimization, and Evaluation*, R. de Neufville and D.H. Marks, eds., Englewood Cliffs, NJ: Prentice Hall. 322–339.

Bodily, S.E. 1977. A multiattribute decision analysis for the level of frozen blood utilization. *IEEE Transactions on Systems, Man and Cybernetics* **SMC-7**, 683–694.

Ozernoy, V.M., Smith, D.R. and A. Sicherman. 1981. Evaluating computerized geographic information systems using decision analysis. *Interfaces* **11**:5, 92–99.

Kirkwood, C.W. 1982. A case history of nuclear power plant site selection. *Journal of the Operational Research Society* **33**, 353–363.

Madden, T.J., Hyrnick, M.S. and J.A. Hodde. 1983. Decision analysis used to evaluate air quality control equipment for Ohio Edison Company. *Interfaces* **13**:1, 66–75.

Fryback, D.G. and R.L. Keeney. 1983. Constructing a complex judgmental model: An index of trauma severity. *Management Science* **29**:8, 869–883.

Brown, C. 1984. The central Arizona water study: A case for multiobjective planning and public involvement. *Water Resources Bulletin* **20**, 331–337.

Renn, O., Stegelmann, U., Albrecht, G. and U. Kotte. 1984. The empirical investigation of citizens' preferences for four energy scenarios. *Technological Forecasting and Social Change*. 26.

Stover, R.D., Teas, R.K. and R.J. Gardner. 1985. Agricultural lending decision: A multiattribute analysis. *American Journal of Agricultural Economics* **67** (August) 513–520.

Pollock, S.M. and K. Chen. 1986. Strive to conquer the black stink: Decision analysis in the People's Republic of China. *Interfaces* **16**:2, 31–37.

Brownlow, S.A. and S.R. Watson. 1987. Structuring multi-attribute value hierarchies. *Journal of the Operational Research Society* **38** (Apri) 309–317.

Keeney, R.L. 1987. An analysis of the portfolio of sites to characterize for selecting a nuclear repository. *Risk Analysis* 7:2, 195–218.

Keeney, R.L., Renn, O. and D. von Winterfeldt. 1987. Structuring West Germany's energy objectives. *Energy Policy* (August) 352–362.

Hyberg, B.T. 1987. Multiattribute decision theory and forest management: A discussion and application. *Forest Science* 33 (December) 835–845.

Tzeng, G.-H. and T.-A. Shiau. 1988. Multiple objective programming for bus operation: A case study for Taipei City. *Transportation Research–B*, **22B**:3, 195–206.

Simloes, V.C. 1988. Portugal and FDI attraction: A multi-criteria approach. *Management International Review* 28:4, 42–52.

Wenstop, R.F. and A.J. Carlsen. 1988. Ranking hydroelectric power projects with multicriteria decision analysis. *Interfaces* 18:4, 36–48.

Peerenboom, J.P., Buehring, W.A. and T.W. Joseph. 1989. Selecting a portfolio of environmental programs for a synthetic fuels facility. *Operations Research* 37 (September–October) 689–699.

Hobbs, B.F. and P. Maheshwari. 1990. A decision analysis of the effect of uncertainty upon electric utility planning. *Energy* 15:9, 785–801.

Hanson, M., Kidwell, S. and D. Ray. 1991. Electric utility least-cost planning: Making it work within a multiattribute decision-making framework. *Journal of the American Planning Association* 57 (Winter) 34–43.

Durance, P.W., Jacobs, L. and C.B. Kerr. 1991. Setting priorities for diverse equipment acquisition and program proposals with automated multiattributed utility functions. *Health Care Management Review* 16 (Spring) 73–85.

Corner, J.L. and C.W. Kirkwood. 1991. Decision analysis applications in the operations research literature, 1970–1989. *Operations Research* 39:2, 206–219.

MAUT Group Decision Making

Dyer, J.S. and R.F. Miles, Jr. 1976. An actual application of collective choice theory to the selection of trajectories for the Mariner Jupiter/Saturn 1977 Project. *Operations Research* 24, 220–244.

Lincoln, D.R. and E.S. Rubin. 1979. Cross–media environmental impacts of coal-fired power plants: An approach using multiattribute utility theory. *IEEE Transactions on Systems, Man and Cybernetics* **SMC-9**, 285–289.

Ulvila, J.W. and W.D. Snider. 1980. Negotiation of international oil tanker standards: An application of multiattribute value theory. *Operations Research* **28**:1, 81–96.

Golabi, K., Kirkwood, C.W. and A. Sicherman. 1981. Selecting a portfolio of solar energy projects using multiattribute preference theory. *Management Science* 27, 174–189.

Dyer, J.S. and R.F. Miles, Jr. 1982. Tinker toys and Christmas trees: Opening a new merchandising package for Amoco Oil Company. *Interfaces* 12:6, 38–52.

Lathrop, J.F. and S.R. Watson. 1982. Decision analysis for the evaluation of risk in nuclear waste management. *Journal of the Operational Research Society* **33**, 407–418.

Torrance, G.W., Boyle, M.H. and S.P. Horwood. 1982. Application of multi-attribute utility theory to measure social preferences for health states. *Operations Research* **30**:6, 1043–1069.

Sarin, R.K. 1983. A social decision analysis of the earthquake safety problem: The case of existing Los Angeles buildings. *Risk Analysis* **3**, 35–50.

Keeney, R.L., Lathrop, J.F. and A. Sicherman. 1986. An analysis of Baltimore Gas and Electric Company's technology choice. *Operations Research* **34**, 18–39.

Kok, M. 1986. The interface with decision makers and some experimental results in interactive multiple objective programming models. *European Journal of Operational Research* **26**, 178–188.

Gillmor, D.A. 1987. Objectives in Irish energy policy. *Energy Policy* (August) 363–375.

Merkhofer, M.W. and R.L. Keeney. 1987. A multiattribute utility analysis of alternative sites for the disposal of nuclear waste. *Risk Analysis* **7**:2, 173–194.

Keeney, R.L. 1987. An analysis of the portfolio of sites to characterize for selecting a nuclear repository. *Risk Analysis* **7**:2, 195–218.

Gregory, R. and S. Lichtenstein. 1987. A review of the high-level nuclear waste repository siting analysis. *Risk Analysis* **7**:2, 219–223.

Thomas, J.B., McDaniel, R.R. Jr. and M.J. Dooris. 1989. Strategic Issue Analysis: NGT + decision analysis for resolving strategic issues. *The Journal of Applied Behavioral Science* **25**:2, 189–200.

Jones, M.R. 1989. The potential of decision analysis as a means of integrating the environment into energy policy decisionmaking. *Environment and Planning A* **21**, 1315–1327.

Jones, M., Hope, C. and R. Hughes. 1990. A multi-attribute value model for the study of UK energy policy. *Journal of the Operational Research Society* **41**:10, 919–929.

Hanson, M., Kidwell, S., Ray, D. and R. Stevenson. 1991. Electric utility least-cost planning: Making it work within a multiattribute decision-making framework. *Journal of the American Planning Association* **57**:1, 34–43.

Nurmi, H. and J. Kacprzyk. 1991. On fuzzy tournaments and their solution concepts in group decision making. *European Journal of Operational Research* **51**, 223–232.

Reagan-Cirincione, P., Schuman, S., Richardson, G.P. and S.A. Dorf. 1991. Decision modeling: Tools for strategic thinking. *Interfaces* **21**:6, 52–65.

Quaddus, M.A., Atkinson, D.J. and M. Levy. 1992. An application of decision conferencing to strategic planning for a voluntary organization. *Interfaces* **22**:6, 61–71.

Vári, A. and J. Vecsenyi. 1991. Experiences with decision conferencing in Hungary. *Interfaces* **22**:6, 72–83.

Kusnic, M.W. and D. Owen. 1992. The unifying vision process: Value beyond traditional decision analysis in multiple-decision-maker environments. *Interfaces* **22**:6, 150–166.

Analytic Hierarchy Process

Overview

Saaty, T.L. 1977. A scaling method for priorities in hierarchical structures. *Journal of Mathematical Psychology* **15**:3, 234–281.

Saaty, T.L. 1980. *The Analytic Hierarchy Process*. 1980. New York: McGraw Hill. 2nd ed. T.L. Saaty.

Saaty, T.L. 1982. *Decision Making for Leaders*. Belmont, CA: Van Nostrand Reinhold. 2nd ed. RWS Publications, 1986.

Saaty, T.L. and K.P. Kearns. 1985. *Analytical Planning*. New York: Pergamon.

Zahedi, F 1986. The analytic hierarchy process-A survey of the method and its applications. *Interfaces* **16** (4), 96–108.

Saaty, R.W 1987. The analytic hierarchy process-What it is and how it is used. *Mathematical Modelling* **9** (3–5), 161–176.

Saaty, T.L. and Alexander. 1987. *A new logic to resolve conflicts: The analytic hierarchy process*.

Shim, J.P. 1989. Bibliographical research on the analytic hierarchy process (AHP) *Socio–Economic Planning Sciences* **23:3**, 161–167.

Vargas, L.G. 1990. Overview of the analytic hierarchy process and its applications *European Journal of Operational Research* **48**, 2–8.

Saaty, T.L. 1990. How to make a decision: The analytic hierarchy process. *European Journal of Operational Research* **48**, 9–26.

AHP Theory

Saaty, T.L. 1977. A scaling method for priorities in hierarchical structures. *Journal of Mathematical Psychology* **15**, 234–281.

Saaty, T.L. and L.G. Vargas. 1979. Estimating technological coefficients by the analytic hierarchy process. *Socio–Economic Planning Sciences* **13**, 333–336.

Johnson, C.R., W.B. Beine and T.J. Wang. 1979. A note on right-left asymmetry in an elgenvector ranking procedure. *Journal of Mathematical Psychology* **19**, 61–64.

Vargas, L.G. 1982. Reciprocal matrices with random coefficients. *Mathematical Modelling* **3** (1), 69–81.

Belton, V. and T. Gear 1983. On a short-coming of Saaty's method of analytic hierarchies. *Omega* **11** (3), 228–230.

Saaty, T.L., L.G. Vargas and R.E. Wendell. 1983. Assessing attribute weights by ratios. *Omega* **11** (1), 9–12.

Saaty, T.L. and L. Vargas 1984. Inconsistency and rank preservation. *Journal of Mathematical Psychology* **28**, 205–214.

Harker, P.T. 1985. The use of expert judgments in predicting interregional migration patterns: An analytic hierarchy approach. *Geographical Analysis*.

Saaty, T.L 1985. Axiomatization of the analytic hierarchy process. In [**H&C**], 91–108.

Takeda, E., Yu, P.L. and K.O. Cogger. 1985. A comparative study of eigen weight vectors. In [H&C], 338–399

Saaty, T.L. 1986. A note on the AHP and expected value theory. *Socio-Economic Planning Sciences* **20** (6), 397–398..

Saaty, T.L. 1987. Rank generation, preservation, and reversal in the analytic hierarchy process. *Decision Sciences* **18** (2), 157–177.

Saaty, T.L. 1987. Absolute and relative measurement with the AHP: The most livable cities in the U.S.. *Socio–Economic Planning Sciences* **20** (6), 327–332.

Harker, P.T. 1987. Derivatives of the Perron root of a positive reciprocal matrix: With applications to the analytic hierarchy process. *Applied Mathematics and Computation* **22** (3), 217–232.

Weiss, E.N. and V.R. Rao. 1987. AHP design issues for large scale systems. *Decision Sciences* **18**:1, 43–61.

Weiss, E.N. 1987. Using the analytic hierarchy process in a dynamic environment. *Mathematical Modelling* **9** (3–5), 211–216.

Harker, P.T. and L.G. Vargas. 1987. The theory of ratio scale estimation: Saaty's analytic hierarchy process. *Management Science* **33** (110), 1383–1403.

Saaty, T.L. and L.G. Vargas. 1987. Uncertainty and rank order in the analytic hierarchy process. *European Journal of Operational Research* **32** (13), 107–117.

Lane, E.F. and W.A. Verdini. 1989. A consistency test for AHP decision makers. *Decision Sciences* **20** (3), 575–590.

Schoner, B. and W.C. Wedley. 1989. Ambiguous criteria weights in AHP: Consequences and solutions. *Decision Sciences* **20** (3), 462–475.

Dyer, J.S. 1990. Remarks on the analytic hierarchy process. *Management Science* **36**:3, 249–258.

Saaty, T.L. 1990. An exposition of the AHP in reply to the paper 'Remarks on the Analytic Hierarchy Process'. *Management Science* **36**:3, 259–268.

Harker, P.T. and L.G. Vargas. 1990. Reply to 'Remarks on the Analytic Hierarchy Process' by J.S. Dyer. *Management Science* **36**:3, 269–273.

Dyer, J.S. 1990. A clarification of 'Remarks on the Analytic Hierarchy Process.' *Management Science* **36**:3, 274–275.

Korhonen, P. and J. Wallenius. 1990. Using qualitative data in multiple objective linear programming. *European Journal of Operational Research* **48**, 81–87.

Millet, I. and P.T. Harker. 1990. Globally effective questioning in the analytic hierarchy process. *European Journal of Operational Research* **48**, 88–97.

Saaty, T.L. 1990. Physics as a decision theory. *European Journal of Operational Research* **48**, 98–104.

Weiss, E.N. 1990. Fly now or fly later? The delayed consumption problem. *European Journal of Operational Research* **48**, 128–135.

Basak, I. 1990. Testing for the rank ordering of the priorities of the alternatives in Saaty's ratio-scale method. *European Journal of Operational Research* **48**, 148–152.

Forman, E.H. 1990. Random indices for incomplete pairwise comparison matrices. *European Journal of Operational Research* **48**, 153–155.

Saaty, T.L. 1990. Eigenvector and logarithmic least squares. *European Journal of Operational Research* **48**, 156–160.

Barzilai, J. and B. Golanyi. 1990. Deriving weights from pairwise comparison matrices: The additive case. *Operations Research Letters* **9**:6, 407–410.

Iz, P. and M.T. Jelassi. 1990. An interactive group decision aid for multiobjective problems: An empirical assessment. *OMEGA* **18**, 595–604.

Zahir, M.S. 1991. Incorporating the uncertainty of decision judgements in the analytic hierarchy process. *European Journal of Operational Research* **53**:2, 206–216.

Iz, P. 1992. Two multiple criteria group decision support systems based on mathematical programming and Ranking Methods. *European Journal of Operational Research* **61**, 245–253.

Dyer, R.F. and E.H. Forman. 1992. Group decision support with the analytic hierarchy process. *Decision Support Systems* **8**, 99–124.

Iz, P. and L. Krajewski. 1992. A comparison of three interactive multiobjective programming techniques as group decision support tools. *INFOR* **30**, 349–365.

AHP Applications

Saaty, T.L. 1977. Scenarios and priorities in transport planning: Applications to the Sudan. *Transportation Research* **11** (5), 343–350.

Saaty, T.L. and J.P. Bennett. 1977. A theory of analytical hierarchies applied to political candidacy. *Behavioural Science* **22**, 237–245.

Saaty, T.L. 1979. The US-OPEC energy conflict: The payoff matrix by the analytic hierarchy process. *International Journal of Game Theory* **8** (4), 225–234.

Saaty, T.L. and R.S. Mariano. 1979. Rationing energy to industries: Priorities and input-output dependence. *Energy Systems and Policy* **3** (1), 85–111.

Wind, Y. and T.L. Saaty. 1980. Marketing applications of the analytic hierarchy process. *Management Science* **26** (7), 641–658.

Ramanujam, V. and T.L. Saaty. 1981. Technological choices in the less developed countries: An analytic hierarchy process. *Technological Forecasting and Social Change* **19** (1), 81–98.

Emshoff, J.R. and T.L. Saaty. 1981. Applications of the analytic hierarchy process to long range planning processes. *European Journal of Operational Research* **10**, 131–143.

Gholamnezhad, H. and T.L. Saaty. 1982. A desired energy mix for the United States in the year 2000: An analytic hierarchy process. *International Journal of Policy Analysis and Information Systems* **6** (1), 47–64.

Saaty, T.L. and M. Wong. 1983. Projecting average family size in India by the analytic hierarchy process. *Journal of Mathematical Sociology* **9** (3), 181–209.

Cook, T., Falchi, P. and R. Mariano. 1984. An urban allocation model combining time series and analytic hierarchy methods. *Management Science* **30** (2), 198–208.

Harker, P.T 1985. The use of expert judgments in predicting interregional migration patterns: An analytic hierarchy approach. *Geographical Analysis.*

Kok, M. and F.A. Lootsma 1985. Pairwise comparisons in a multiobjective energy model. In **[H&C]**, 457–474.

Mitchell, K.H. and T. Bingham. 1986. Maximizing the benefits of Canadian forces equipment overhaul programs using multiobjective Optimization. *INFOR* **24** (4), 251–264.

Bard, J. 1986. A multiobjective methodology for selecting subsystem automation *Management Science* **32** (12), 1628–1641.

Lauro, G.L. and A.P.J. Vepsalainin. 1987. Assessing technology portfolios for contract competition: An analytic hierarchy process. *Socio–Economic Planning Sciences* **20** (6), 4071–411.

Liberatore, M.J. 1987. An extension of the AHP for industrial R and D project selection and resource allocation. *IEEE Transactions on Engineering Management* **34**, 12–18.

Pay, P.S., K. Tsuji and Y. Suzuki. 1987. Comprehensive evaluation of new urban transportation systems by AHP. *International Journal of Systems Science* **18** (6), 1179–1190.

Anselin, A., Meire, P.M. and L. Anselin. 1989. Multicriteria techniques in ecological evaluation: An example using the analytic hierarchy process. *Biological Conservation* **49**:3, 215–229.

Bard, J.F. and S. Sousk. 1990. A tradeoff analysis for rough terrain cargo handlers using the AHP: An example of group decision making. *IEEE Transactions on Engineering Management* **EM–37**:3, 222–228.

Roper-Lowe, G.C. and J.A. Sharp. 1990. The analytic hierarchy process and its application to an Iiformation technology decision. *Journal of the Operational Research Society* **41**:1, 49–59.

Bard, J.F. 1990. Using multicriteria methods in the early stages of new product development. *Journal of the Operational Research Society* **41**, 755–766.

Arbel, A. and Y.E. Orgler. 1990. An application of the AHP to bank strategic planning: The mergers and acquisitions process. *European Journal of Operational Research* **48**, 27–37.

Azis, I.J. 1990. Analytic hierarchy process in the benefit-cost framework: A post-evaluation of the trans-Sumatra project. *European Journal of Operational Research* **48**, 38–48.

Cook, D.R., Staschak, S. and W.T. Green. 1990. Equitable allocation of livers for orthotopic transplantation: An application of the analytic hHierarchy process. *European Journal of Operational Research* **48**, 49–56.

Dobias, A.P. 1990. Designing a mouse trap using the analytic hierarchy process and expert choice. *European Journal of Operational Research* **48**, 57–65.

Hamalainen, R.P. 1990. A decision aid in the public debate on nuclear power. *European Journal of Operational Research* **48**, 66–76.

Hegde, G.G. and P.R. Tadikamalla. 1990. Site selection for a 'sure service terminal'. *European Journal of Operational Research* **48**, 77–80.

Srinivasan, V. and P.J. Bolster. 1990. An industrial bond rating model based on the analytic hierarchy process. *European Journal of Operational Research* **48**, 105–119.

Steenge, A.E., Bulten, A. and F.G. Peters. 1990. The decentralization of a sales support department in a medium-large company: A quantitative assessment based on ideas of Thomas L. Saaty and Stafford Beer. *European Journal of Operational Research* **48**, 120–127.

Zahedi, F. 1990. A method for quantitative evaluation of expert systems. *European Journal of Operational Research* **48**, 136–147.

Vellore, R.C. and D.L. Olson. 1991. An AHP application to computer system selection. *Mathematical and Computer Modelling* **15**:7, 83–93.

Selection Techniques

Other Weighting Methods

Eckenrode, R.T 1965. Weighing multiple criteria. *Management Science* **12** (3), 180–192.

Fischer, G.W. 1977. Convergent validation of decomposed multiattribute utility assessment. *Organizational Behavior and Human Performance* **18**, 295–315.

Novoa, J.I. and A.H. Halff 1977. Management of flooding in a fully-developed low-cost housing neighborhood. *Water Resources Bulletin* **13** (6).

Shoemaker, P.J.H. and C.C. Waid 1982. An experimental comparison of different approaches to determining weight in additive utility models. *Management Science* **28**, 182–196.

Watson, S.R. and A.N.S. Freeling. 1982. Assessing attribute weights. *Omega* **10** (6), 582–583.

Dombi, J. 1982. Basic concepts for a theory of evaluation: The aggregative operator. *European Journal of Operational Research* **10**, 282–293.

Watson, S.R. and A.N.S. Freeling 1982. Comment on: Assessing attribute weights by ratios. *Omega* **11** (1), 13.

Jensen, R.E. 1984. An alternative scaling method for priorities in hierarchical structures. *Journal of Mathematical Psychology* **28** (3), 317–322.

Kmietowicz, A.W. and A.D. Pearman 1984. Decision theory, linear partial information and statistical dominance. *Omega* **12**, 391–399.

Choo, E.U. and W.C. Wedley 1985. Optimal criterion weights in multicriteria decision making. In [**H&C**], 345–357.

Lockett, G., Hetherington, B. and P. Yallup. 1985. Subjective estimation and its use in MCDM. In [**H&C**], 358–374.

Belton, V. and A.E. Gear. 1985. The legitimacy of rank reversal-A comment. *Omega* **13** (3), 143–144.

Vargas, L.G. 1985. A rejoinder. *Omega* **13** (4), 249.

Belton, V. and A.E. Gear. 1985. A series of experiments into the use of pairwise comparison techniques to evaluate criteria weights. In [**H&C**], 375–387.

Crawford, G. and C. Williams. 1985. A note on the analysis of subjective judgement matrices. *Journal of Mathematical Psychology* **29**, 387–405.

Belton, V. 1985. A comparison of the analytic hierarchy process and a simple multi-attribute value function. *European Journal of Operational Research* **26**, 387–405.

Belton, V. and A.E. Gear. 1986. Assessing weights by means of pairwise comparisons. *Proceedings of the Operational Research* **26**, 7–21.

Solymosi, T. and J. Dombi. 1986. A method for determining the weights of criteria: The centralized weights. *European Journal of Operational Research* **26**, 35–41.

Vansnik, J.-C. 1986. On the problem of weights in multiple criteria decision making (The Noncompensatory Approach). *European Journal of Operational Research* **24**, 288–294.

Barzilai, J., Cook, W.D. and B. Golanyi. 1987. Consistent weights for judgments matrices of the relative importance of alternatives *Operations Research Letters* **6** (3), 131–134.

Krovak, J. 1987. Ranking alternatives - comparison of different methods based on binary comparison matrices. *European Journal of Operational Research* **32** (13), 86–95.

Weber, M., Eisenfuhr, F. and D. von Winterfeldt. 1988. The effects of splitting attributes on weights in multiattribute utility measurement. *Management Science* **34** (4), 431–445.

ELECTRE

Benayoun, R., Roy, B. and B. Sussman. 1966. ELECTRE: Une methode pour guider le choixe en presence de points de vue multiples. *SEMA* Note 49, June.

Roy, B. 1968. Clessement et choix en presence de criteres multiples. *RIRO* **8**, 57–75.

Roy, B. 1973. La Methode ELECTRE II, Une Application au Media–Planning. *Operational Research '72*, M. Ross, ed., Amsterdam, North-Holland.

Roy, B. 1978. ELECTRE III: Une algorithme de classement fonde sur une representation floue des preferences en presence de criteres multiple. *Cahiers du Centre Etudes Recherche Operationelle* **20**, 3–24.

Roy, B. 1978. ELECTRE III: Un algorithme de classement fonde sur une representation floue des preferences en presence de criteres multiple. *Cahiers du Centre Etudes Recherche Operationelle* **20**, 3–24.

Skalka, J.M., Bouyoussou, D. and Y.A. Bernabeu. 1983. ELECTRE III et IV: Aspect methodologique et guide d'utilisation. *Cahier du LAMSADE 25*, Universite Paris–Dauphine.

Brans, J.P. and Ph. Vincke. 1985. A preference ranking organization method, The PROMETHEE Method. *Management Science* **31**, 647–656.

Brans, J.P., Vincke, P. and B. Mareschal. 1986. How to select and how to rank projects: The PROMETHEE Method. *European Journal of Operational Research* **24**, 228–238.

Mladineo, N. and J. Margeta. 1987. Multicriteria ranking of alternative locations for small scale hydro plants. *European Journal of Operational Research* **31**, 215–222.

Mareschal, B. and J.-P. Brans. 1988. Geometrical representations for MCDA. *European Journal of Operational Research* **34**, 69–77.

DuBois, P., Brans, J.P., Cantraine, F. and B. Mareschal. 1991. MEDICIS: An expert system for computer-aided diagnosis using the PROMETHEE multicriteria method. *European Journal of Operational Research* **52**, 224–234.

Pasche, C. 1991. EXTRA: An expert system for multicriteria decision making. *European Journal of Operational Research* **52**, 224–234.

Mareschal, B. and J.P. Brans. 1991. BANKADVISER: An industrial evaluation system. *European Journal of Operational Research* **54**, 318–324.

Brans, J.P. and B. Mareschal. 1992. PROMETHEE V: MCDM problems with segmentation constraints. *INFOR* **30**:2, 85–96.

Preference Cones

Zionts, S. and J. Wallenius. 1980. Identifying efficient vectors: Some theory and computational results *Operations Research* **28**:3, 785–793.

Zionts, S. 1981. A multiple criteria method for choosing among discrete alternatives. *European Journal of Operational Research* **7**, 143–147.

Korhonen, P. and M. Soismaa. 1981. An interactive multiple criteria approach to ranking alternatives. *Journal of the Operational Research Society* **32**, 577–585.

Koksalen, M., Karwan, M.H. and S. Zionts. 1984. An improved method for solving multiple criteria problems involving discrete alternatives. *IEEE Transactions on Systems, Man & Cybernetics* **SMC–14** (1).

Korhonen, P., Wallenius, J. and S. Zionts. 1984. Solving the discrete multiple criteria problem using convex cones. *Management Science* **30** (11), 1336–1345.

Korhonen, P.J. 1986. A hierarchical interactive method for ranking alternatives with multiple qualitative criteria. *European Journal of Operational Research* **24**, 265–276.

Ramesh, R., Karwan, M.H. and S. Zionts. 1988. Theory of convex cones in multicriteria decision making. *Annals of Operations Research* **16**, 131–148.

Malakooti, B. 1988. A decision support system and a heuristic interactive approach for solving discrete multiple criteria problems. *IEEE Transactions on Systems, Man, and Cybernetics* **18**:2, 273–284.

Koksalan, M., Karwan, M.H. and S. Zionts. 1988. An approach for solving discrete alternative multiple criteria problems involving ordinal criteria. *Naval Research Logistics* **35**:6, 625–642.

Koksalan, M.M. 1989. An improved method for solving multiple criteria problems involving discrete alternatives. *Naval Research Logistics* **36**, 359–372.

Malakooti, B. 1989. Theories and an exact interactive paired-comparison approach for discrete multiple-criteria problems. *IEEE Transactions on Systems, Man, and Cybernetics* **19**, 365–378.

Malakooti, B. 1989. Multiple objective facility layout: A heuristic to generate efficient alternatives. *International Journal of Production Research* **27**:7, 1225–1238.

Malakooti, B. 1989. A hierarchical, multi-objective approach to the analysis, design, and selection of computer-integrated manufacturing systems. *Robotics & Computer–Integrated Manufacturing* **6**:1, 83–97.

Malakooti, B. 1989. An interactive multiple criteria approach for parameter selection in metal cutting. *Operations Research* **37**, 805–818.

Malakooti, B. 1991. An interactive on-line multi-objective optimization approach with application to metal cutting turning operation. *International Journal of Production Research* **29**:3, 575–598.

Taner, O.V. and M.M. Koksalan. 1991. Experiments and an improved method for solving the discrete alternative multiple-criteria problem. *Journal of the Operational Research Society* **42**, 383–391.

Frazier, G., Gaither, N. and D.L. Olson. 1991. A procedure for dealing with multiple objectives in cell formation decisions. *Journal of Operations Management* **9**:4, 465–480.

Koksalan, M.M. and P.N.S. Sagala. 1991. An interactive approach for choosing the best of a set of alternatives. *Journal of the Operations Research Society* **43**:3, 259–263.

Koksalan, M.M. and O.V. Taner. 1992. An approach for finding the most preferred alternative in the presence of multiple criteria. *European Journal of Operations Research* **60**, 52–60.

Other

Schenkerman, S. 1977. Multi-attribute decision making using constrained criteria. *Computers & Operations Research* **4**, 139–145.

Einhorn, H.J. and W. McCoach. 1977. A simple multiattribute utility procedure for evaluation. *Behavioral Science* **22**, 270–282.

Martel, J.M. and G.R. d'Avignon. 1982. Projects ordering with multicriteria analysis. *European Journal of Operational Research* **10**, 56–69.

Mehrez, A. and Z. Sinuany–Stern. 1983. An interactive approach for project selection. *Journal of the Operational Research Society* **7**, 621–626.

Levine, P. and J.-C. Pomeral. 1986. PRIAM, an interactive program for choosing among multiple attribute alternatives. *European Journal of Operational Research* **25**, 272–280.

Larichev, O.I., Naginskaya, V.S. and A.I. Mechitov. 1987. An interactive procedure for industrial building design choice. *Journal of Applied Systems Analysis* **14**, 33–40.

Harvey, C.M. 1991. Models of tradeoffs in a hierarchical structure of objectives. *Management Science* **37**:8, 1030–1042.

Larichev, O.I. and H.M. Moshkovich. 1991. ZAPROS: A method and system for ordering multiattribute alternatives on the base of a decision-maker's preferences. All–Union Research Institute for Systems Studies.

Wang, M.-J., Singh, H.P. and W.V. Huang. 1991. A decision support system for robot selection. *Decision Support Systems* **7**, 273–283.